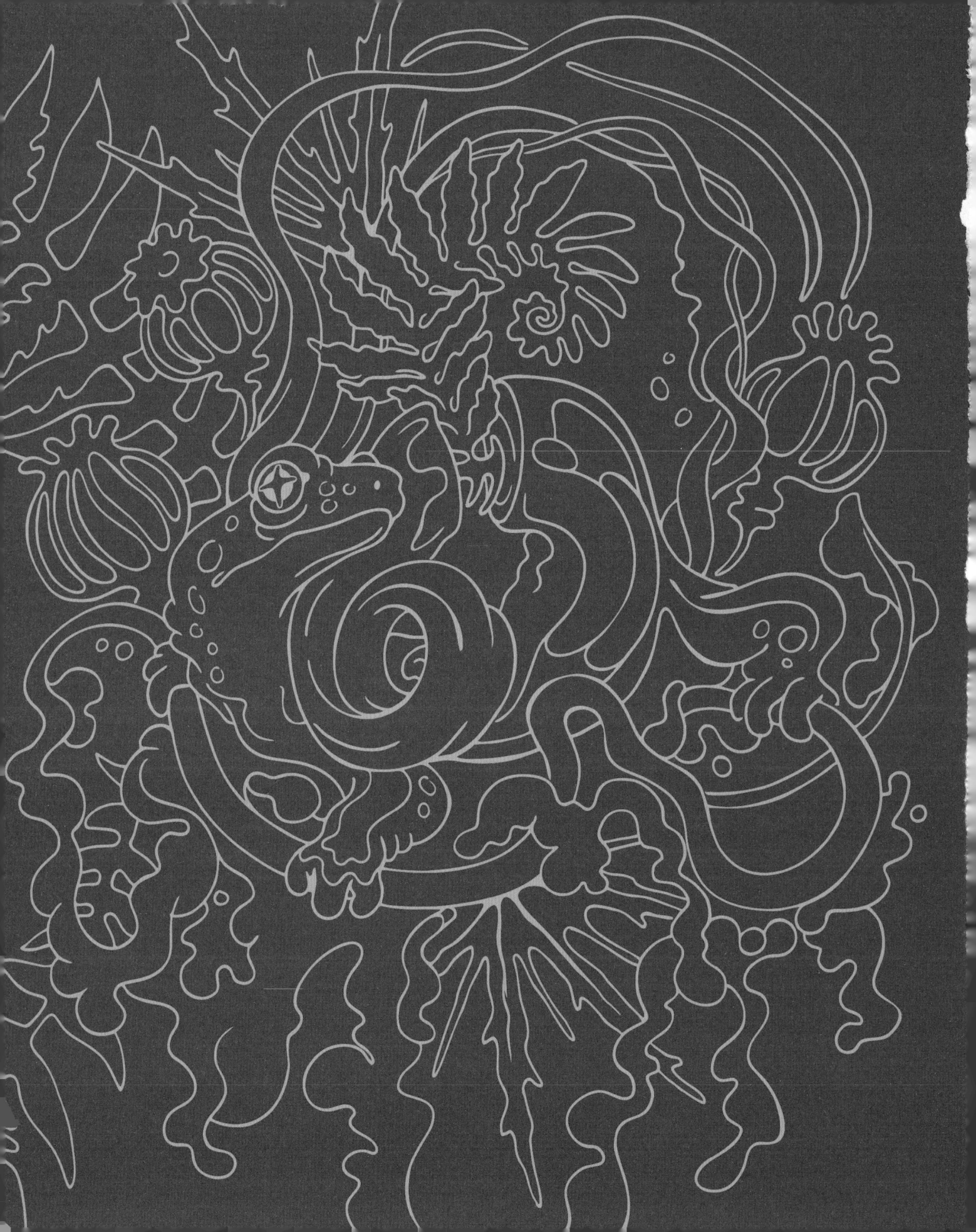

Unfurl

The Art of Christina Tyzhuk

3dtotalPublishing

Correspondence: publishing@3dtotal.com
Website: store.3dtotal.com

First published in the United Kingdom, 2026, by 3dtotal Publishing.

Address: 3dtotal.com Ltd,
6 Sansome Street, Worcester,
WR1 1UH, United Kingdom.

Hard cover ISBN: 978-1-915992-38-3

Printed and bound in China
by C&C Offset Printing Co., Ltd

Visit store.3dtotal.com for a complete list of available book titles.

Editorial Project Manager: Rhiannon Joseph
Lead Editor: Samantha Rigby
Lead Designer: Joseph Cartwright
Studio Manager: Simon Morse
Managing Director: Tom Greenway

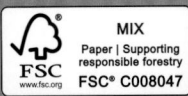

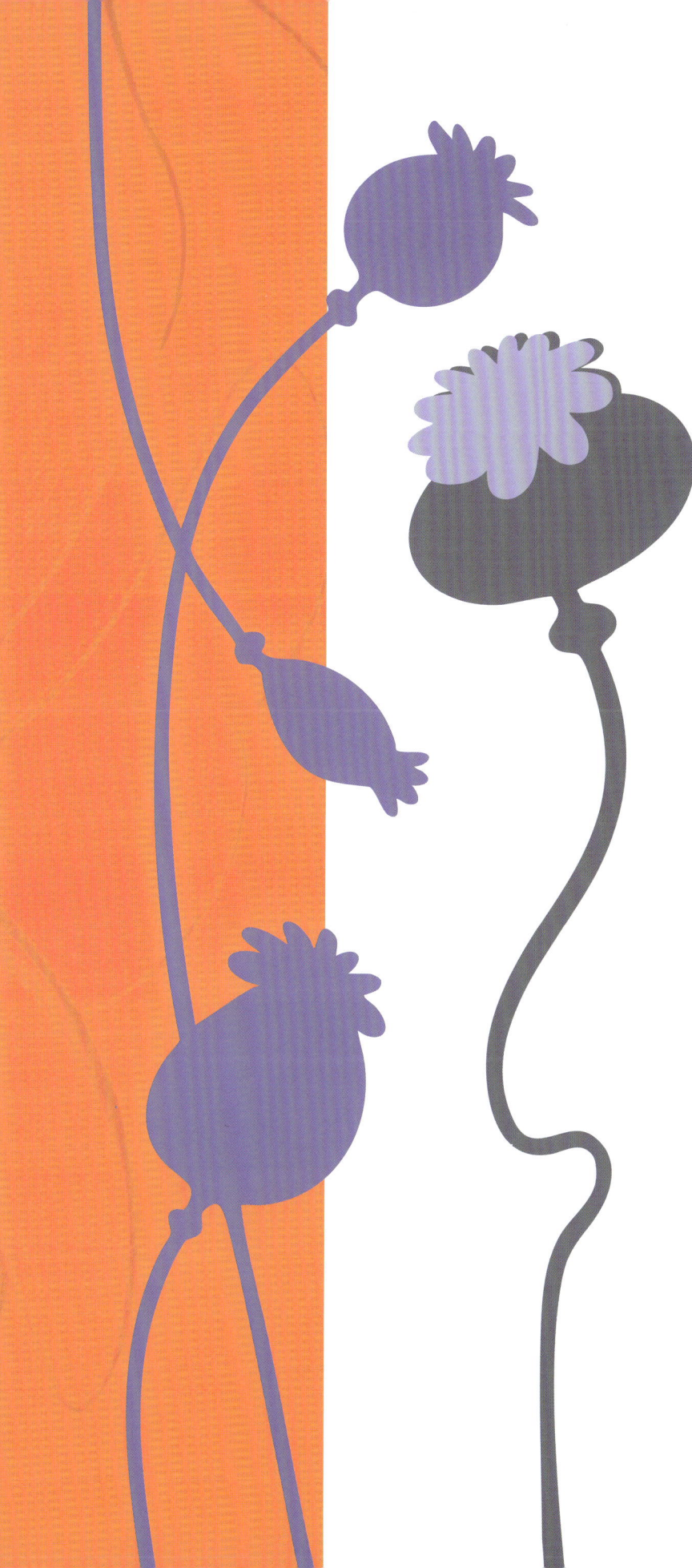

50%
of net profits donated
TO CHARITY

In 2022, 3dtotal Publishing became successful enough to make a pledge to **donate 50% of its net profits to charity.** This continues to be possible due to the incredible support from all our customers, employees, and partners. At the time of printing, we have donated over $1.62 million (USD) to charity.

We focus our giving on three charitable areas: **environmental, humanitarian, and animal welfare.** We use organizations such as Effective Altruism and Founders Pledge to guide who we help within these causes. Some ways of doing good are over 100 times more effective than others, so donating this way hugely increases the impact of our contributions.

See **3dtotal.com/charity** for full details.

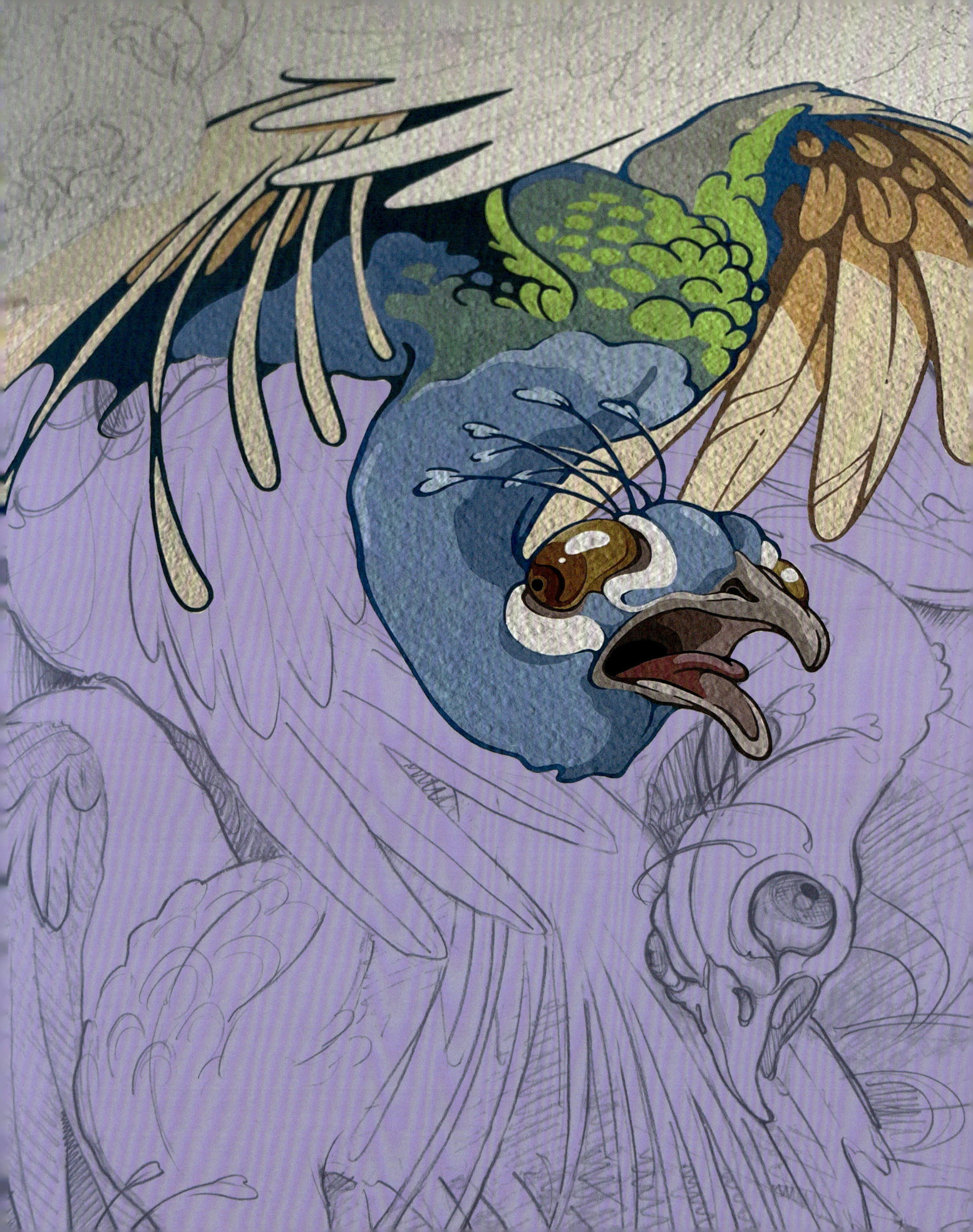

Contents

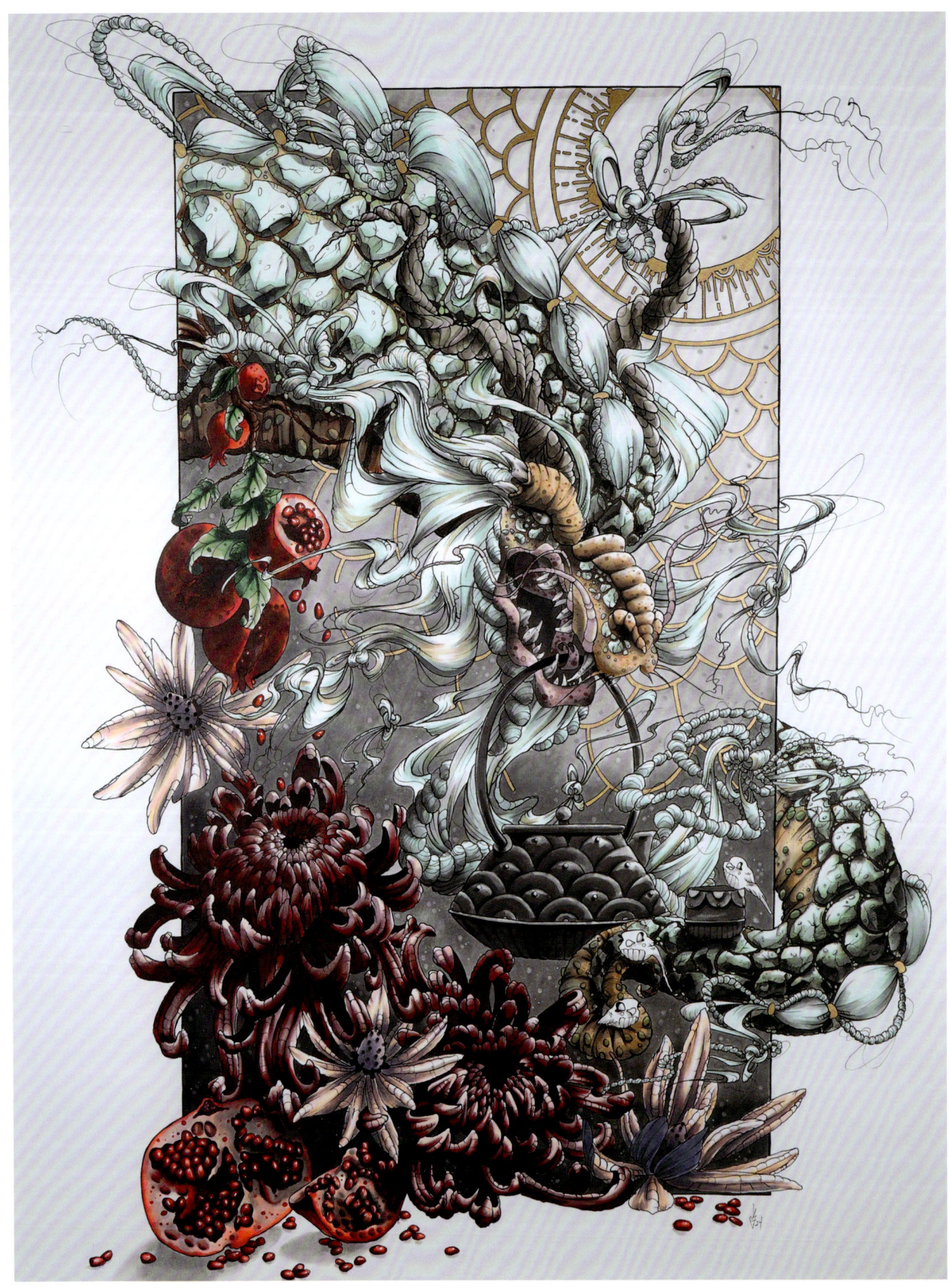

Foreword
by Mallarie Bundy

Christina's creative process is truly mesmerizing. Her fast-paced social-media videos expertly capture viewers' attention, which is so crucial for artists today. However, these quick glimpses only hint at the immense time, effort, and meticulous detail that go into her vibrant and imaginative creations. It's truly rare to find such a combination of precision and boundless creativity. Beyond her artistic talent, Christina is a kind and bright individual who deeply connects with her community, a quality I've experienced first-hand. Her work has been a profound influence on my own artistic journey; I'm fortunate to have several of her original pieces in my home, which serve as a daily source of inspiration and a reminder of the unique beauty every artist brings to the world.

Christina's latest work further showcases her incredible versatility as an artist. Her exploration of new mediums demonstrates a commitment to continuous learning and innovation, yet her distinctive style remains instantly recognizable. I'm certain that fans, including myself, will thoroughly enjoy this book. As an artist and a devoted admirer of Christina's work, I believe having her collected works in one place, along with the added insight into her creative process, is an invaluable resource.

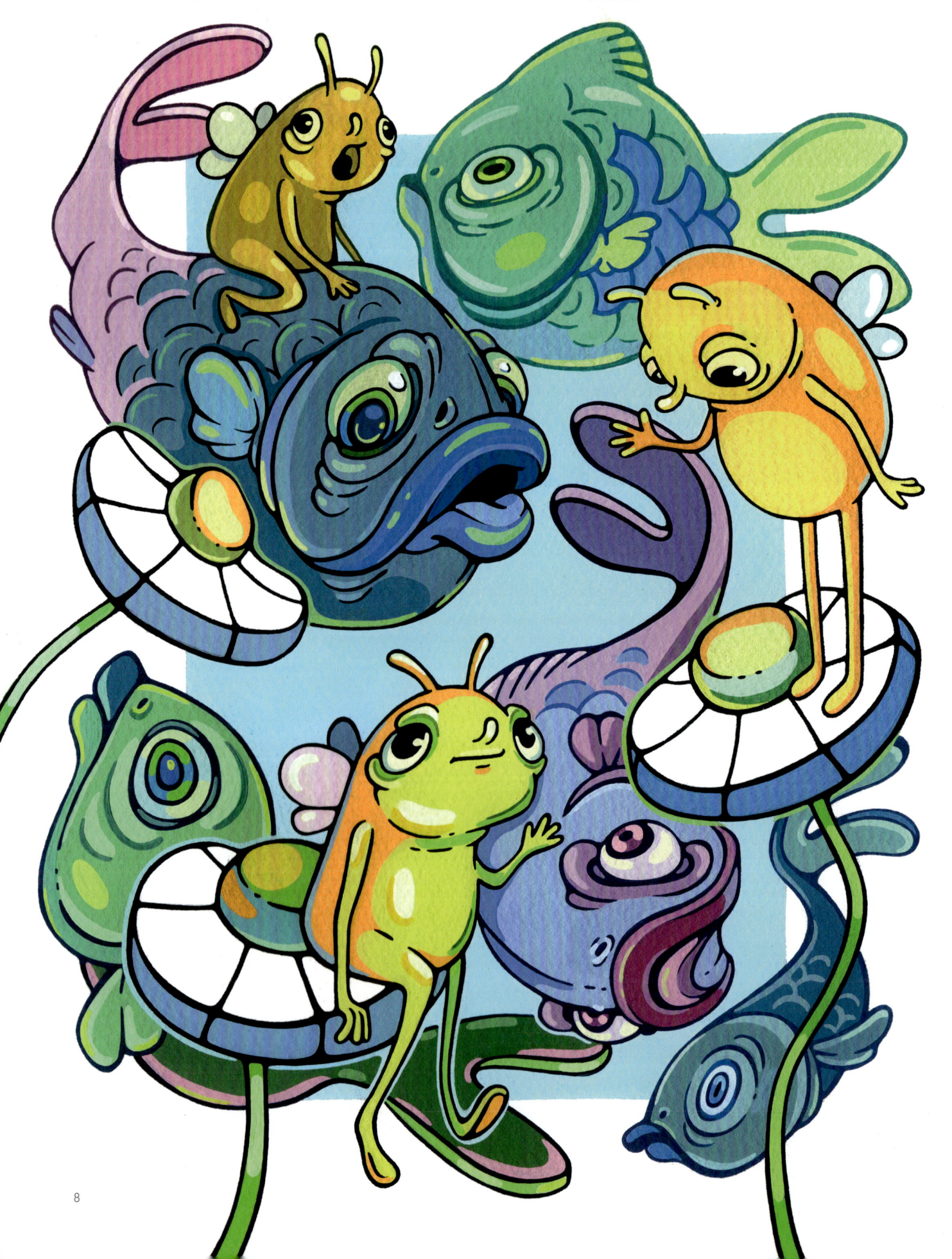

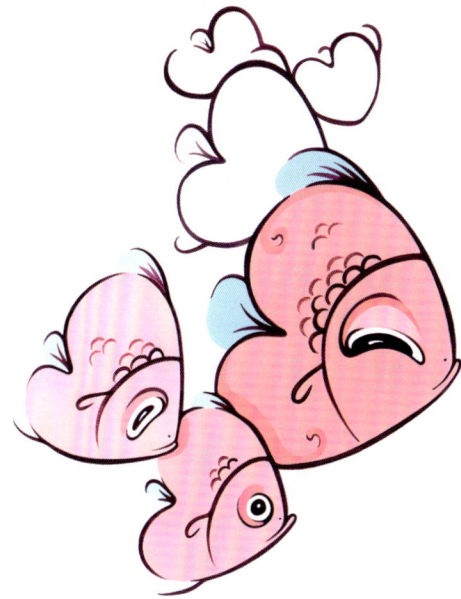

Introduction

Some works of art speak for themselves, requiring no need for verbal or written explanation. Viewers can use their imaginations to fill in the gaps, interpreting colour to evoke emotion and composition to understand story. However, what is often lost in translation is what is found *behind* a painting; the personality that inspires these feelings. This book has been an incredible opportunity for me to reveal my inner world more deeply – all my illustrations to date and all the emotions that fuelled their creation.

While piecing *Unfurl* together, I was fascinated by the process of self-reflection. I revisited cherished memories and looked through my childhood drawings with feelings of warmth and nostalgia. I remembered the moments where it all began and traced the path to where and who I am today. And although it is much easier for me to draw than to write, I was able to communicate and reveal a lot across these pages, surprising even *me*. For the first time, I traced the evolution of my art and shared thoughts that I normally keep to myself: what motivates me, my inner fears, and my small victories, to name a few.

For those who have already seen my illustrations, or those just coming across them for the first time, this book is both a story and an invitation to join a journey that's only just beginning. I hope it will give you the motivation to pursue your own creative dreams.

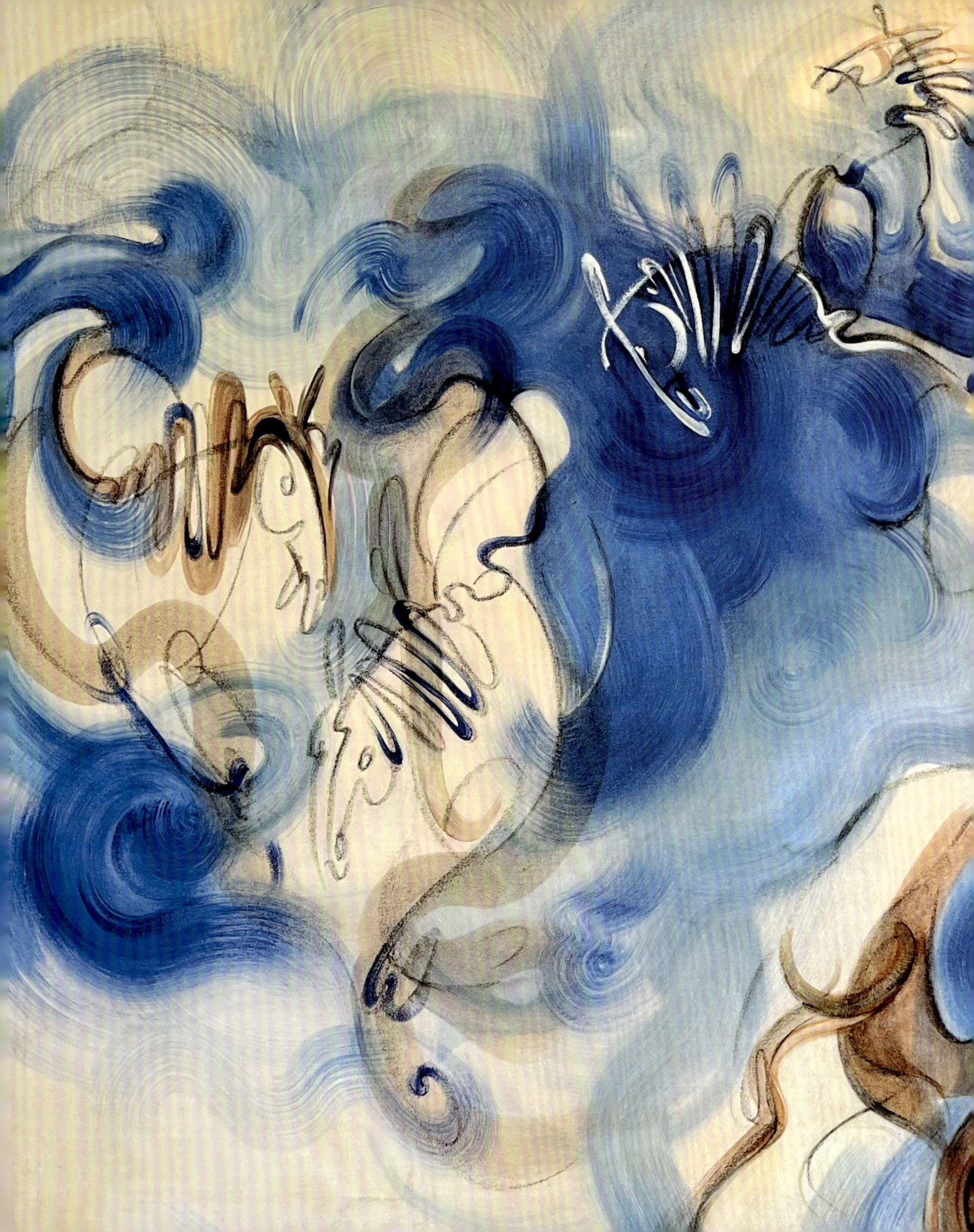

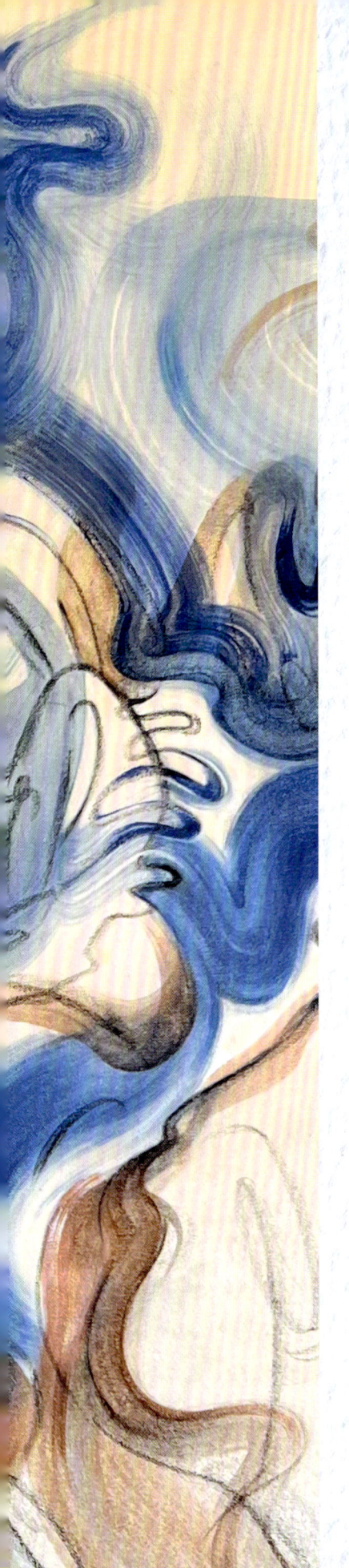

Creative journey

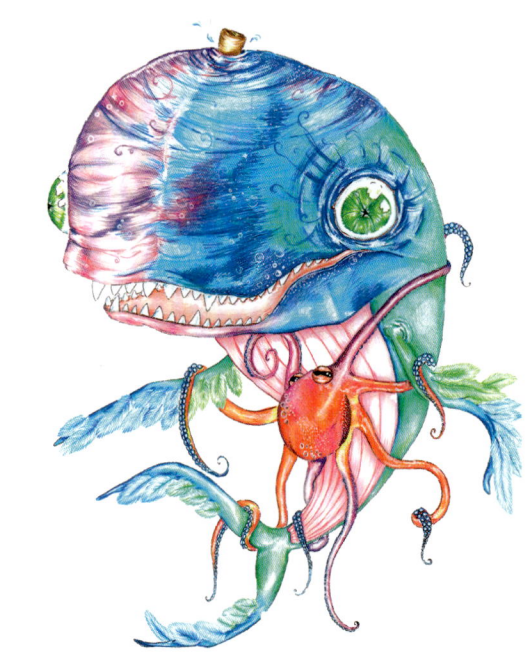

BEGINNINGS

My childhood was full of creativity. Both of my
parents studied visual art, so I grew up watching
them bring their imaginations to life. As a theatre
designer, my mother curated the spaces, costumes,
scale models, and props for stage shows. The
theatre was a special place for me. I had the unique
opportunity not only to watch a performance,
but also to look behind the scenes, watching how
costumes and backdrops were created based on my
mother's sketches. It still fascinates me to this day.
At home, she would make her own dolls, thinking
over each little detail from facial expressions to
clothes and poses.

My father worked more with painting, exploring
different techniques and genres, which eventually
led him to a career in architecture and design.
My home was a truly inspiring place and fostered a
healthy appreciation for artistry in all its many forms.

Although my parents were passionate about their
careers, they never imposed their interests on me.
I had complete freedom of choice. I don't
even recall wanting to pursue art as a career when I
was a child. Back then, it was just an easy way for me
to express my emotions.

Books, however, had a significant influence on
my early worldview. I loved fairy tales, poems,
and legends, especially the ones with beautiful
illustrations. I spent countless hours flipping
through pages, travelling between the lines and
immersing myself in new stories and worlds.

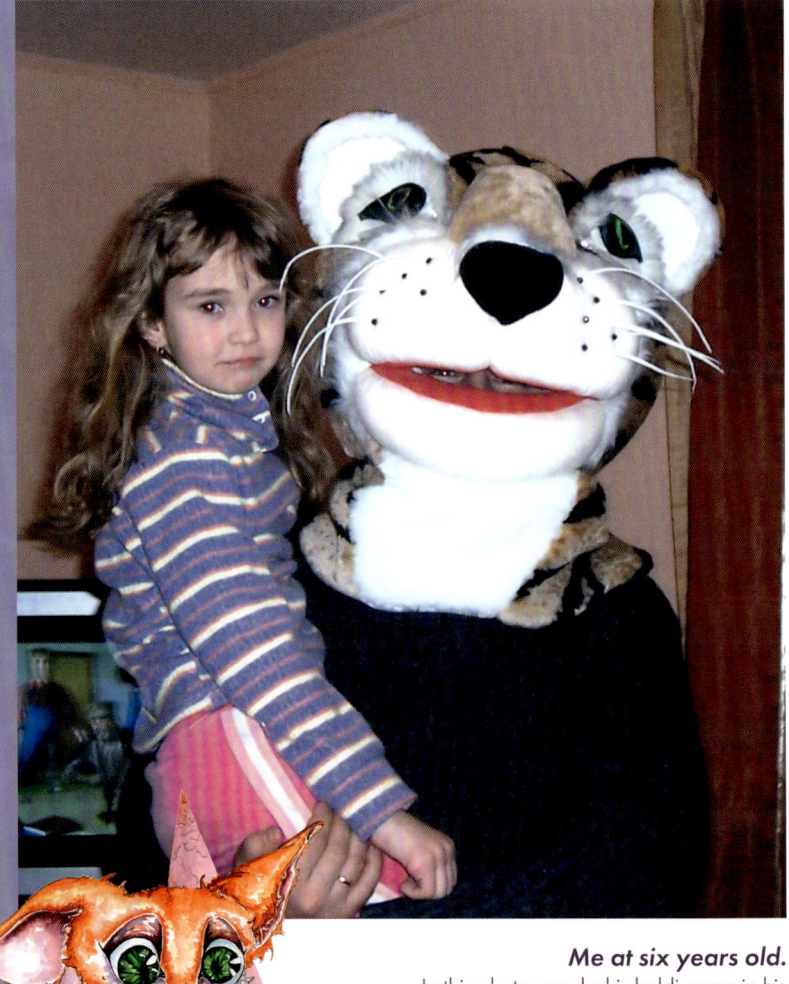

Me at six years old.
In this photo, my dad is holding me in his
arms while wearing a tiger head that my
mom made for the theatre

12

I re-read these children's books many times over, each time finding something new in the artwork that had previously gone unnoticed. At the age of six, my favourite series was the *Beechwood Bunny Tales* by French author Geneviève Huriet and illustrator Loïc Jouannigot.

Eventually, I was inspired to create my own stories and illustrations. Of course, I didn't have a 'style' in those days. But one detail remained the same in most of my drawings: big, round eyes. For some reason, that feature was inherent in all my characters.

Around the same age, I joined a creative group led by Ukrainian artist, teacher, and writer Angelina Turak. She had a strong love of nature, and one day took our little class on a trip to the mountains. It's usually hard for me to remember the details of moments from so long ago, but that day is forever etched in my memory: the bus ride, warm sun, old villages, and sea of trees. I remember walking through flower-speckled meadows and drawing our beautiful surroundings. I spent many years with the group, strengthening my love of art. We were encouraged to try different artistic techniques and mediums, which sometimes even involved needlework and crafting.

One of my fondest memories of my time with Angelina was when she instructed our group to draw a subject using a black pen and repetitive graphic elements. It took hours, but it was a fascinating experience. I chose to draw an owl, and loved it so much that I continued to draw in a similar style at home. Using references found online, I started with simple images until I grew good enough to tackle more complex ones in both appearance and size. Drawing in this style almost felt like a form of meditation. Its intricate and detailed nature taught me valuable lessons like patience, perseverance, and accuracy. The elements and influence of this art style can definitely be seen in my works today.

In high school, I had a hard time adjusting to my new surroundings. I wasn't necessarily withdrawn, but I was certainly quiet, so it was difficult to find friends. However, I discovered there was a girl in one of my classes who was

also creative, and we quickly found common ground. It was a relief to be around a kindred spirit. We doodled in each other's notebooks constantly, creating whimsical sketches or caricatures of our teachers. It didn't take long for our peers to perceive us as the school's 'artists'.

The obsession with drawing didn't stop at the end of the school day. At home, I'd sit at the small table in my room and immerse myself in my own imagination, watching the real world around me slowly dissolve into a fantastical one. Over time, I accumulated enough works from these sessions to become the basis for my first exhibition at the age of thirteen. One of my teachers had suggested the idea to me, and so a little stand was placed near my school entrance showcasing my artworks. I wasn't thrilled about the idea at first. It was one thing to draw for friends and family, but displaying my works for everyone else to see was a different story. These artworks were insights into my thoughts and feelings, a reflection of very personal experiences. In retrospect, exhibiting them publicly forced me to convey ideas of mine that were not yet fully formed. I was certainly not ashamed of my imagination and love of fantasy, but revealing such intimacies about myself might have distorted what I was still trying to learn about myself.

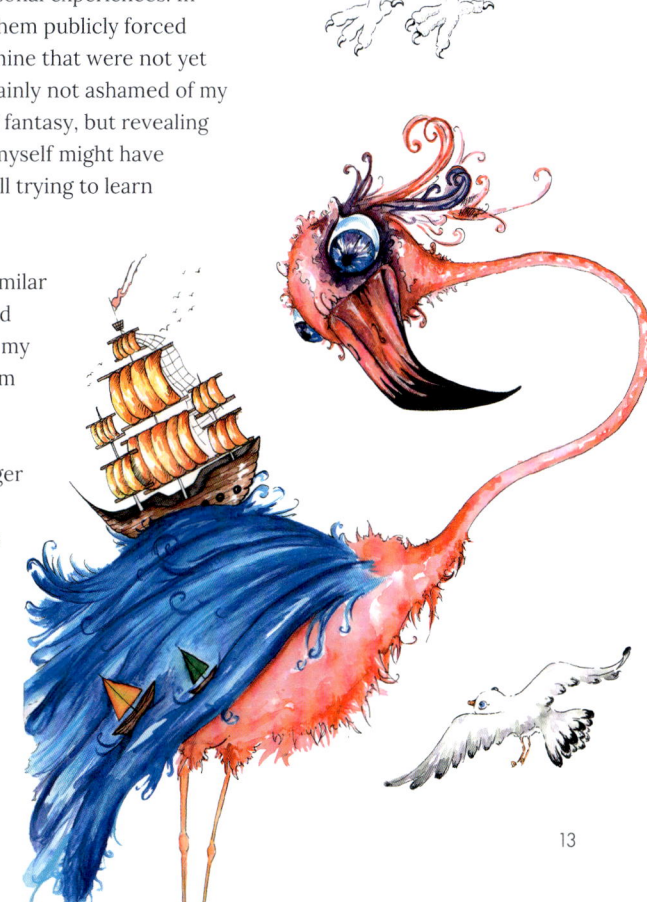

I continued to create similar works until I was around fifteen. I am grateful to my mother for keeping them safe. My interest in my own finished art never lasted long, as I was eager to focus on my newer ideas. It's not that I was indifferent to these older projects, but the process of creating was just more exciting to me.

ART EDUCATION

My hometown in Western Ukraine, Uzhhorod, is home to the Adalbert Erdeli Professional Art College, and it's where my father once studied. At the age of fifteen, I decided to follow in his footsteps and begin my formal art education there. The decision marked a turning point in my life, dividing it into a 'before' and 'after'.

At the time, I wasn't sure which major to pursue. Design seemed like the most promising direction – in-demand, practical, and progressive. I went to the interview thinking that it was the best option for me. The committee reviewed my portfolio and instead advised me to choose the Fine Arts programme. I hesitated at their words – sure, design was something that offered a tangible future, but painting … could I really make a successful career out of it? Fortunately, I didn't have clear enough arguments to defend my initial choice, so I listened to their recommendation. Of course, they were correct, and that path turned out to be the right one.

Before the programme officially started, I attended preparatory courses under the guidance of a painter and graphic artist, which helped me adapt to my new environment. During this period, I realized that my bizarre illustrations were a far cry from the requirements of the course, so I shelved them to focus on discovering new subjects and learning advanced methods and techniques. I wasn't sad about it – it was interesting to test my strengths and weaknesses in new ways.

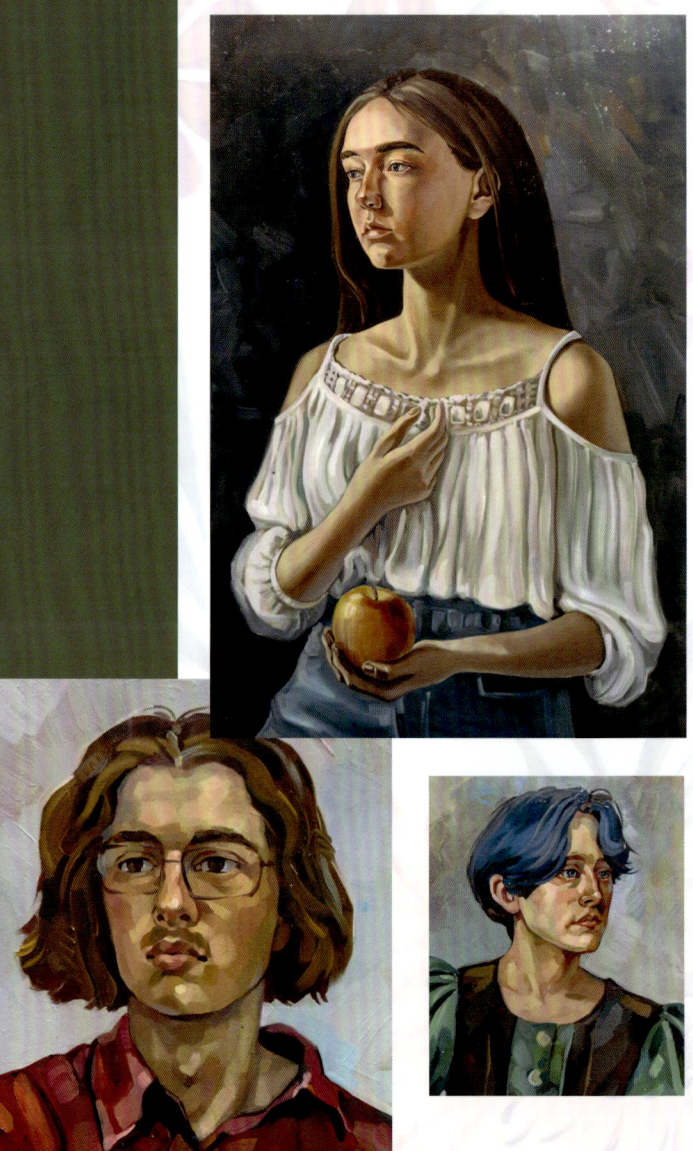

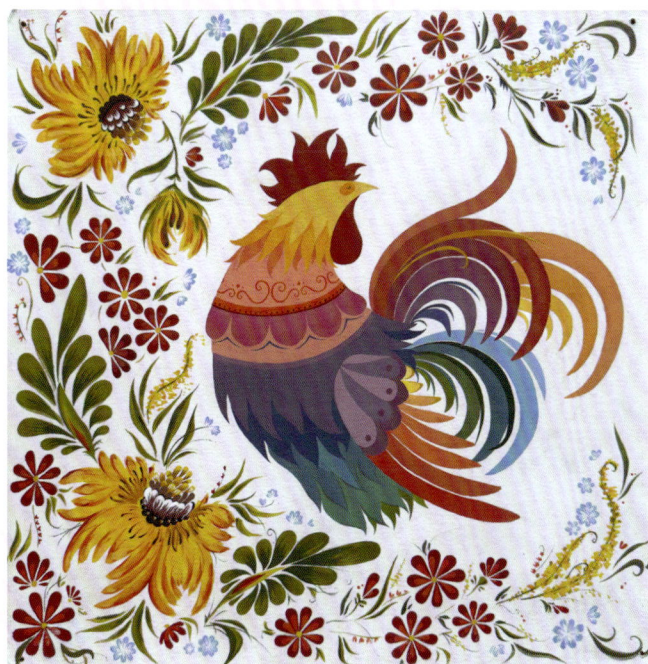

Rooster with Ukrainian motifs, one of my first works using tempera paints when I was fifteen years old

For the first few years, I drew exclusively what was required of me. Although sometimes there were students who felt dissatisfied by the limitations of their own artistic vision, I understood the importance of fundamental knowledge.

During that first year, it felt like we only drew cubes. I still see them in my sleep! These are memories full of tears and failures, but each tough time and rough patch hardened me. That was the whole point: it wasn't really about drawing what was in front of us, it was about understanding the basic principles of construction.

The 'Transcarpathian School of Painting' is an artistic movement that originated in the Transcarpathian region of Ukraine in the first half of the twentieth century, and it formed the basis for the culture of my college and the Transcarpathian Academy of Arts, where I later continued my studies. This movement has a unique history that began in my small town. Its full story would require another book, but for general understanding, it combines early modernist artistic movements and folk art. Our teachers taught in the same spirit. We didn't always strive for the ideal academic styles taught in the central institutions of art. Often, we were allowed to explore things on a deeper level. For example, if a life model had a big nose, we could emphasize and exaggerate this striking feature to achieve a more expressive look. Teachers frequently held masterclasses or drew with us, and as a result, my work gradually adopted a recognizable style – in particular, my attention to detail and love for bright colours.

The hardest thing for me was drawing people. I wasn't really interested in it. However, in college, portraiture held considerable weight and it was impossible to move forwards without understanding human anatomy. I wasn't inspired to delve into all the nuances, so my ability to visually judge proportions saved me. Eventually, with constant practice, my work improved and the process of drawing human faces and bodies became more enjoyable. Today, I no longer draw people realistically. In fact, I am increasingly attracted to what people of different cultures put on their faces, such as Japanese Oni masks. I feel like masks can effectively embody a human characteristic, sometimes even more than a facial expression.

There is also a special attitude towards plein air where I live. Going out into nature with a canvas and paint is an old tradition of Transcarpathian artists. But, I must admit, I didn't really like it at first. I would often find myself irritated and unable to relax with so much open space and people around. Additionally, working with oil paints in such conditions was not the best for me. Being used to the comfort of studio work, I found it difficult to paint neatly with oils in the rain, wind, or bright sunlight. Regardless of my frustration, we painted in all seasons. Outdoors, the light constantly changed, forcing me to quickly analyse and reproduce what was in front of me. It was no easy feat, but plein air painting eventually became a calming practice for me. After all, I had always loved observing nature, and it helped me step beyond my comfort zone.

This period became an invaluable experience for me. I don't think I would have learned so much on my own, or had the same sense of perseverance. My time here amounted to six eventful years, and when it was over, I felt ready to build my own path.

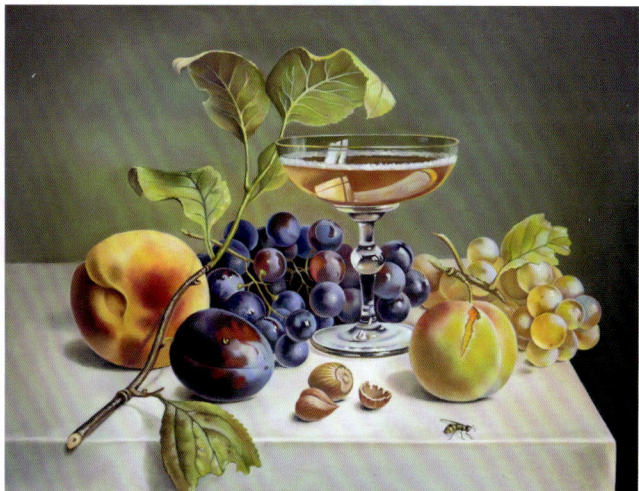

Dutch still-life (copy), painted when I was eighteen years old. In college, we were regularly given assignments to create copies of paintings in different genres and styles

FINDING
THE PATH

I would say that my career as an artist began in 2019, when I first posted my work on social media during my third year of college. This was made possible thanks to the support of close friends, who convinced me to create profiles on Instagram and TikTok. I was sceptical at first – how could my work be noticed in such a saturated space? Without clear plans or grandiose expectations, I took the plunge anyway, which eventually became the impetus for my own art revival.

I taught myself how to shoot videos, take photos, and present my work online. Each new post was an opportunity to analyse previous posts for improvement. As I did this during college, and later while I was at the Academy, my internal conflict grew. My creativity seemed to be divided into two opposite halves: the academic process on one hand and my own ventures on the other, which I wanted to develop further but lacked the time. It was hard for me to harmoniously combine these two directions.

In 2022, I was getting closer to my current style and my social-media audience was growing. That was when I first dared to accept commissions. A year later, my Instagram followers reached 400,000. However, that victory was shortlived because my account was hacked. For the first time, I was overcome with a feeling of utter devastation; what I had been creating for the past few years had disappeared in an instant. That day, I experienced all the stages of grief, accepted the inevitable, and allowed myself the evening to suffer before starting all over again the next day.

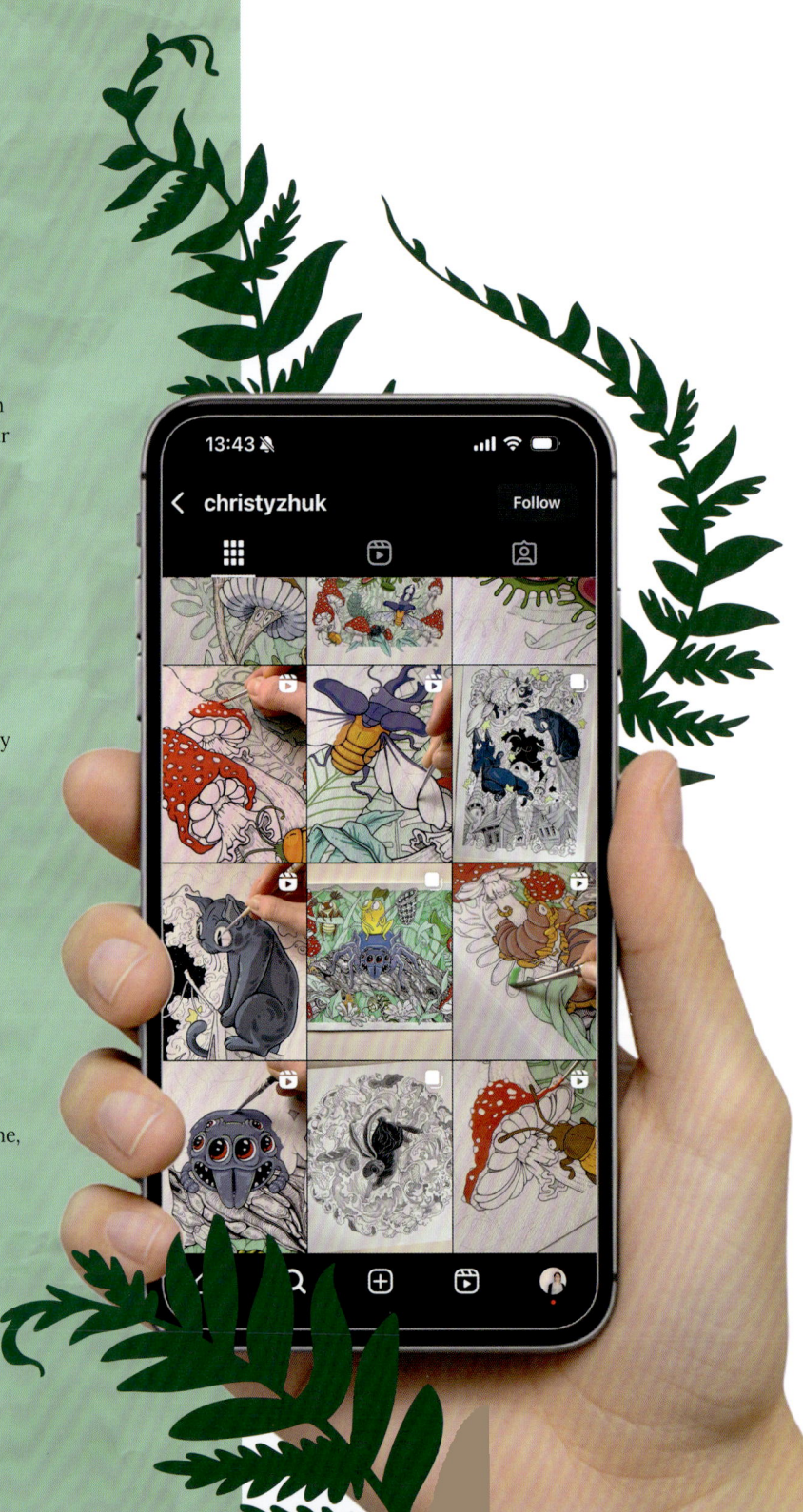

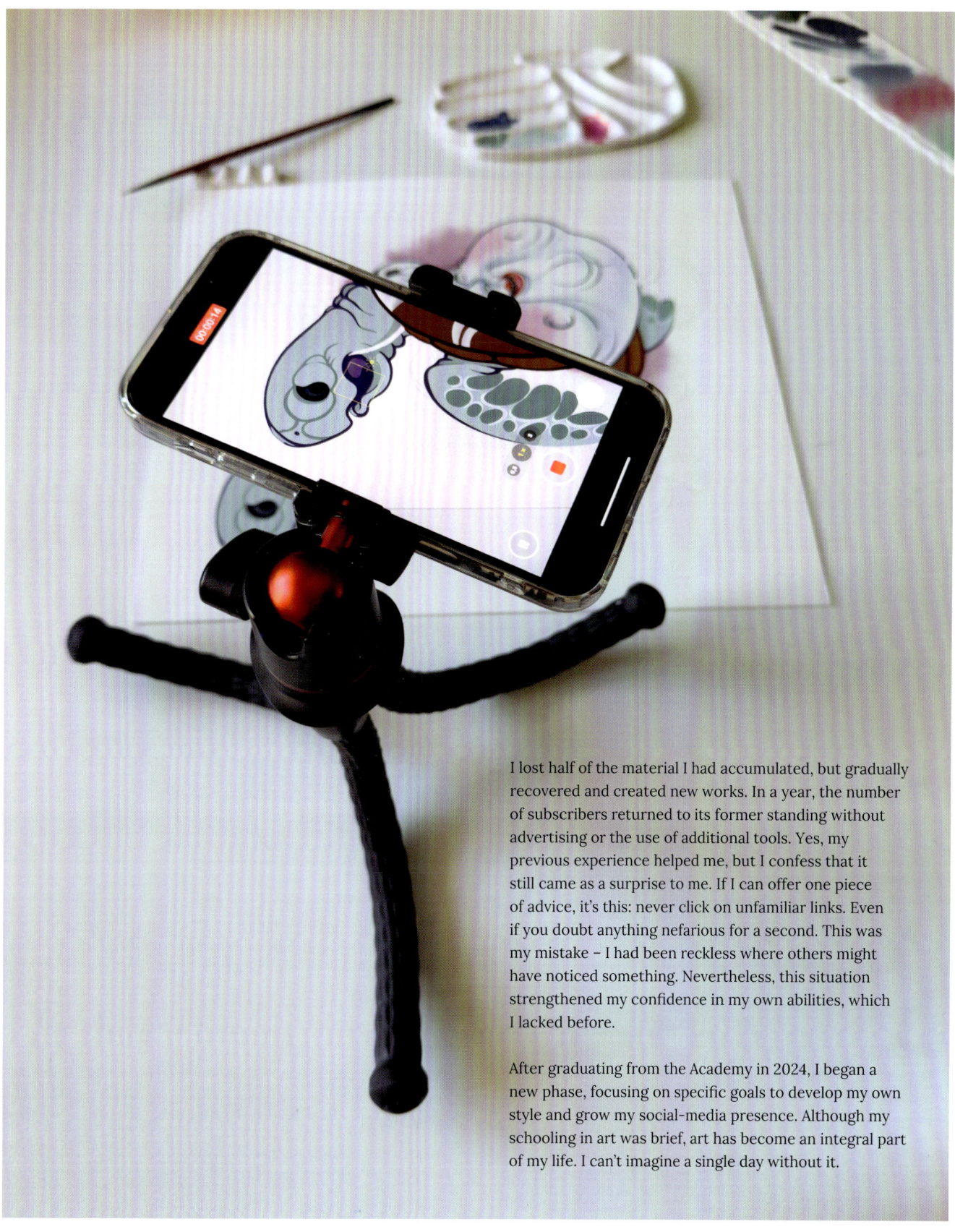

I lost half of the material I had accumulated, but gradually recovered and created new works. In a year, the number of subscribers returned to its former standing without advertising or the use of additional tools. Yes, my previous experience helped me, but I confess that it still came as a surprise to me. If I can offer one piece of advice, it's this: never click on unfamiliar links. Even if you doubt anything nefarious for a second. This was my mistake – I had been reckless where others might have noticed something. Nevertheless, this situation strengthened my confidence in my own abilities, which I lacked before.

After graduating from the Academy in 2024, I began a new phase, focusing on specific goals to develop my own style and grow my social-media presence. Although my schooling in art was brief, art has become an integral part of my life. I can't imagine a single day without it.

THE PRICE OF ART

The first time I sold a painting was to a customer from Switzerland. The theme revolved around mermaids and an underwater world. As I mentioned previously, I tended to avoid human features in my illustrations, but since this was the only request from the buyer, I didn't hesitate for long. The other details were left to my discretion, so I felt quite free to express my imagination. The difficult part was deciding on a price. At the time, I thought that only artists with a respected 'name' in the industry could value their art at a higher price point. I still partially have this opinion, but looking back, the effort and time I invested in this illustration could have been worth a little more than the sixty euros I chose to charge.

For many artists, the topic of pricing is a painful one. No one has ever devalued my work – I did that to myself. For some reason, it seemed to me that the work could not be worth more, and that I had to sell it as soon as possible in order to create something better and worthy of higher appreciation. Ultimately, valuing art is a vague concept. There is no universal formula, because there is no artwork that would appeal to everyone without exception. Over time, I realized that the value of art is determined not only by the creator's experience or opinion of others, but also by the artist's ability to appreciate their own work.

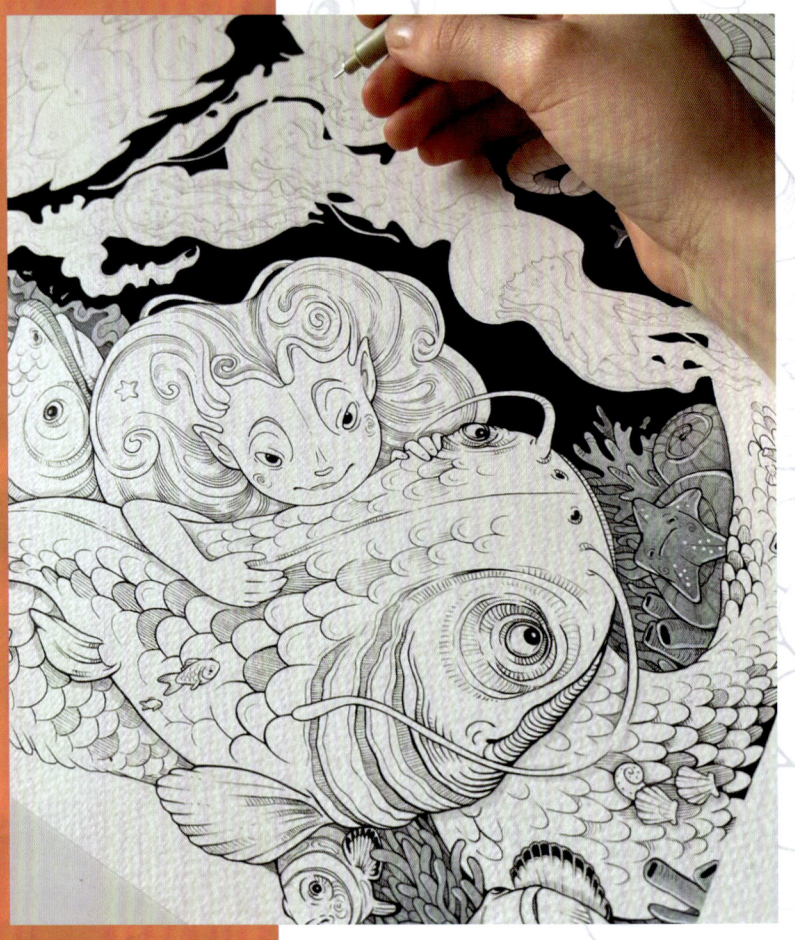

The Mystery of the Deep Sea, created when I was nineteen years old

TIPS FOR BEGINNERS

First of all, I want to emphasize that there is no universal advice. What worked for me may not work for you or another artist, and vice versa.

At the same time, I understand how valuable someone else's experience can be as a source of knowledge and inspiration. I hope that among my recommendations everyone will find something that resonates with their creative nature.

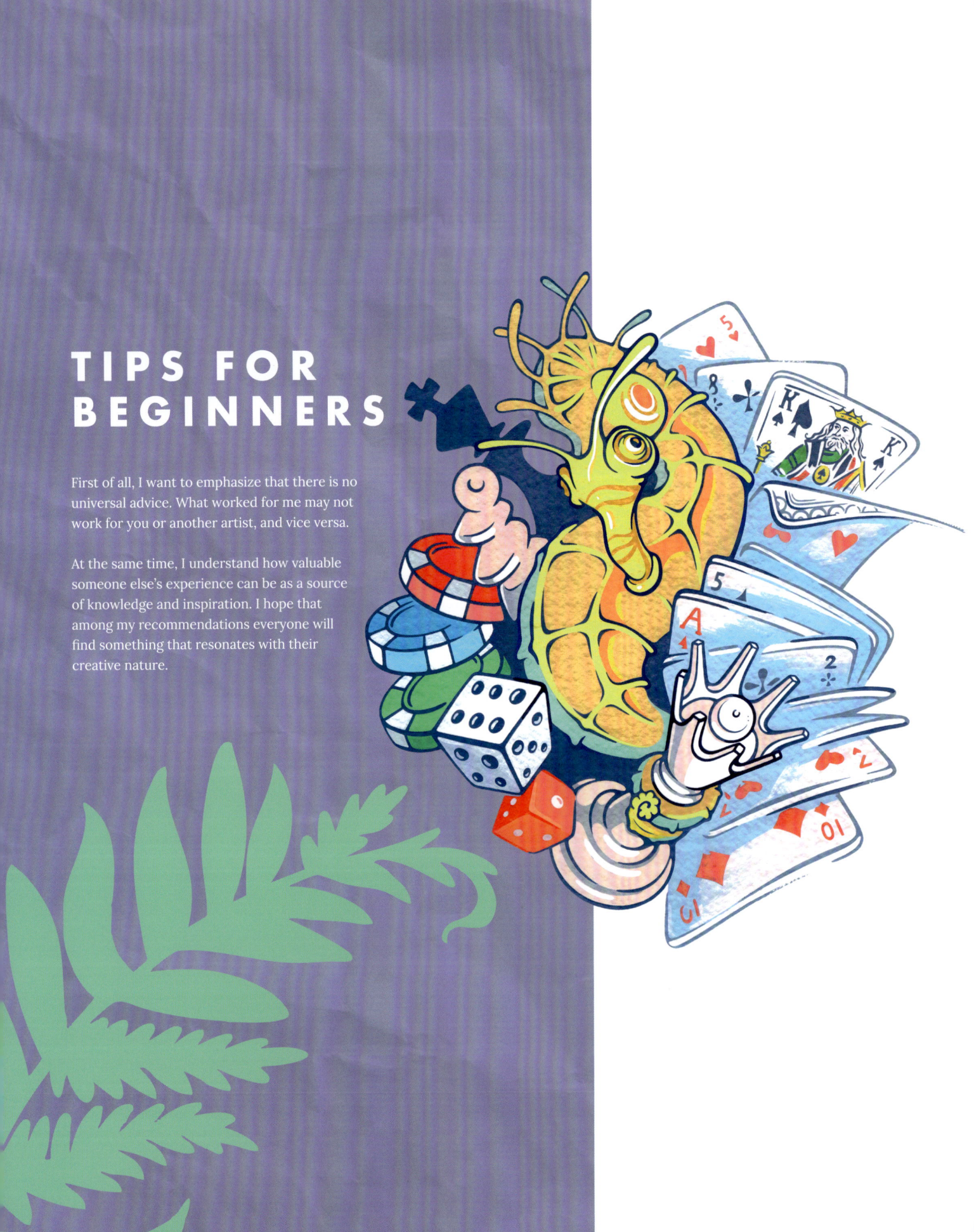

1. LOVE DRAWING

Cultivate a real passion for it, and then build your goals and ambitions around it. Don't immediately dive into learning a lot of theory, as this can easily discourage you from creating.

2. GET TO KNOW YOURSELF

Find out why you love to draw and what inspires you. For me, the first source of inspiration was detailed illustrations that evoked a sense of warmth and nostalgia.

3. DETERMINE YOUR DIRECTION

Don't try to become a master of all techniques right out of the gate. It's good to experiment, but focus on what you're good at and develop your strengths. You're not a bad artist if you don't master a particular technique or style. By focusing on a specific area, you can hone your skills much more effectively.

4. GET ORGANIZED

Discipline may feel restrictive, but creativity is often accompanied by chaotic thoughts. To avoid feeling scatter-brained and uncertain, create a habit of drawing regularly. Learn to balance your enthusiasm to work with your rest time. Organize your time and resources.

5. STUDY

Learning and self-improvement often require significant amounts of effort, and it can be frustrating when something doesn't work out on the first try. It's important to understand the value of this process: learning never ends, it only deepens and expands. Even when it comes to your own artistic vision, there will come a time when you feel that you lack knowledge. Begin to gradually master the basics of composition, colour, anatomy, perspective, and other aspects.

6. SEEK FEEDBACK

Don't be afraid to ask experienced artists for constructive criticism. Over time, your eyes become accustomed to your own work, and you lose the ability to objectively assess your efforts. A fresh perspective from an expert can help you identify weaknesses and encourage development.

7. CREATE YOUR OWN ARCHIVE OF INSPIRATION

Keep samples of inspirational paintings, illustrations, and photographs that serve as your guidelines and sources of energy. Over time, as your own journey begins, this archive may lose its relevance, but you can always refer to it when you need a new perspective.

8. STUDY OTHER WORKS

The practice of copying will help you better understand the techniques, methods, and thought processes of other artists. This is not about passing off other people's work as your own or mindlessly redrawing it, but about expanding your own artistic horizons.

10. PRESENT YOURSELF

Start showcasing your work, focusing on the enjoyment of creating instead of external expectations. Analyse what other artists are doing and introduce your own unique elements that reflect your personality.

9. CHOOSE THE RIGHT PROJECTS

Try to find opportunities to make money from the art you truly enjoy. Sometimes, it can be hard to turn down commissions when there are few of them, but if a project is motivated only by financial gain, it can negatively affect your attitude towards creativity and, as a result, also affect your productivity and overall morale.

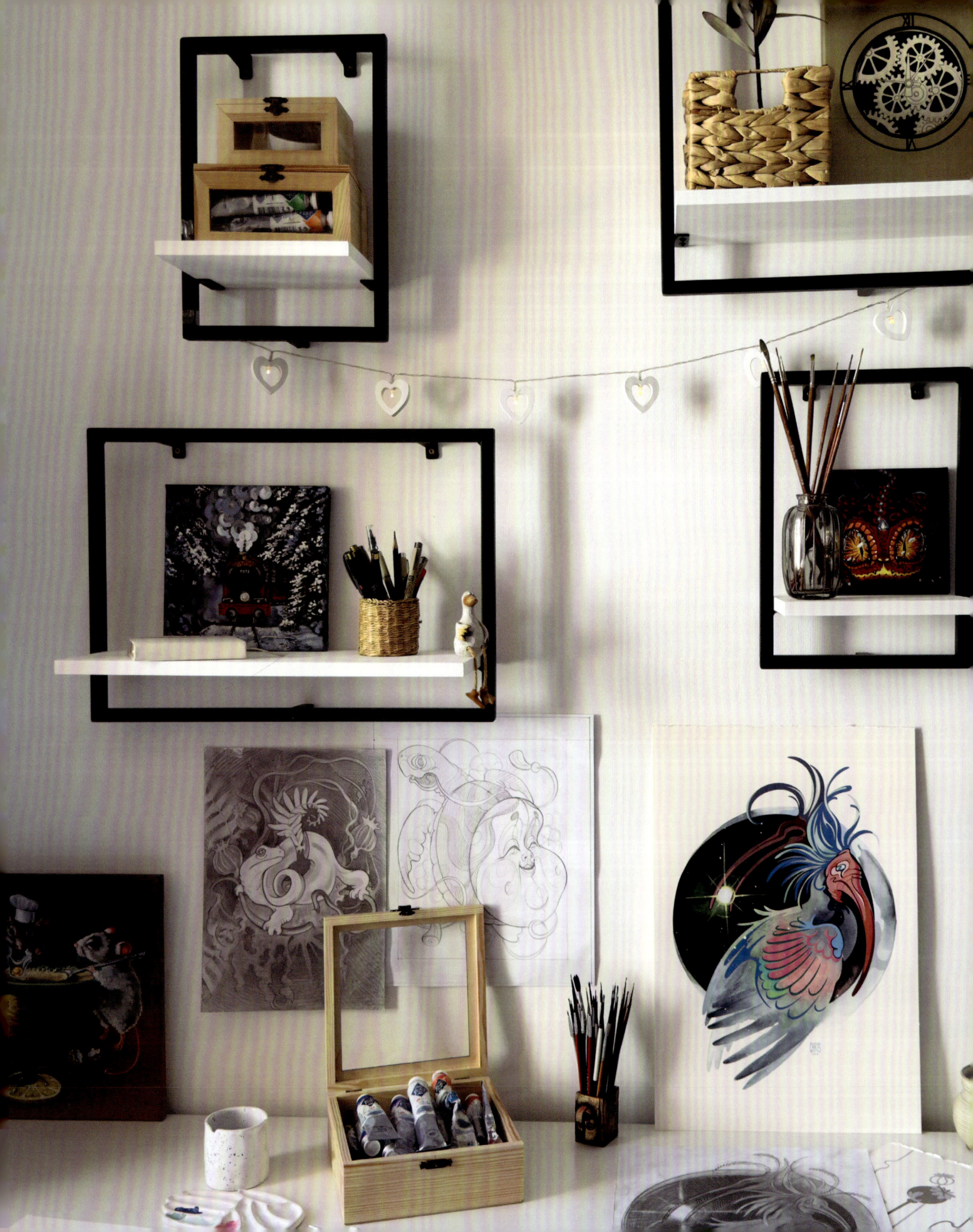

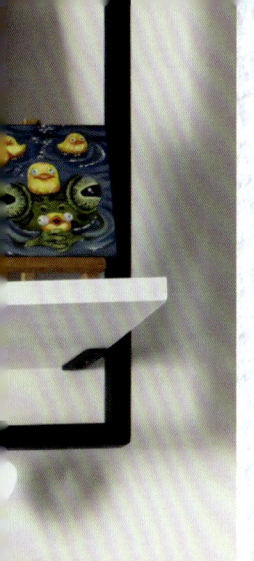

Behind the scenes

WORKSPACE

During my studies, my workspace became super chaotic. I'm not a fan of creative clutter, and working with oil paints or charcoal didn't exactly help the situation. Today, I've made sure the spaces I work in have 'breathing room'. I always put away all tools and materials I'm not using, leaving only what is necessary for my current work.

It's a small space, but I'm happy with it – it has everything I need to meet my main criteria.

LIGHTING

One of the most important things for my workspace is a good lighting set-up. Too much light can negatively impact my work just as much as a lack of light can. That's why placing my desk to sit opposite a window that doesn't get direct sunlight is the perfect solution. When working with colour, and especially when choosing a palette, it's crucial for me to be able to see all the shades in natural light. I learned this lesson in college when I painted at night with artificial lighting and had to redo everything during daylight hours.

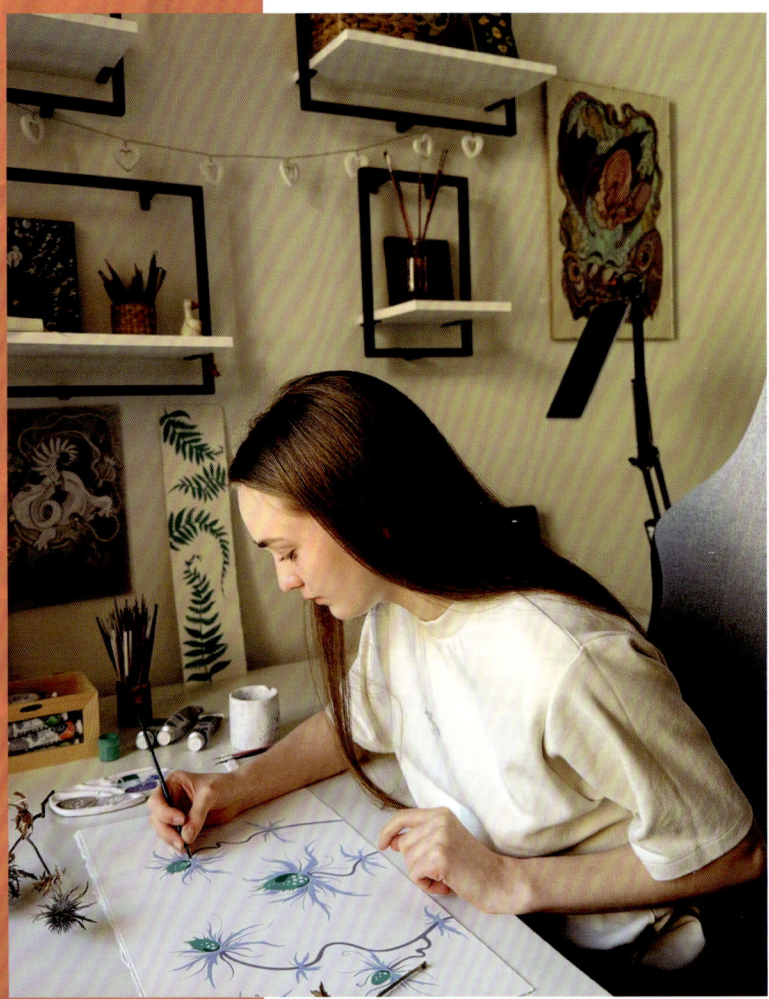

ORDER

As I mentioned above, my creative space can't be overloaded with unnecessary trifles, so all unneeded materials are stored on their respective shelves. I work with the bare minimum laid out on the table, and I always find time to thoroughly clean up after I'm done. It's a little ritual that helps me recharge and organize my thoughts.

COMFORT

Working in the same position hour after hour can take its toll on your body. For me, a comfortable, supportive chair makes all the difference, saving me from back pain that can occur after several hours of constant painting. The same applies to materials: do yourself a favour and arrange your tools so that the process is more enjoyable and, hopefully, pain-free. Though it is a stationary endeavour, creating art does not exempt artists from developing ailments like wrist, arm, or neck pain, which can happen at any age.

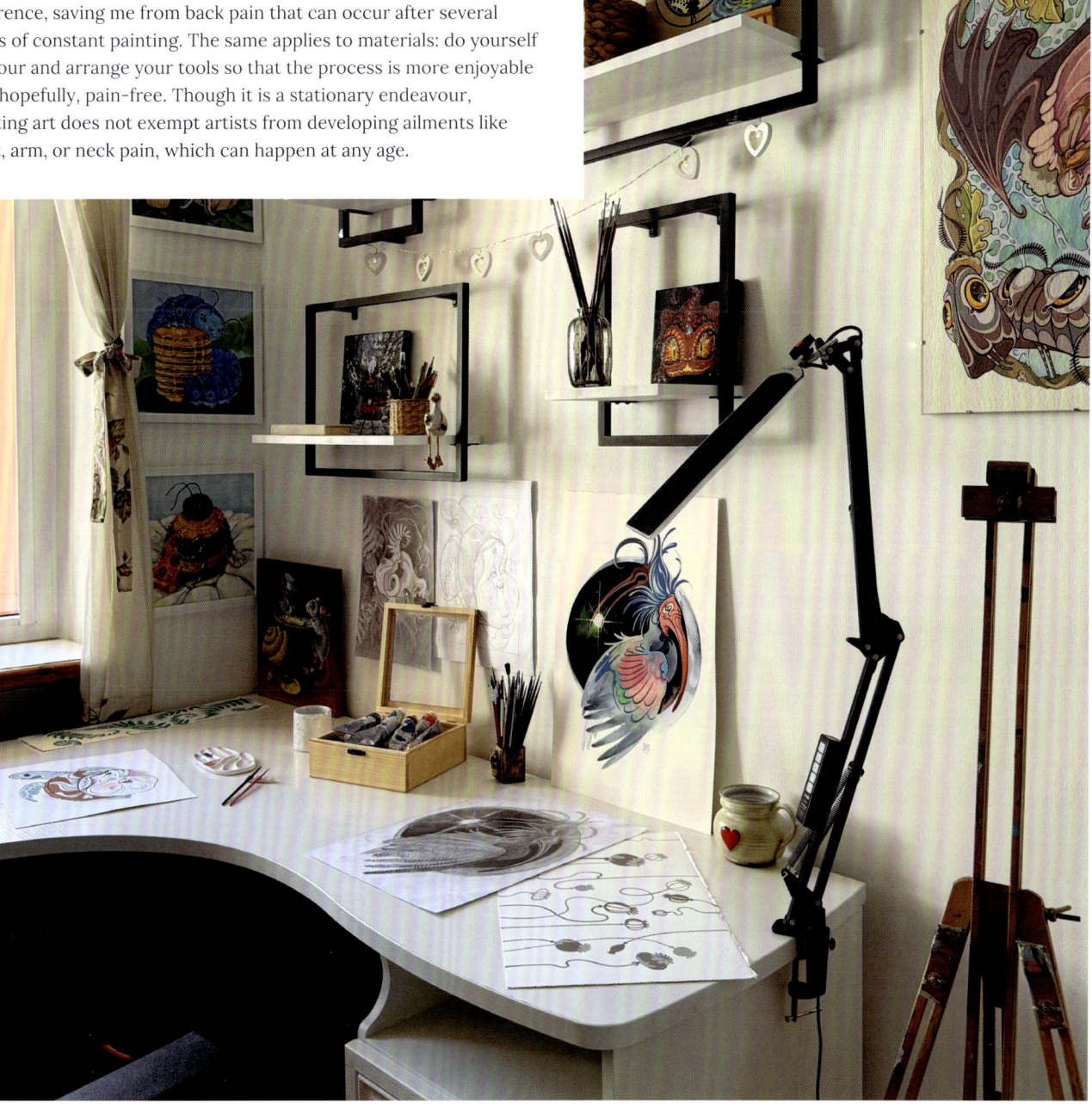

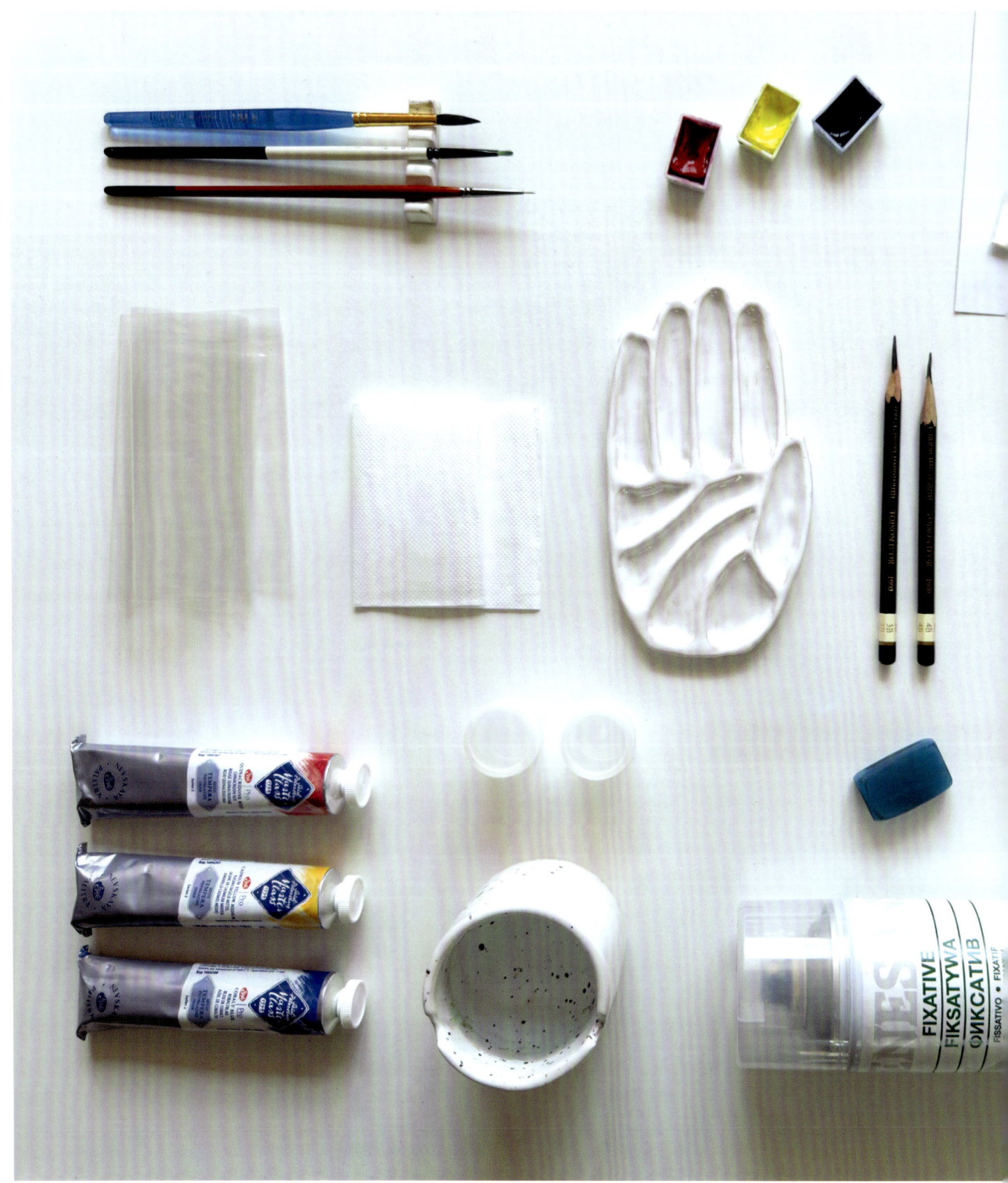

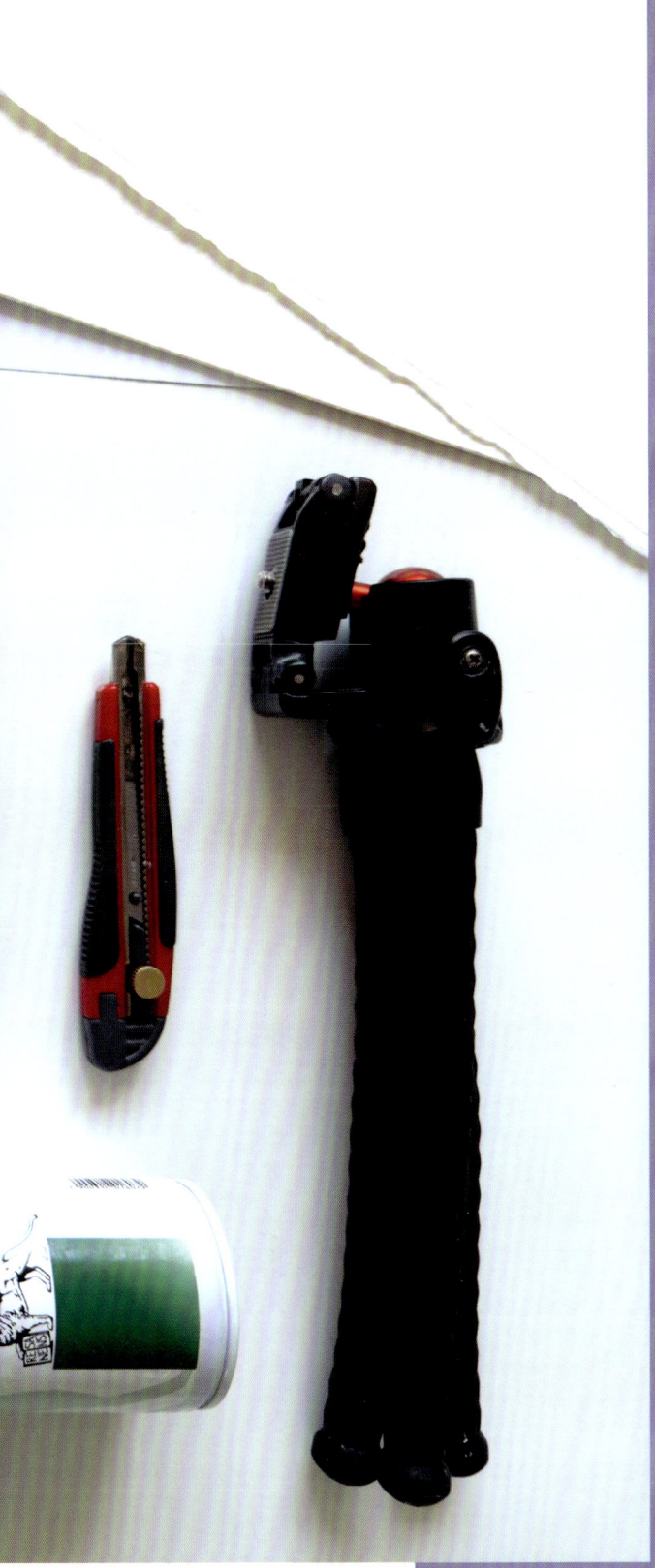

TOOLS & MATERIALS

1. PALETTE. I use a glazed ceramic palette, which doesn't absorb pigment and is easy to clean, even when the paint fully dries.

2. BRUSHES. I prefer synthetic brushes. Natural ones (made from animal fur) are usually too soft for tempera paints.

3. TEMPERA PAINT. I use tempera from the brand Master Class.

4. WATERCOLOUR PAINTS. I don't use them often, but sometimes watercolour is the best medium to evoke feelings of lightness and background depth.

5. JARS. For storing mixed colours when working on large areas or pieces.

6. PENCILS. I prefer 4B and 3B, as they are soft but also provide a controlled line.

7. ERASER. For erasing pencil marks, of course.

8. STATIONERY KNIFE. A versatile tool for sharpening pencils and cutting paper into the desired size.

9. PAPER TOWEL. Always at hand to remove excess water from the brush.

10. FILM. I use this to cover the palette while painting to prevent premature drying.

11. TRIPOD. A compact, tabletop tripod to make filming easier.

12. PAPER. For sketching, I use ordinary drawing paper. For painting, I prefer watercolour paper made of 100% cotton and 640 gsm density – mostly hot-pressed, smooth, and great for details. Sometimes, I choose a coarse-grain paper to experiment with texture.

13. RENESANS FIXATIVE. This is for additional protection of finished works. Before buying this product, make sure you're getting the correct one for your needs. For example, the fixative variety that I use is suitable for pencils and paints.

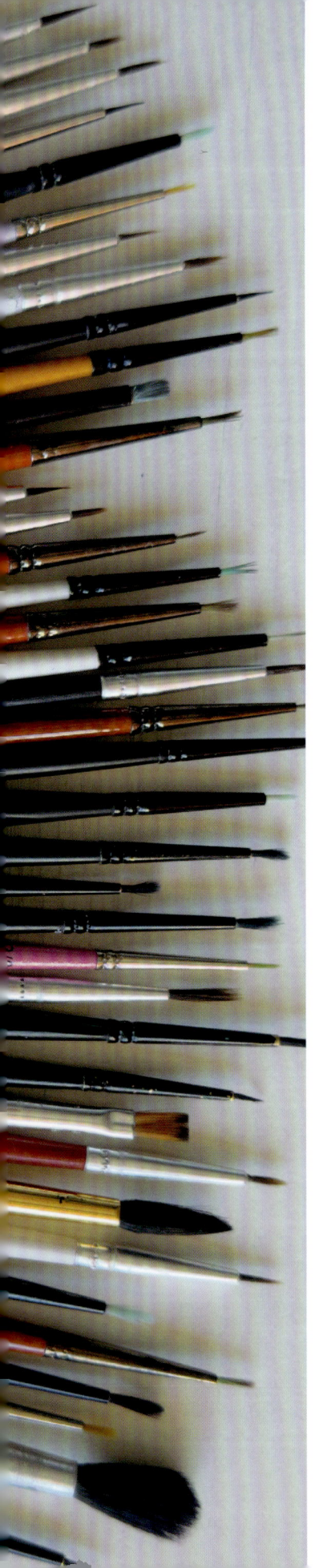

TEMPERA PAINTS

Traditionally, tempera paint is made by combining water, egg yolks, and pigment. Just like with baking, the egg works as a binder, while the pigment supplies the colour. My father used tempera when he painted, making the mixture himself and using it alongside store-bought paints. When I started college, he gave me his box of materials, and I haven't looked back since. However, this type of paint isn't often made with egg yolks anymore and there are different synthetics available.

That being said, tempera was not popular among my peers. They opted for the usual acrylics and gouaches for their academic work. Of course, I tried them too, but I never felt as strong a connection to those paints as I did with tempera. It laid differently; *felt* different. As I got more and more used to it, I continued exploring its possibilities in college and on my own.

However, tempera doesn't come without its obstacles. Sometimes, the compositions don't seem to work and I end up sitting on them for a long time, or the colours don't match my vision and I have to find a way to fix them. It's not an easy medium to master – definitely not as easy as it looks in the videos I post to social media. I often read comments like 'It looks so easy!' or 'You don't make mistakes.' But in reality, the process is much slower than it looks, and yes, of course I make mistakes.

Despite the difficulties, I am motivated to keep moving forwards through discipline, support from the closest people around me, and the strong desire to bring the rest of my ideas to life. Those things make up the core reason why I continue to do what I do.

> 'Traditionally, tempera paint is made by combining water, egg yolks, and pigment'

FEATURES OF TEMPERA

Tempera paints are water soluble and the binders are either natural or, more commonly, synthetic. There are many types of tempera, each with its own character, so in this book I will focus only on the one I use – a synthetic tempera based on PVA (polyvinyl acetate) as a binder. Unlike natural tempera (the egg-yolk variety), it does not have a strong odour. Tempera can be applied in both a thick, saturated layer and a thin, translucent layer. It dries quickly, which is another advantage for me. However, there are nuances: different pigments behave differently. Some colours harden almost instantly, while others take longer.

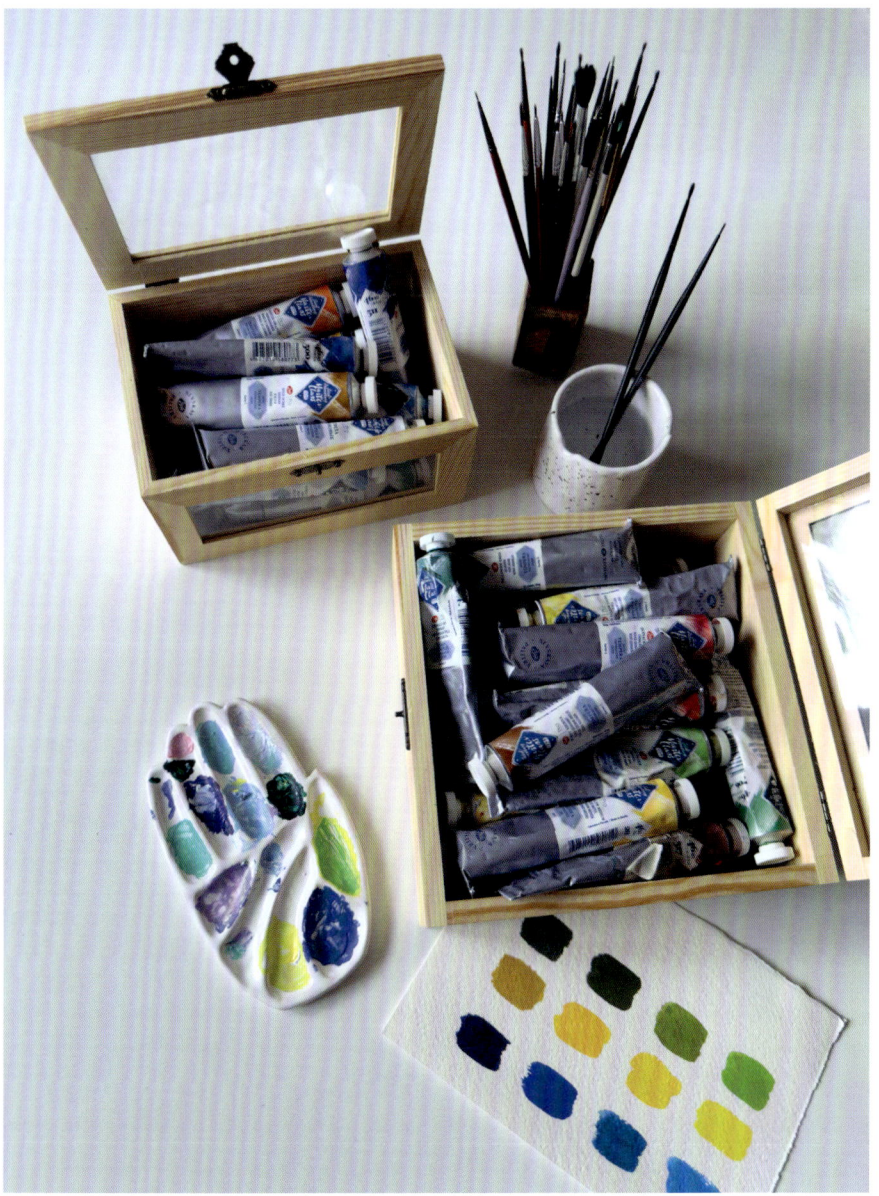

CHANGING COLOURS

Tempera paint colours tend to change when they dry. Light and medium tones usually become darker and dark tones lighten slightly. Over time, I learned to intuitively predict these changes, but just in case, I always keep a sheet of paper nearby to test how a particular shade will settle. Tempera has a wonderful matt texture that gives the finished work a nice velvety appearance.

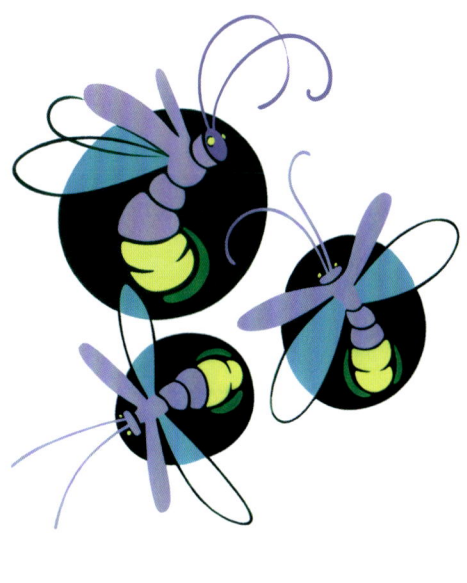

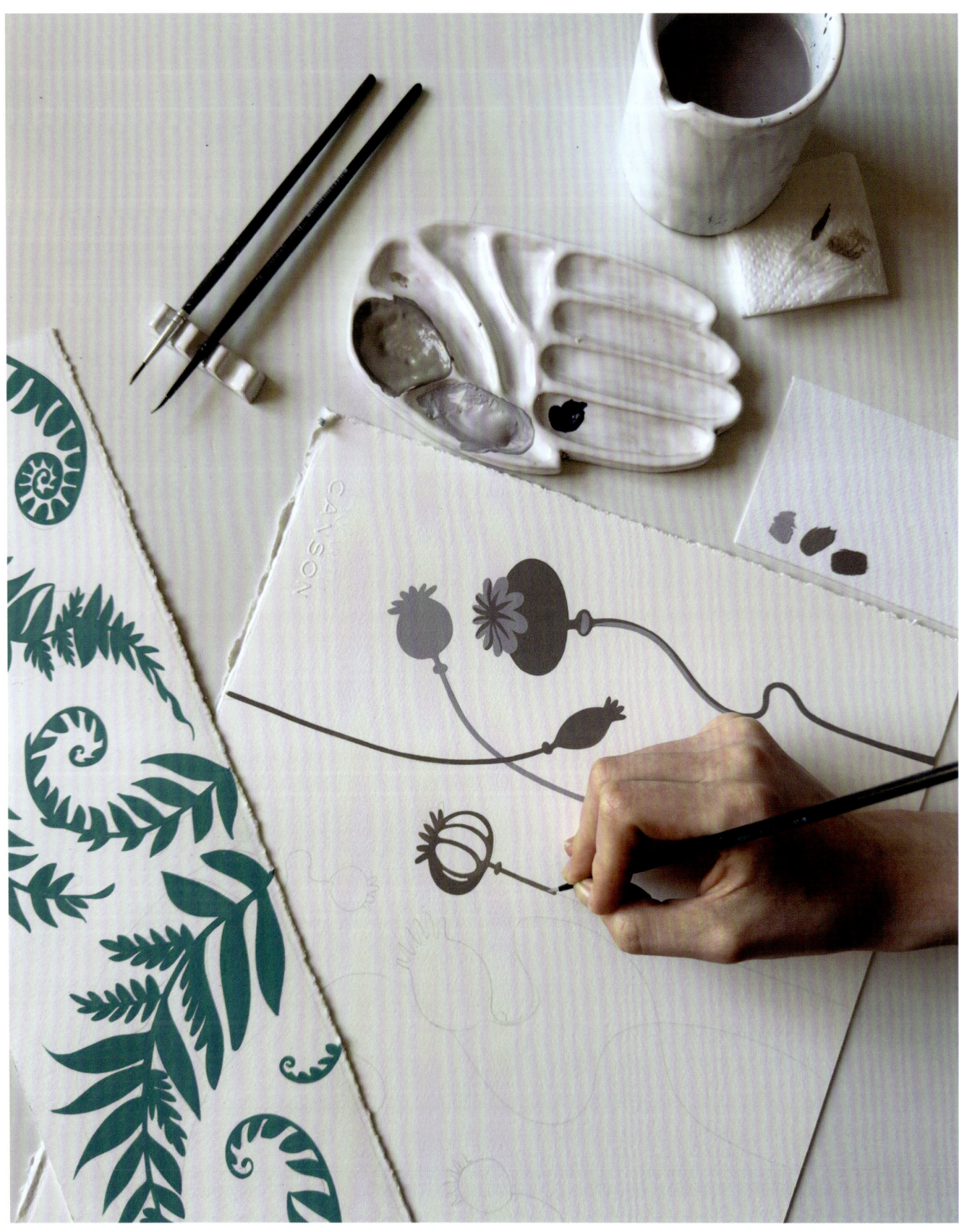

'After finishing the painting, the brushes must be washed with soap and water'

BRUSH CARE

Tempera can easily destroy brushes if you don't keep an eye on their condition. To avoid this happening, I always make sure my brushes are wet while working. I use several brushes at a time, keeping the warm, cold, light, and dark shades separate. While working with one colour, I dip the others in clean water. After finishing the painting, the brushes must be washed with soap and water, otherwise they will quickly deteriorate.

HOW IT DIFFERS FROM GOUACHE

The key difference is that tempera forms a dense film after drying. Technically, you can try to dissolve it using water, but it harms the structure of the paper. Instead, if the colour doesn't work, it's best to cover it with a new layer. This is especially convenient for me, as I can apply clear lines and stains on top of the existing layers.

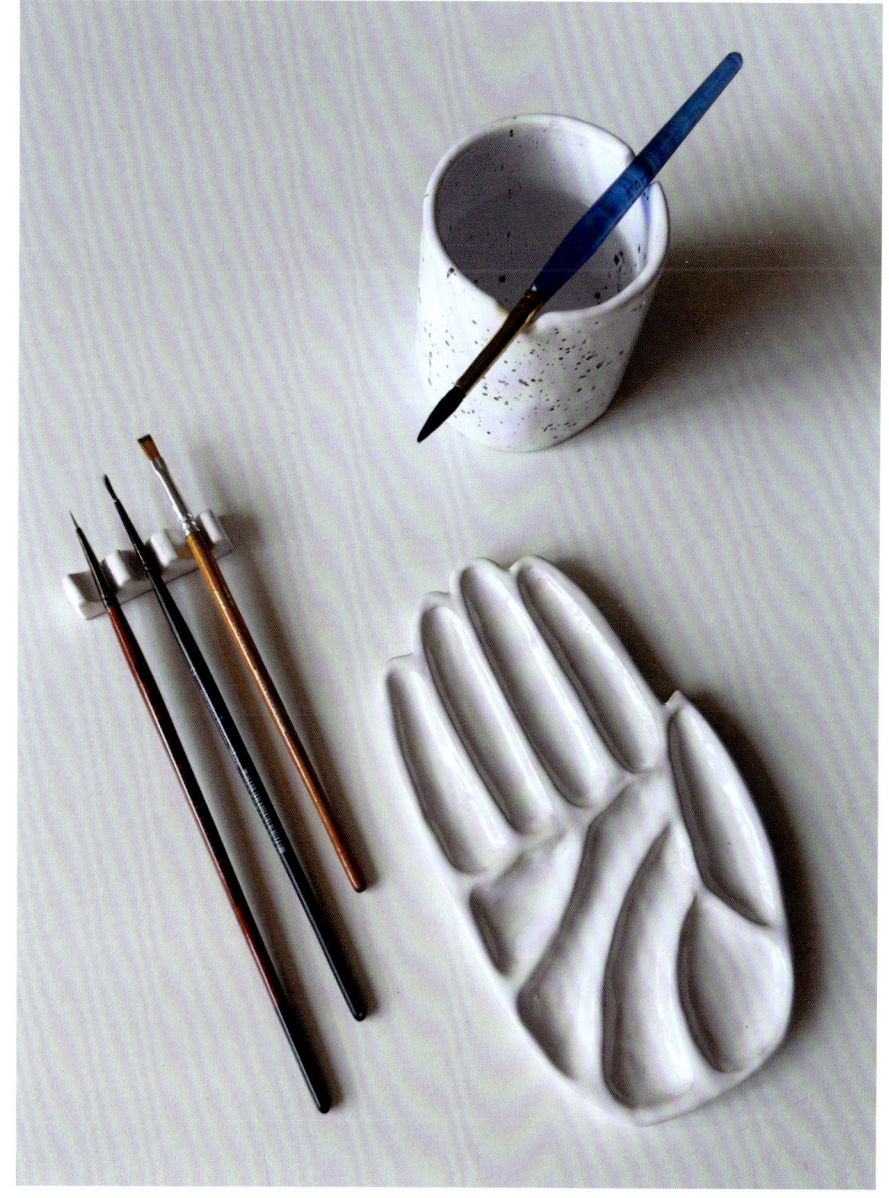

VIDEO PRODUCTION

Social-media promotion is not my favourite thing. I must admit, forming business strategies and communicating with the public on a daily basis tends to exhaust me. During my studies, I really wanted to exclusively devote my remaining time to something I was passionate about. I didn't have time to draw as often as I would have liked, but my online audience continued to grow. Each new video I posted brought thousands, sometimes tens of thousands of new followers and subscribers and, as a result, potential commissions. This has shown me that while account management is important, sincerity and authenticity of content can also catch people's attention.

My first videos were slow, more about the atmosphere than the process itself. I was experimenting, filming everything, trying different formats, spying on interesting ideas from other artists. Sometimes I painted portraits and other times I made small illustrations based on characters suggested by my followers. Over time I gained experience, and as I got closer to my current art style, my filming approach also became more refined. My goal was to show the whole painting process, from the first stroke to the final result. If a colour seemed perfect in the process shot but turned out differently after drying, I would correct it off-screen.

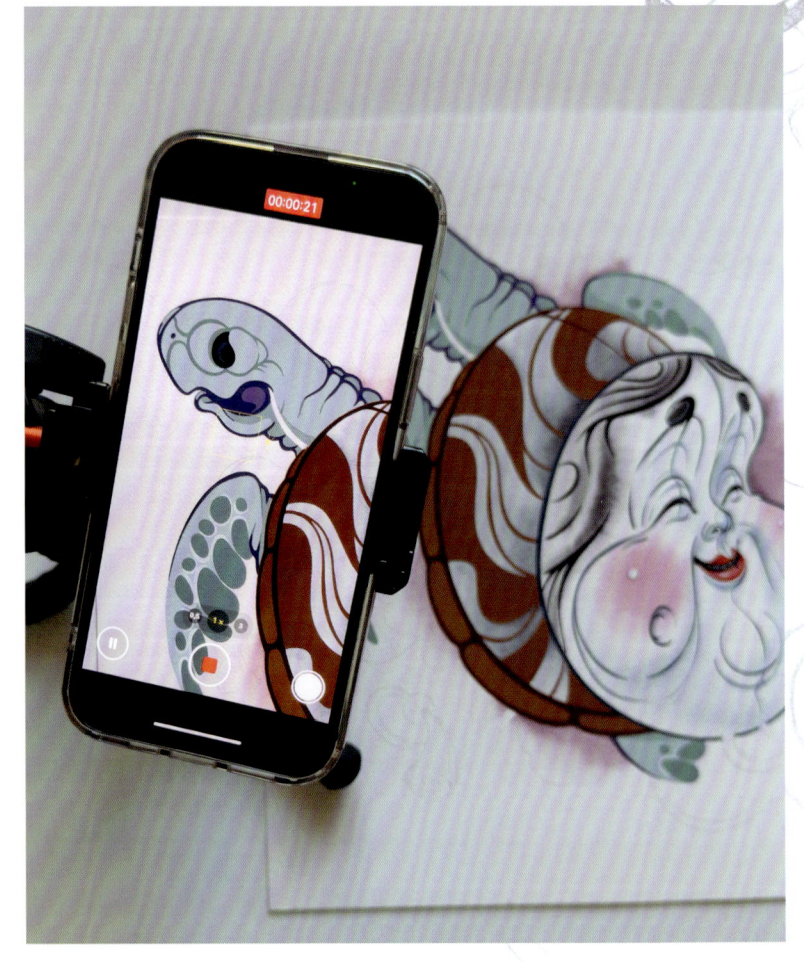

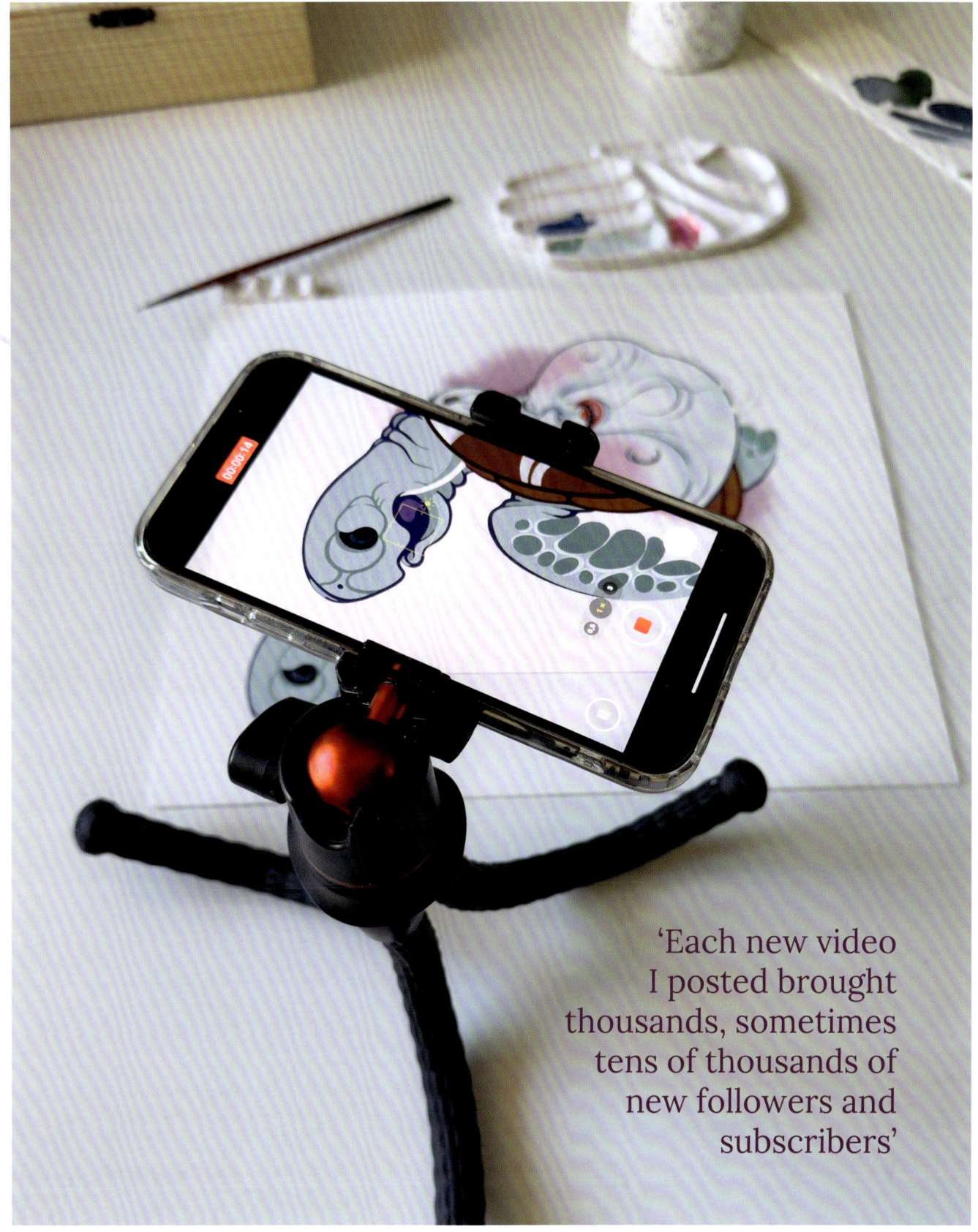

'Each new video
I posted brought
thousands, sometimes
tens of thousands of
new followers and
subscribers'

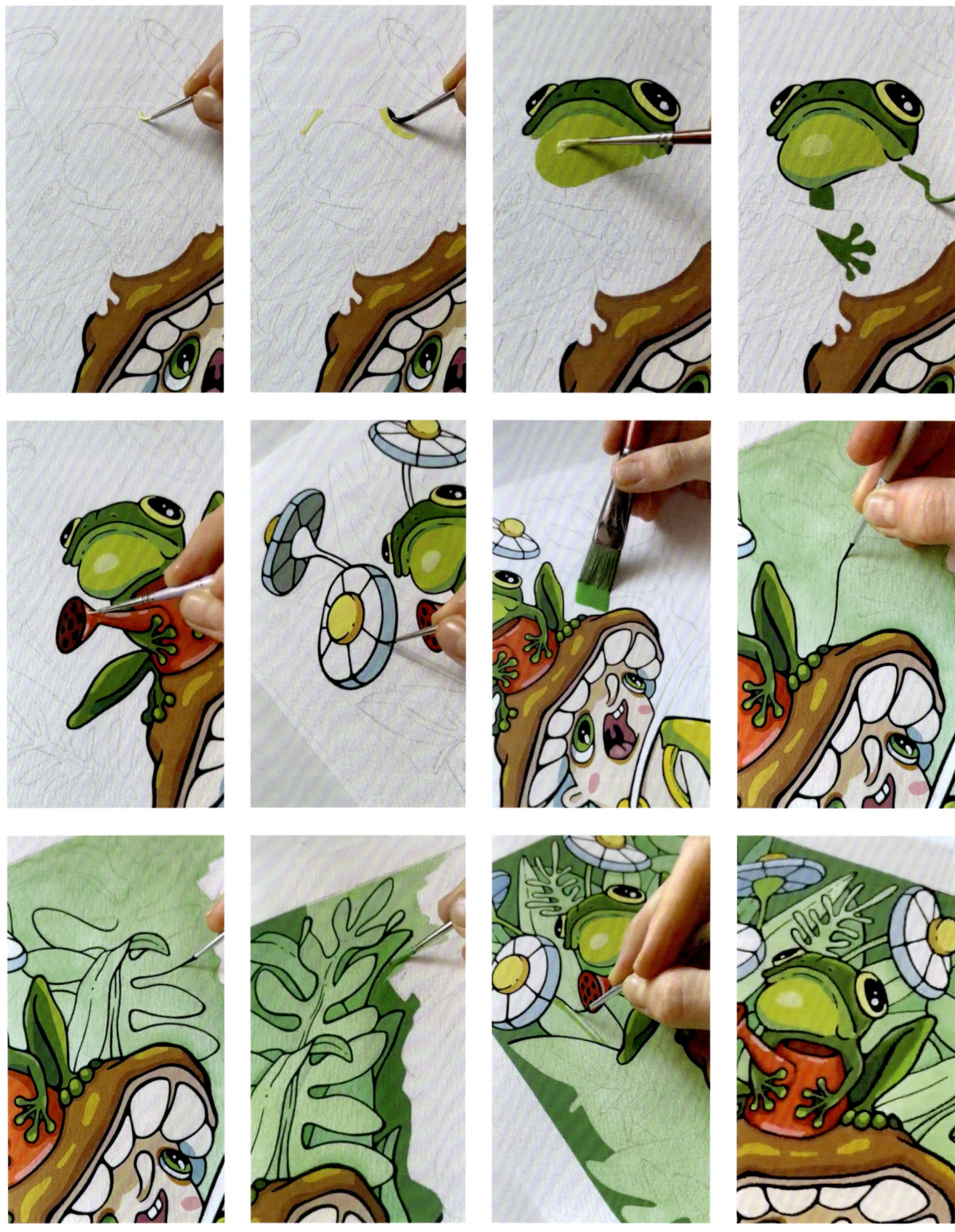

How I record videos

My videos mainly consist of short snippets where I try to capture just one brushstroke at a time. I will record the first frame, then stop filming to continue a small part of the work off-camera. When I resume filming, I keep the same camera angle. I will sometimes zoom in closer during the editing stage, and sometimes I'll mix things up and change perspective, but I always try to have several shots in a row from the same place.

Editing

Editing is super time-consuming. In order to not overload myself, I tend to edit gradually, taking my time just as I would with the painting itself.

I normally end up with about 100 to 200 frames. From each frame, I select one stroke and cut the shot to make it look like my hand never lifts from the canvas. This creates a smooth transition between frames and gives the illusion of lightness.

I also speed up all my videos. I want to show the most interesting shots, and without a dynamic pace, many viewers will simply skip to the final result.

Music

A good piece of music can add emotional context and help keep viewers' attention. First of all, it should be in harmony with the visuals and enhance perception. Most of my videos are quite dynamic due to the constant change of frames, so I usually choose music with a fast pace and bright rhythm. However, it's important that the music does not overpower the artwork and distract viewers. Sometimes I manage to find tracks that resonate with the theme of the painting, and that seems to work really well. There are also trending songs on social media that artists use often because it helps attract new viewers. I understand this logic, but in my opinion, these songs are not always suitable for art content, or can make the videos feel more monotonous than they're supposed to be. It's important to choose music that you like. Everyone has their own taste, so trying to always adapt to the preferences of others is unrealistic.

RECEPTION

Despite the fact that filming takes a long time and can affect the work, it has become an integral part of my process. I created videos that I wanted to watch myself and believed there would be viewers who would share my enthusiasm. As I later learned from the comments on my social-media platforms, watching my videos has a calming effect for many people. It motivates me to produce more and reach new people, all in a way that feels organic and authentic to me.

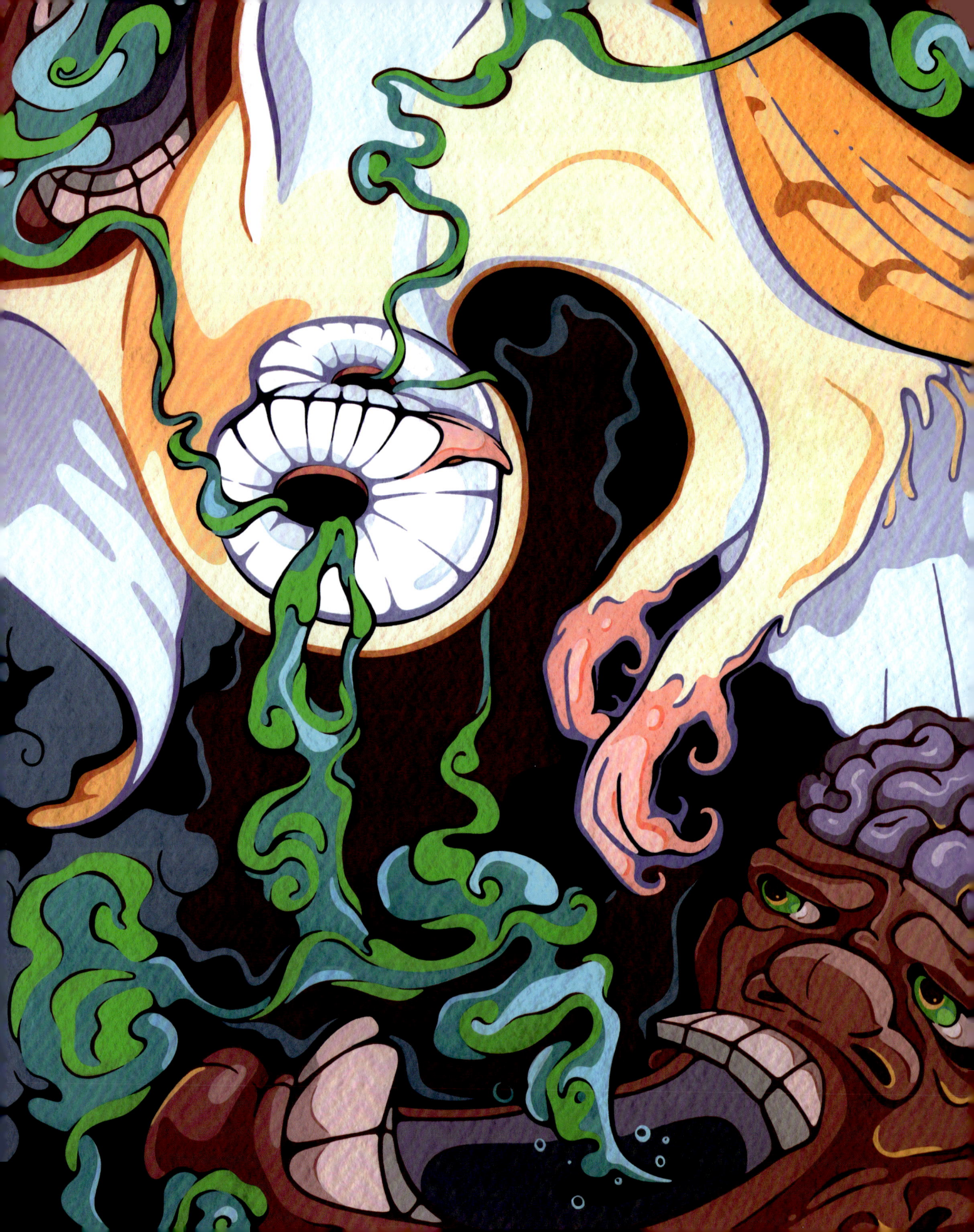

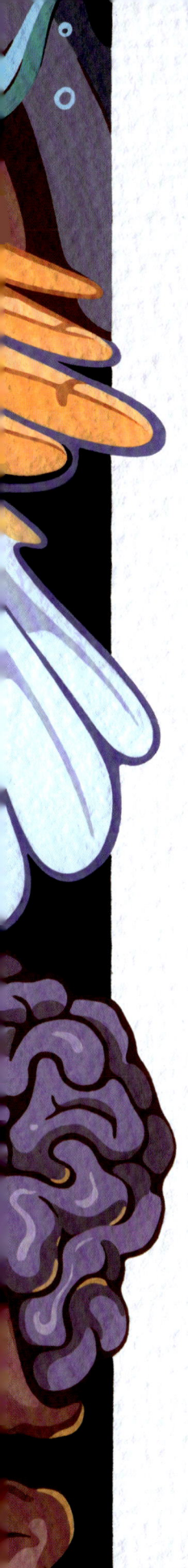

Creative
process

SELF-EXPRESSION

For me, self-expression in art is a way to make your inner world visible; to reflect the workings of the human soul.

INDIVIDUALITY

The way I create art has always depended on my attitude towards life. Both negative and positive experiences have shaped my techniques and become a part of my artistic style. Since what I feel is invisible to others, my goal is to convey my deepest emotions through my artwork; thoughts and desires I normally keep to myself. Consciously or not, everyone expresses their individuality in one way or another.

CAPTURING EMOTION

Shyness is something I struggle with. Sometimes I can be withdrawn, other times indecisive. But when it comes to art, I feel the opposite: emboldened and in my element. Art is where I find my strength. As such, I try to convey a variety of repressed emotions by using rich colours to paint thought-provoking images. It's not the animal or creature I draw that is the thing of importance, but rather the emotion they reflect. That's where my interest in illustration lies.

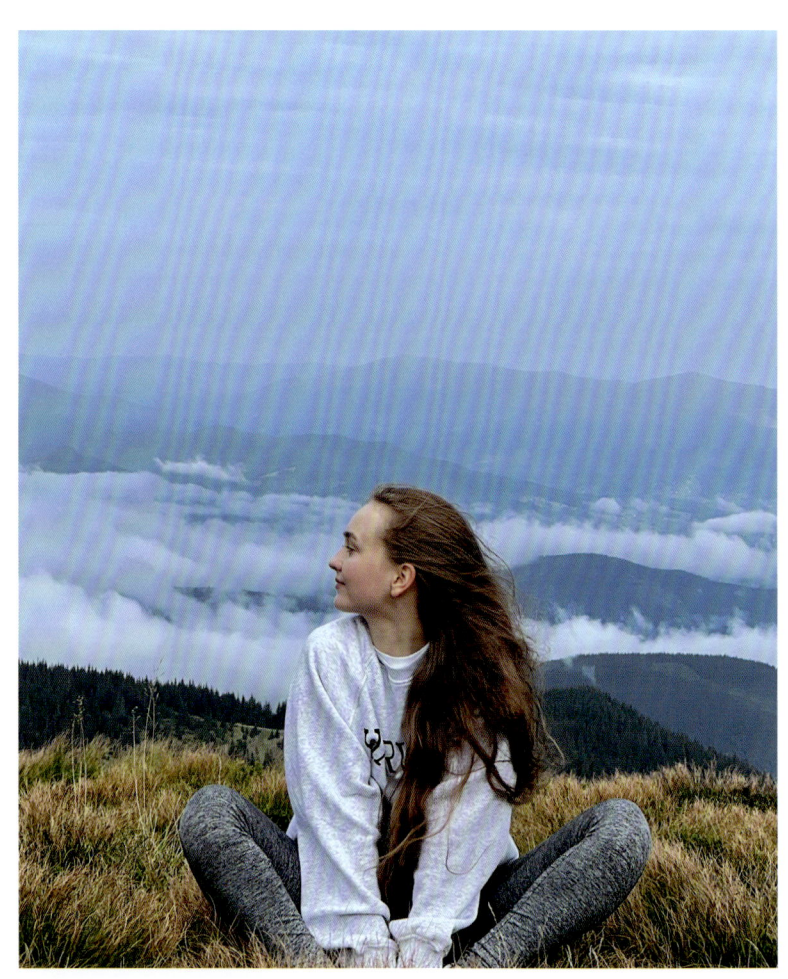

MAKING MISTAKES

Mistakes don't scare me. Of course, it wasn't always that way, but over time I learned to accept them. Now, I might get a little mad at myself for messing up, but then I can continue the process as if nothing happened. Each mistake becomes a tool to help me grow. If the paint spreads in a way I didn't intend or the brush slips out of my hand, I will treat it like a lesson. I'm not a perfectionist in life and don't strive for perfection in art, either. For me, flaws mean there is room to grow.

However, I do still try to make my paintings as clean and controlled as possible – after all, the sharp lines, precise shapes, and smooth layers of paint are what have drawn many people to my work. But this style, with its level of precision and attention to detail, can make me feel bogged down at times. I can easily get lost in reworking little things that no one else will notice.

Now, after many years of a consistent approach, I feel a strong desire to explore and experiment with new techniques. I have started to try combining tempera with watercolour, and this feels like an exciting venture into uncharted territory. I love to see the orderliness of tempera meeting the chaos of watercolour. You can see some of my experimentation with this new (to me) technique in the tutorials on pages 108 and 116.

TRADITIONAL VS DIGITAL

I've noticed that sometimes my illustrations are likened to digital art, which I find quite funny. Perhaps it's because they are primarily viewed on screens. These comparisons don't bother me at all; in fact, I find it fascinating how digital tools have evolved to replicate the nuances of traditional mediums. The ability to imitate the look of brushstrokes, pencil marks, watercolour bleeds, and paper textures is remarkable and blurs the lines between digital and traditional art.

However, my creative process remains deeply rooted in the physical world. Each illustration is the direct result of a tangible connection with brushes, paint, and paper. I believe that if I were to try and create these pieces digitally, the outcome would be different – the work would have a different feel for me personally. Even when my lines appear very clean, almost resembling those in a digital painting, they still possess a certain liveliness that I truly value and wouldn't exchange for anything else.

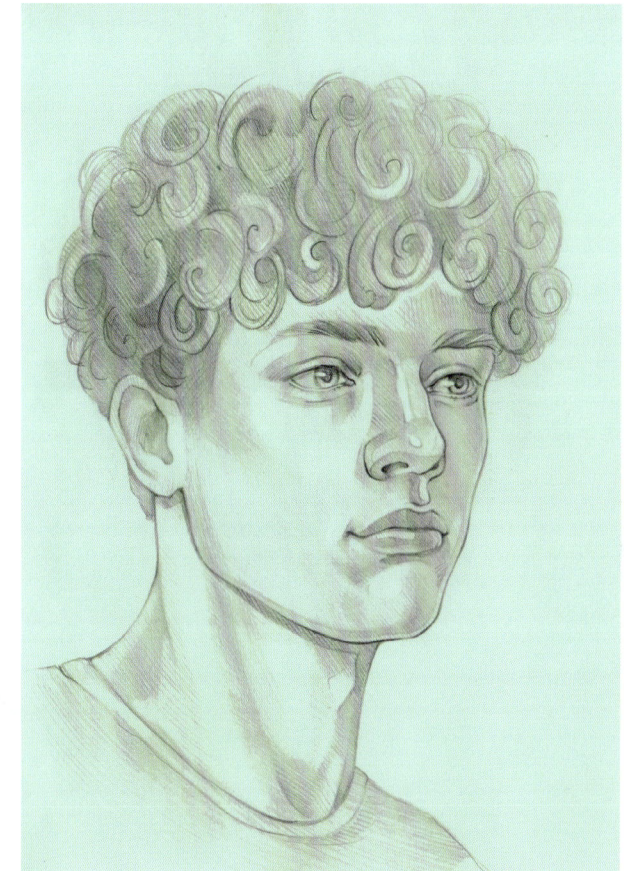

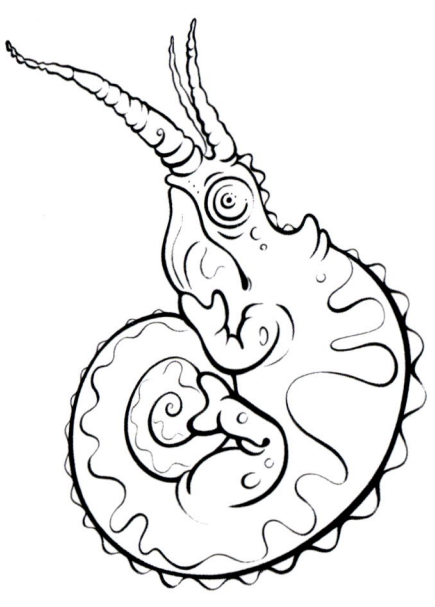

SOURCES OF INSPIRATION

Starting a piece used to be the hardest part for me. But once I found momentum and began to discover my style, inspiration came more easily.

During the period between college and university, as I searched for my artistic direction, I realized I needed time to reconnect with the creative process. It felt as though I had lost the imaginative freedom I experienced as a child. Gradually, I rediscovered this part of myself by making it a habit to paint what truly inspired me at least once a week. My desire to share my art and connect with others became a powerful driving force.

Now, my approach is different. Instead of waiting for inspiration to strike, I've found that drawing every day allows me to cultivate it more deliberately. The act of creation itself has become a source of inspiration. At any moment, I can sit down to work, and the process seems to unfold on its own.

MUSIC

My creative process is always accompanied by music. It helps me focus, sets my mood, gives me energy, and intensifies my emotions. It's the easiest way to ignite inspiration without any extra effort.

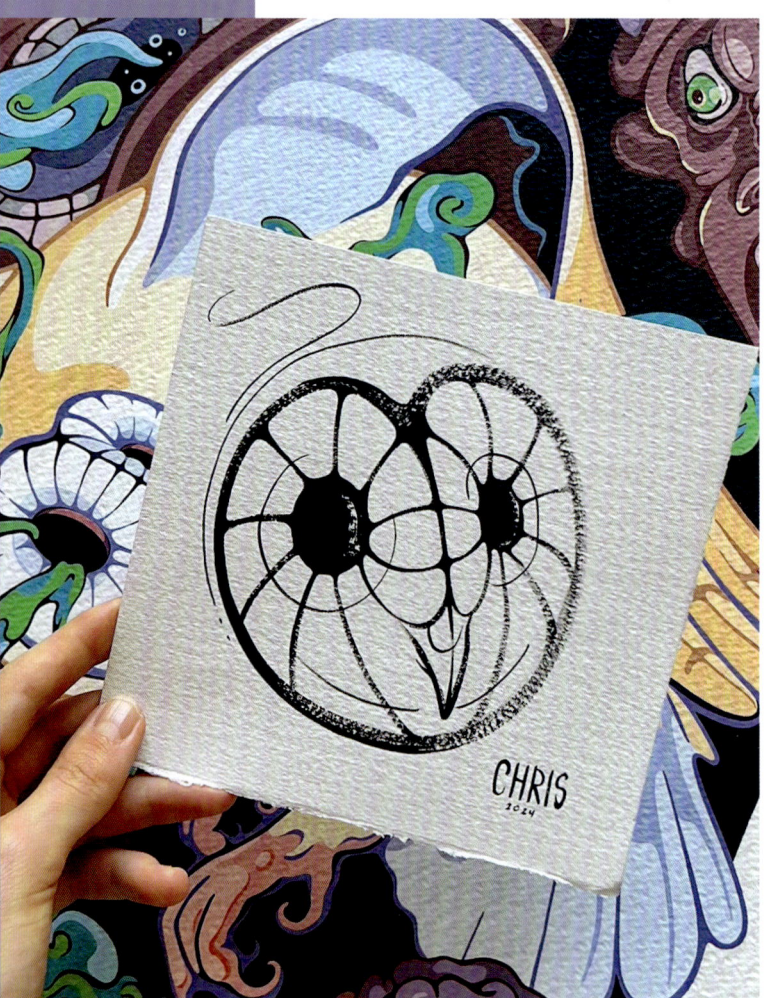

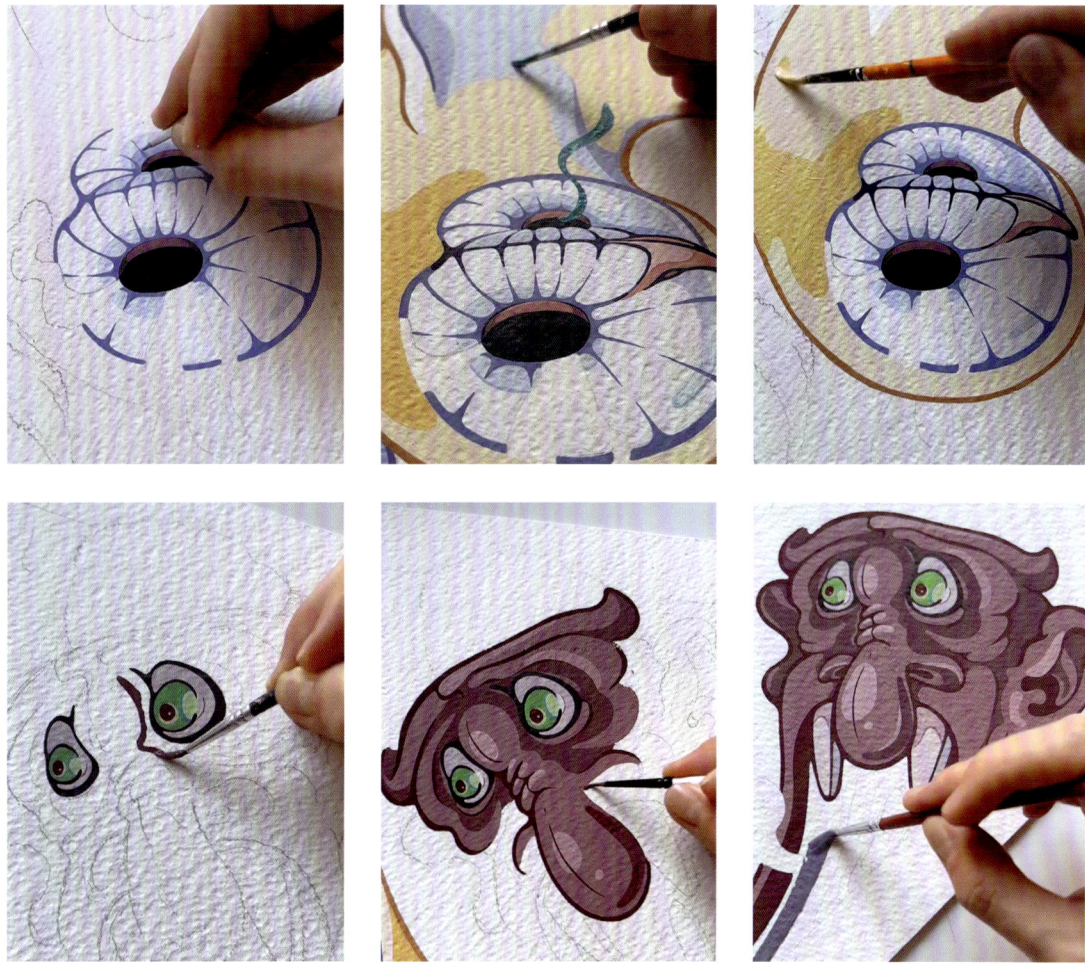

NATURE

I feel a deep connection with nature. As I mentioned previously, I grew up near the mountains, so the wilderness is an endless source of inspiration for me. One time, my friends and I climbed Mount Hoverla, the highest mountain in Ukraine, and the experience was worth the effort – challenging but beautiful. Moments like these give you the power to create. But you also don't need to climb a mountain to feel inspired by nature. For instance, there is a park near my house where I often walk my dog. For me, it's a time for observation and reflection where I can just stop and take in the world around me. Sometimes, creativity and motivation can be found in quieter, humbler spaces, too.

SPORTS

Going to the gym helps me disconnect for a little while. Now that it's become a habit, I've noticed how much easier it is to recover from intense periods of creative work. I try to avoid artistic burnout at all costs.

ART

While the need for external stimuli varies with my state of mind, I'm constantly absorbing interesting things around me. It's fascinating how a fleeting detail, particular colour palette, or the composition of an artwork can lodge itself in my memory. These elements then resurface later, often during period of reflection, and transform into new ideas. It's like a subconscious library that I draw upon when seeking fresh perspectives.

I also find that cinema, theatre, animation, illustration, and many other art forms leave a lasting impression on me. In particular, as a child, I adored the cartoon *The Three Robbers* (*Die drei Räuber*), which was brimming with imaginative concepts and wonderfully strange (and often quite distracting!) background elements.

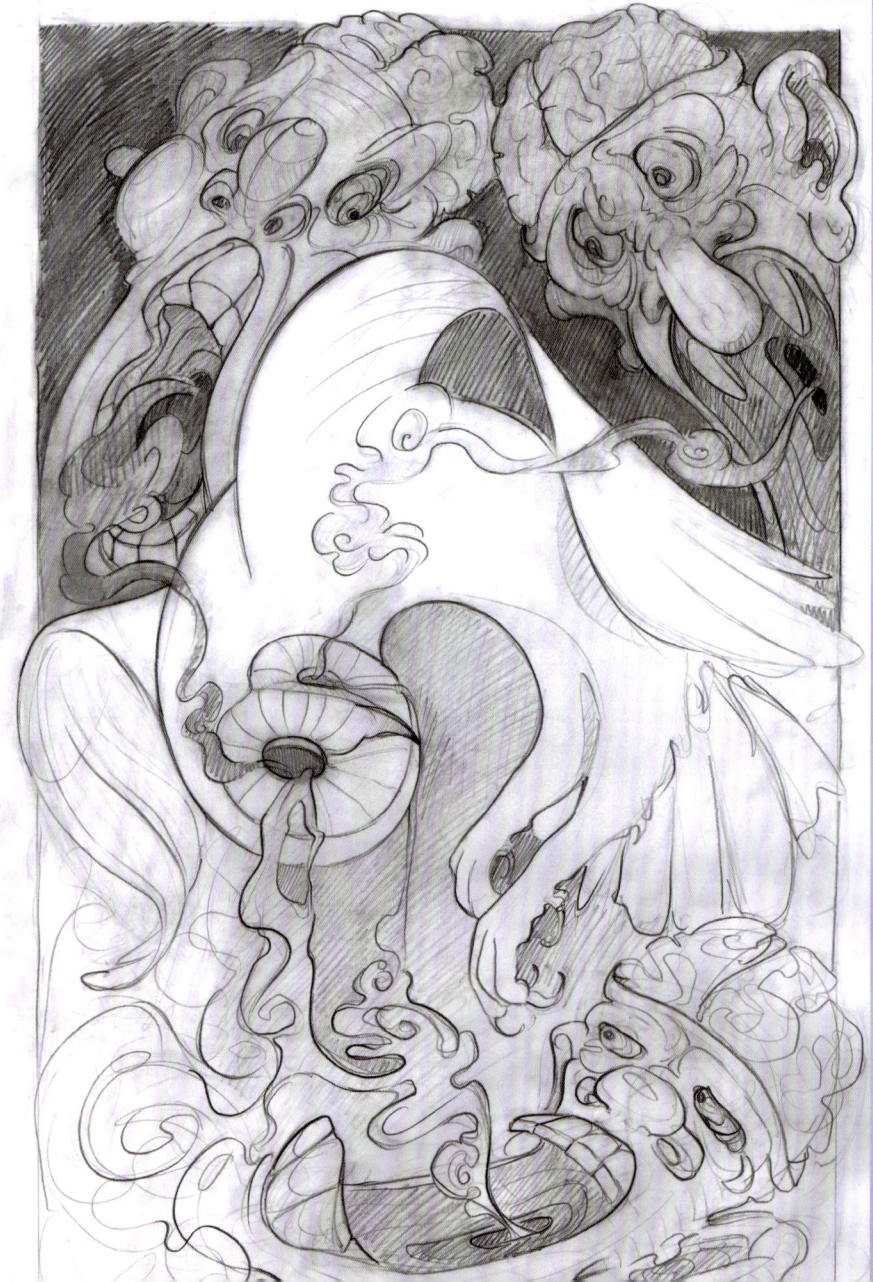

Emptiness, tempera, 2024.
The inspiration for this piece struck me quite unexpectedly after reading a novel by Stephen King. I was initially at a loss for a new subject and began sketching aimlessly. Soon, unsettling images began to surface, culminating in the silhouette of a creature with an exposed brain.

I embraced this moment and continued to draw similar figures, with the creative process unfolding naturally from there. While I found these faces intriguing, I felt they needed a grounding element to become the central focus. To contrast their emptiness, I decided to introduce an owl, which in many cultures symbolises wisdom. Ultimately, a narrative developed: the creatures are attempting to absorb the owl's mind, highlighting the dichotomy between those who possess knowledge and those who do not.

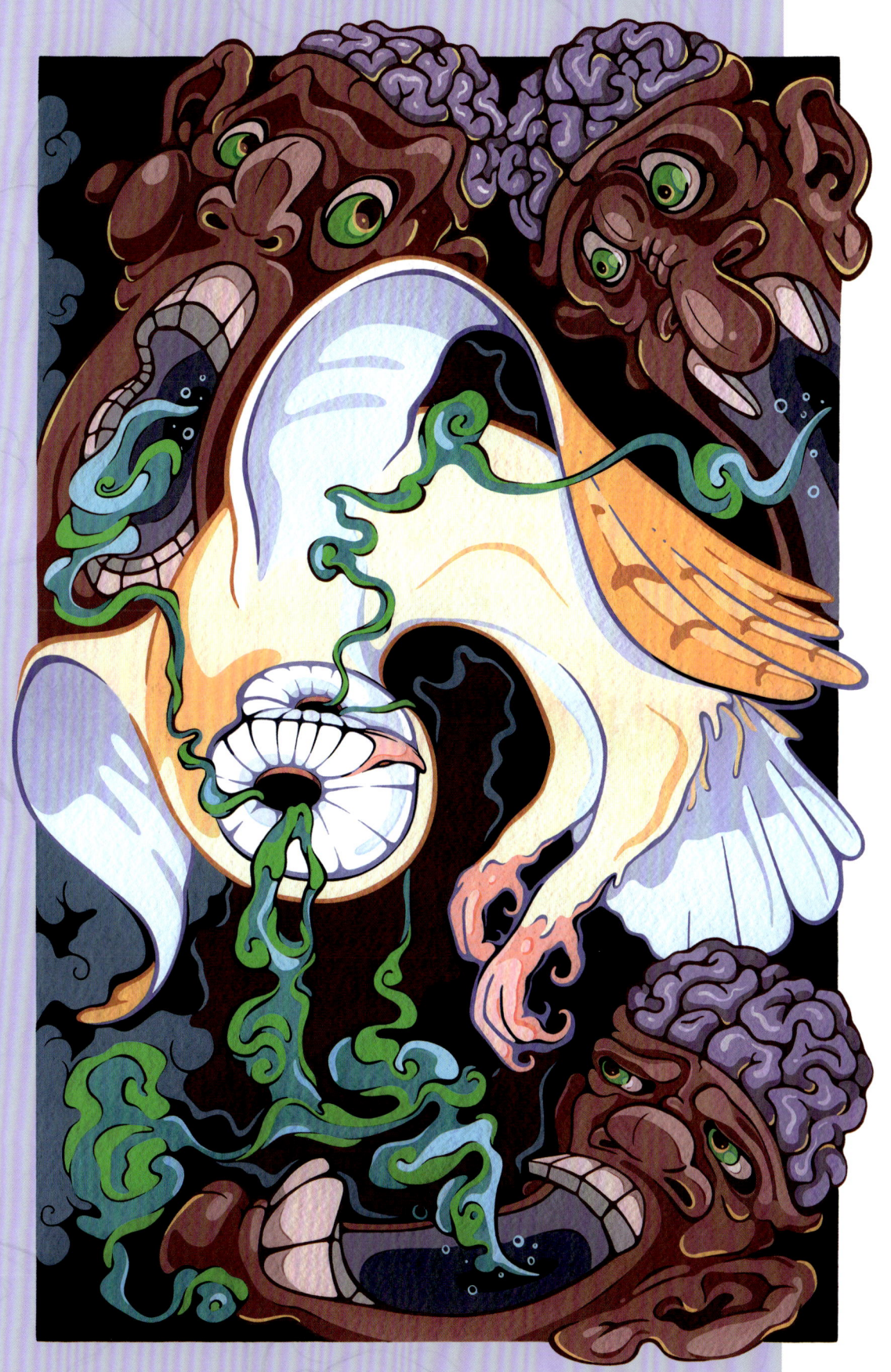

STYLE TRANSFORMATION

I believe an artist's style naturally emerges from their individual experiences, inner thoughts, and how they view the world. Because of this, finding one's style isn't a sudden event but rather an ongoing journey that evolves as the artist grows. The main challenge, I think, lies in the patience and dedication this process demands.

In the following section, I will discuss some key phases that shaped by own artistic transformation and guided me towards what now feels like my unique style.

FINDING A DIRECTION

Instead of seeking a specific style, I was aiming to understand my personal artistic inclinations. The influence of my formal studies was significant, making it difficult to understand my own preferences.

I've found that continually broadening my visual experiences and knowledge of the art world is key to self-discovery. While my college education provided a classical foundation, I initially lacked exposure to diverse, contemporary perspective. Discovering this variety has been instrumental in shaping my artistic viewpoint. Analysing elements like composition, colour palettes, forms, and subjects helps me pinpoint what resonates with me in the art I admire.

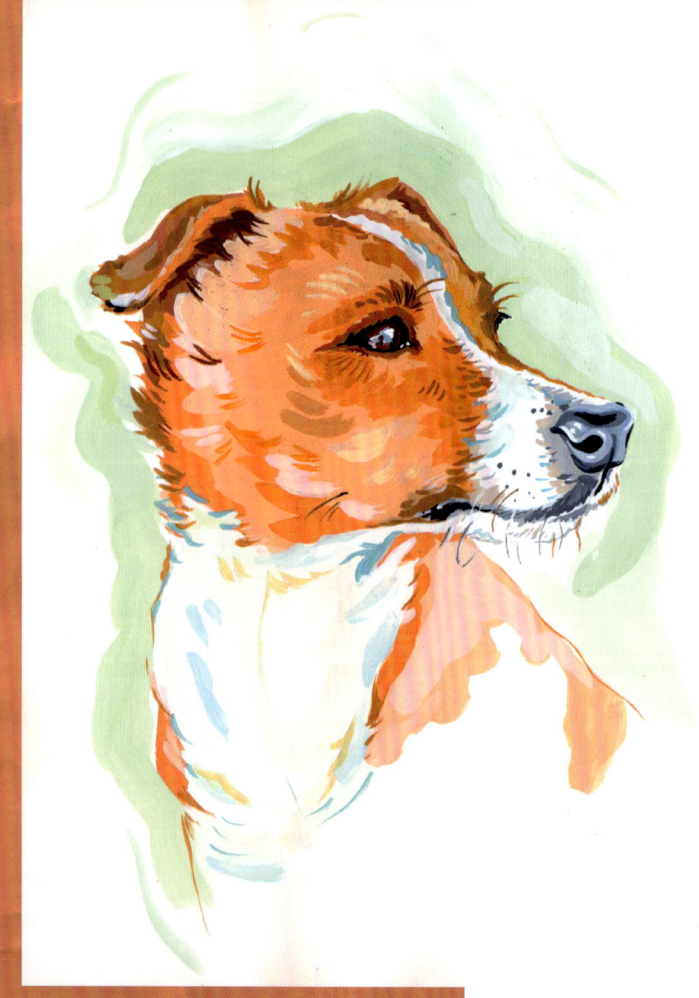

I've been inspired by many artists, even if my focus with each was brief: James Jean for his surrealistic imagery and layered colours; Wylie Beckert for her mystical atmospheres, deep muted tones, and enigmatic figures; and Kerby Rosanes for his intricate worlds built from countless small details.

Another significant revelation has been reconnecting with my past, specifically the uninhibited creativity of my childhood. Recalling childhood dreams, important events, and sources of genuine happiness can form the basis of a personal artistic language. I've recognized a lifelong passion for creating whimsical characters and a particular affinity for the world of flora and fauna.

Oil paintings, 2021. In these early works, it's clear that I was strongly influenced by the chiaroscuro techniques I learned in college. My approach was very traditional in that sense. As time passed, I developed an internal desire for something more decorative, stylized, and imbued with a sense of dreaminess

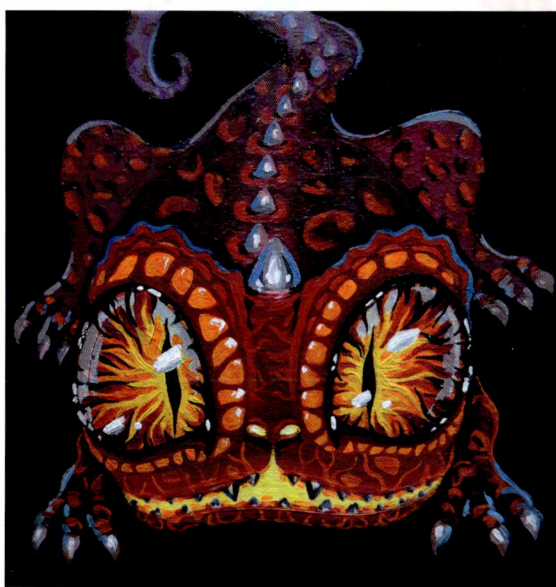

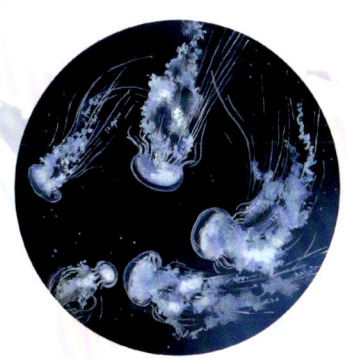

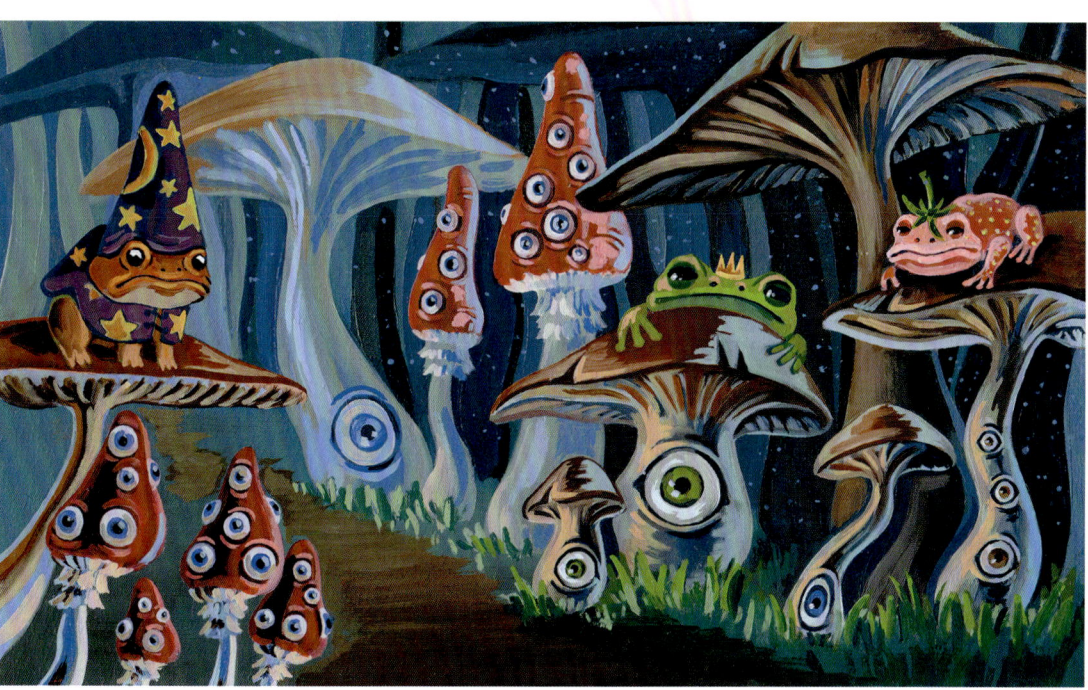

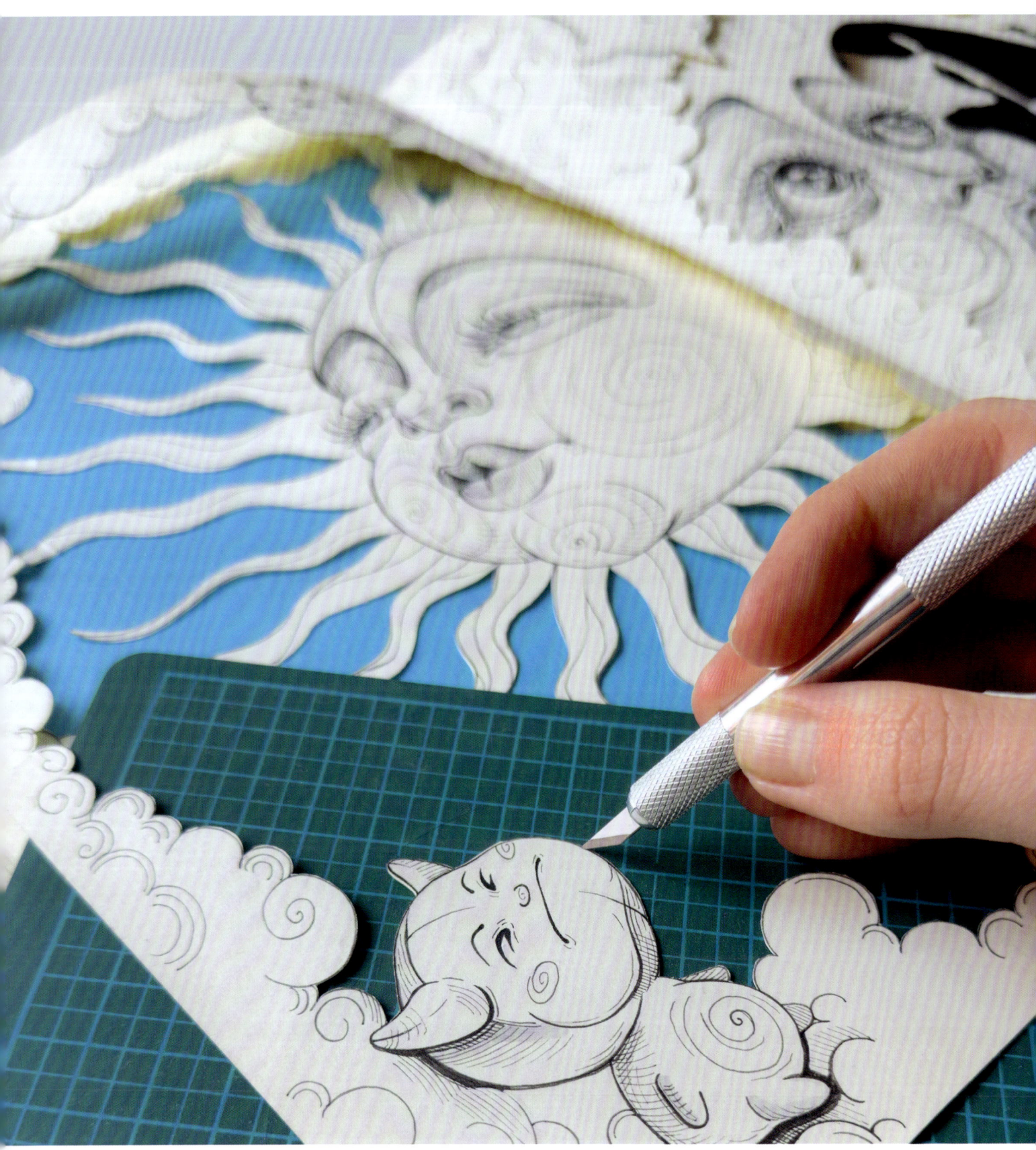

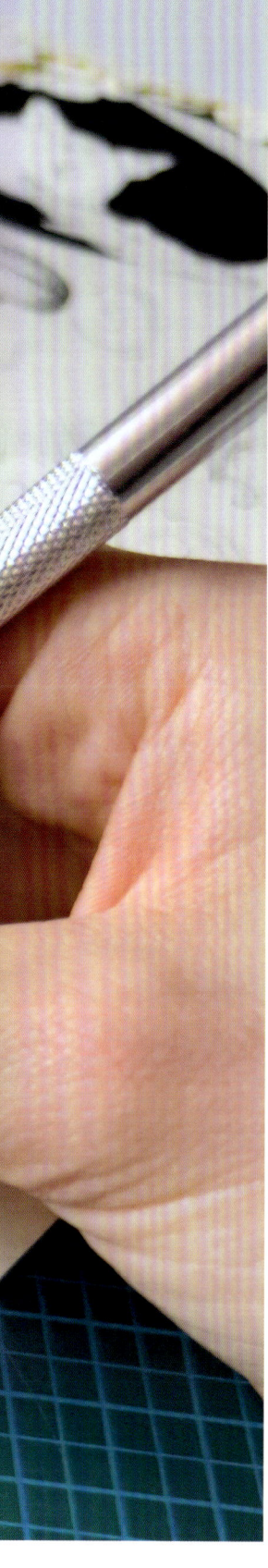

PRACTICE AND EXPERIMENTATION

Developing a unique style comes from consistently practising and revisiting your ideas. It's crucial to regularly draw, take a critical look at your work, identify what works well, and then build upon those successes. Experimentation is also essential in this process. Don't hesitate to try out different methods, combine them in unexpected ways, use a variety of paper types, and play with new colour palettes.

To further expand my abilities, I focused on teaching myself graphic illustration. This led me to spend more time on line work, gradually incorporating colour with mediums like coloured pencils, watercolour, or tempera. As I progressed, I transitioned from using sketchbooks to creating more substantial pieces on watercolour paper.

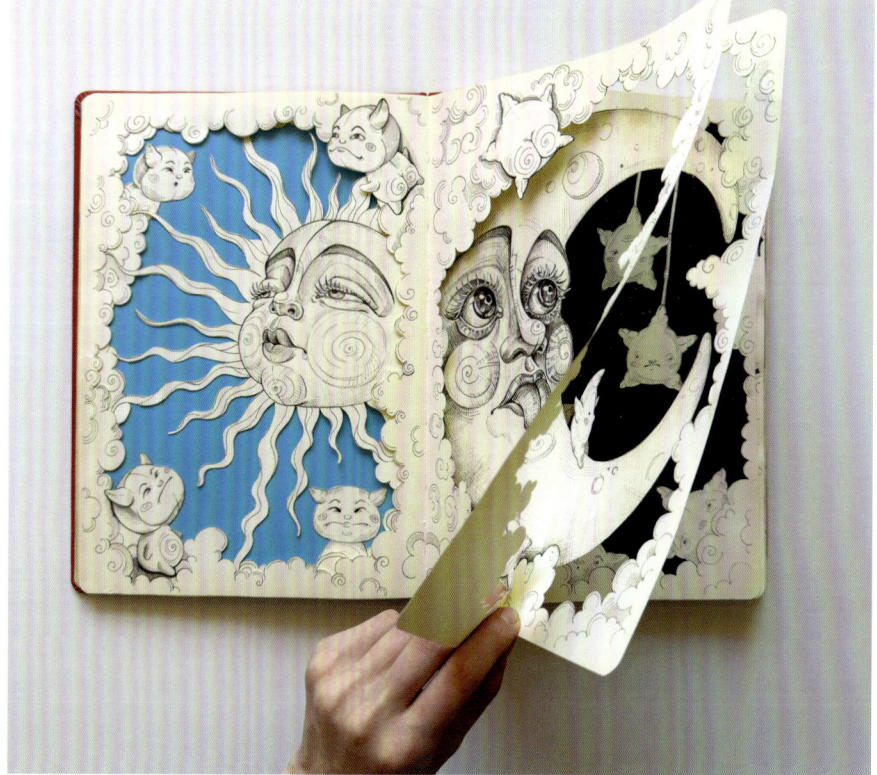

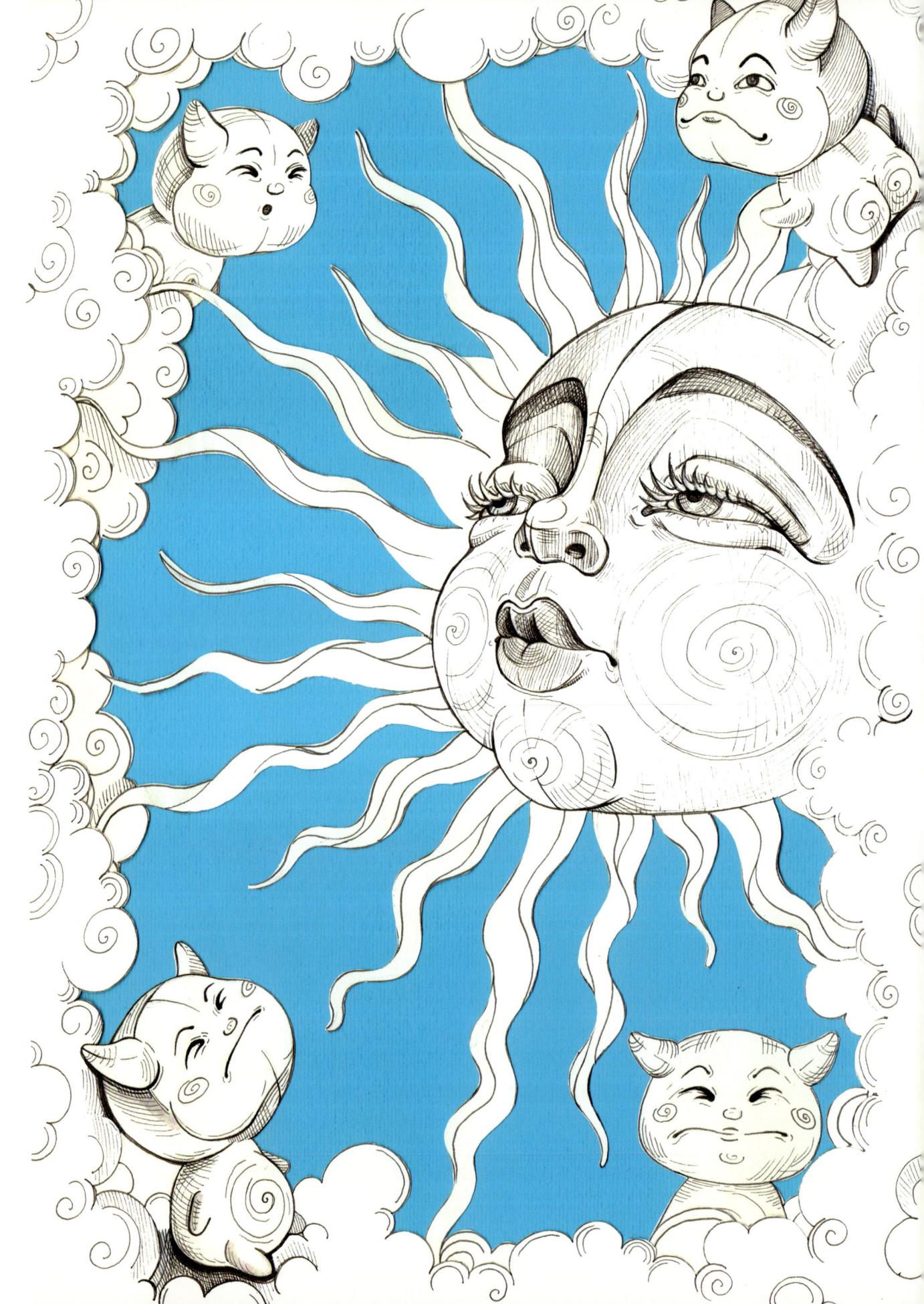

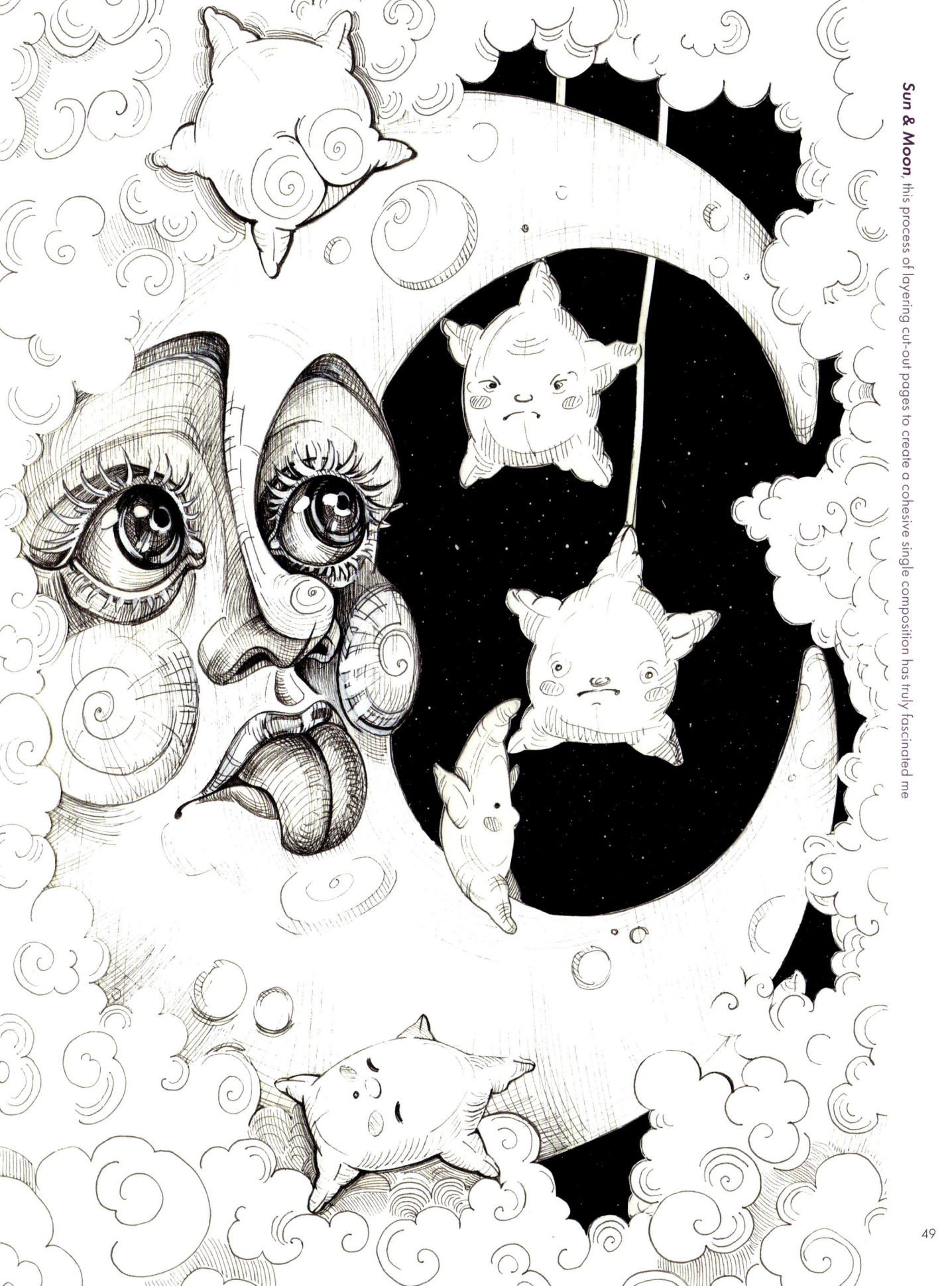

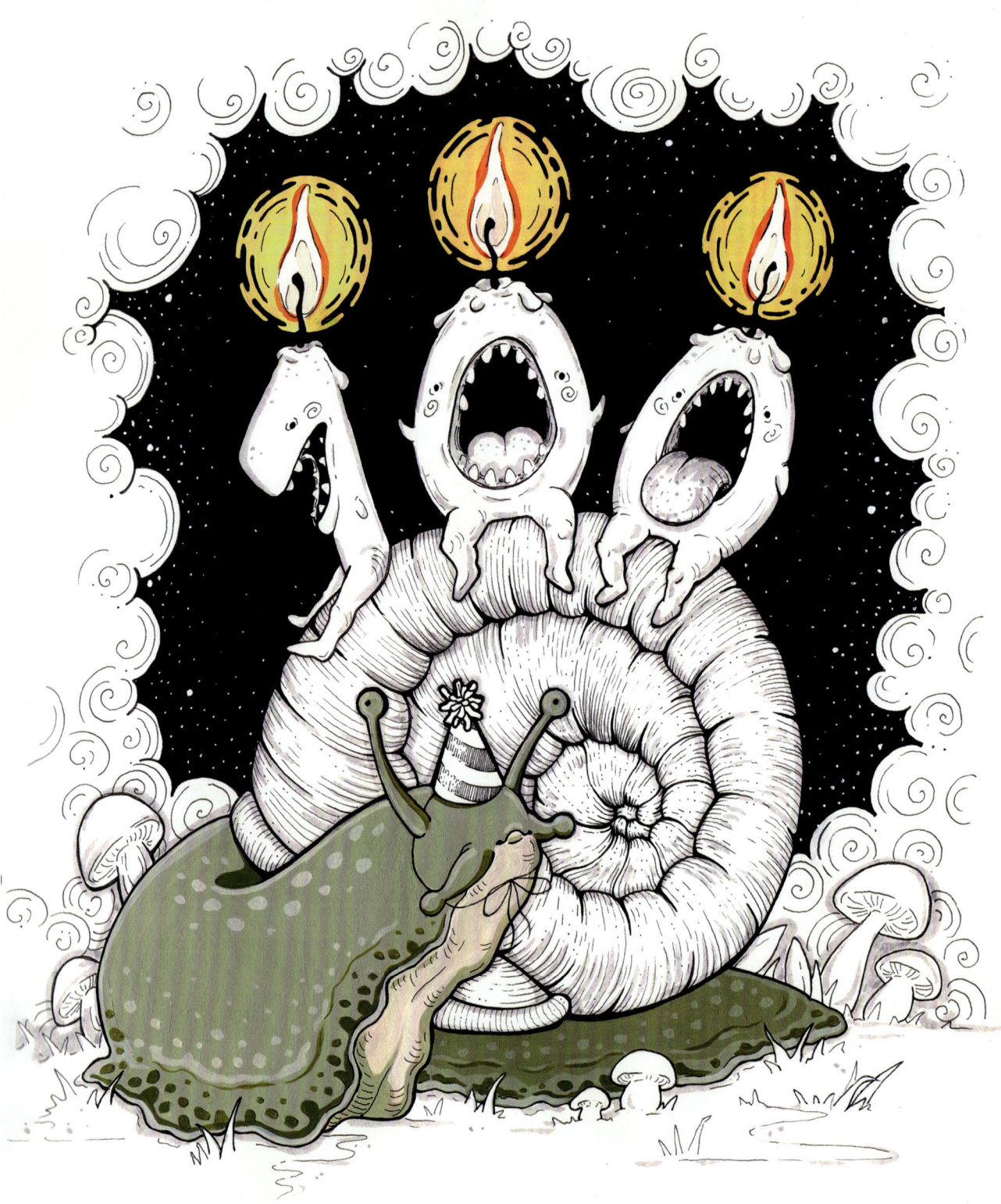

Illustration for 100K followers, tempera and fineliners, 2022

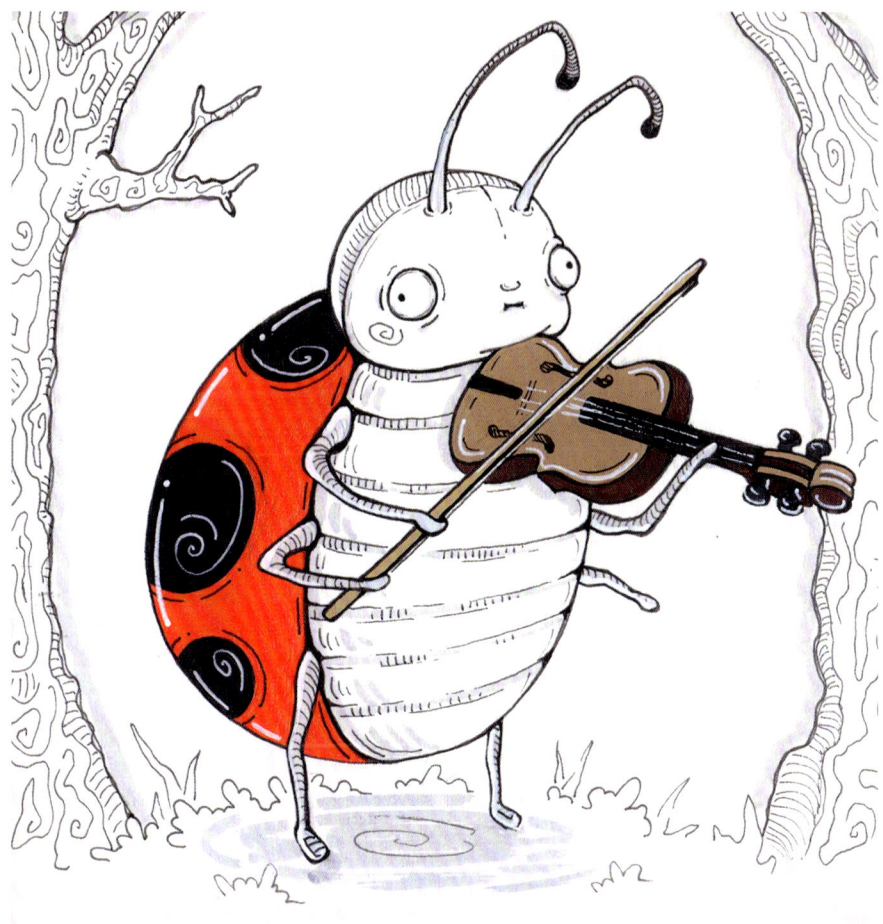

Ladybug, tempera and fineliners, 2022

FLEXIBILITY & EVOLUTION

Style is a constantly evolving aspect of art, shaped by an artist's vision, experiences, and growing skills. It's important to give yourself the freedom to explore.

For example, I initially used only thin black liners for contour lines. Later, I transitioned to using tempera paints. This change, incorporating colour and varying stroke thickness, added significant expressiveness and character to the lines. While this made the process more complex, it ultimately brought a sense of wholeness to my compositions. I also find it fascinating to experiment with the interplay of large shapes and subtle details, as well as to adjust my colour palettes – sometimes narrowing them, sometimes expanding them – to enhance the visual richness and move away from a purely realistic depiction.

I'm curious to see how my style will continue to transform in the future. Each new piece is an exploration, an attempt to discover a new form, a different way of thinking, or a fresh approach. These changes might be subtle for viewers in the short term, but for me, each new work represents a personal journey of discovery. The more I explore, the more I become aware of the vastness of what remains to be learned.

HOW I INTERPRET A BRIEF:
THE PEARL

For this painting, the client asked me to paint flamingos and gave me complete creative freedom, which I appreciated. I immediately wanted to convey the tenderness and connection of these birds, which always stay together.

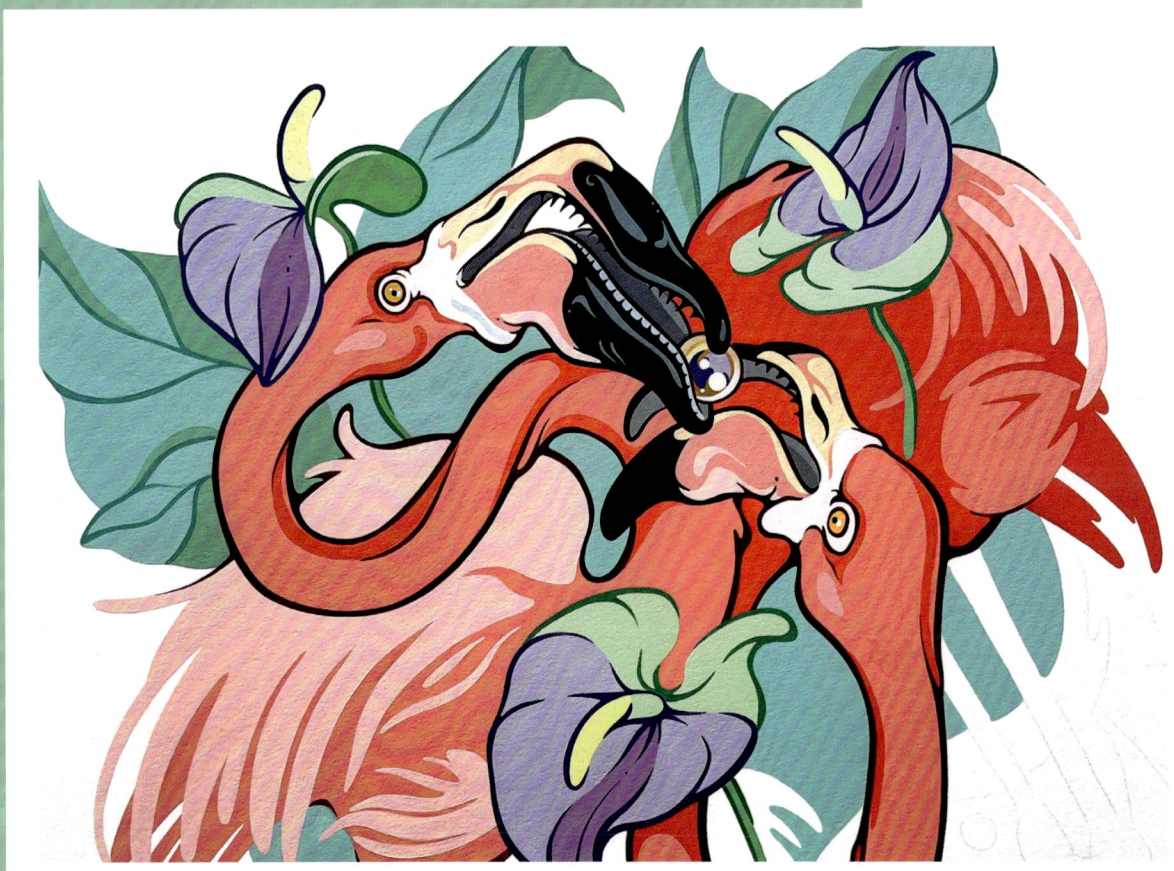

In this painting, flamingos pass each other a pearl, a symbol of purity, loyalty, and devotion. Anthuriums bloom around them. They are graceful and beautiful plants, but poisonous, which reminds me that threats are always lurking in the world. However, the real value lies in what we invest in each other and how we continue to protect it.

I like being able to add mood, memory, or thought to my work. You can just draw a bird, or you can give it context. Then it's no longer just a bird; it's a way to express yourself. However, I don't try to make viewers see my ideas exactly as I intended. Many of my ideas aren't deeply thought out; they simply reflect my preferences.

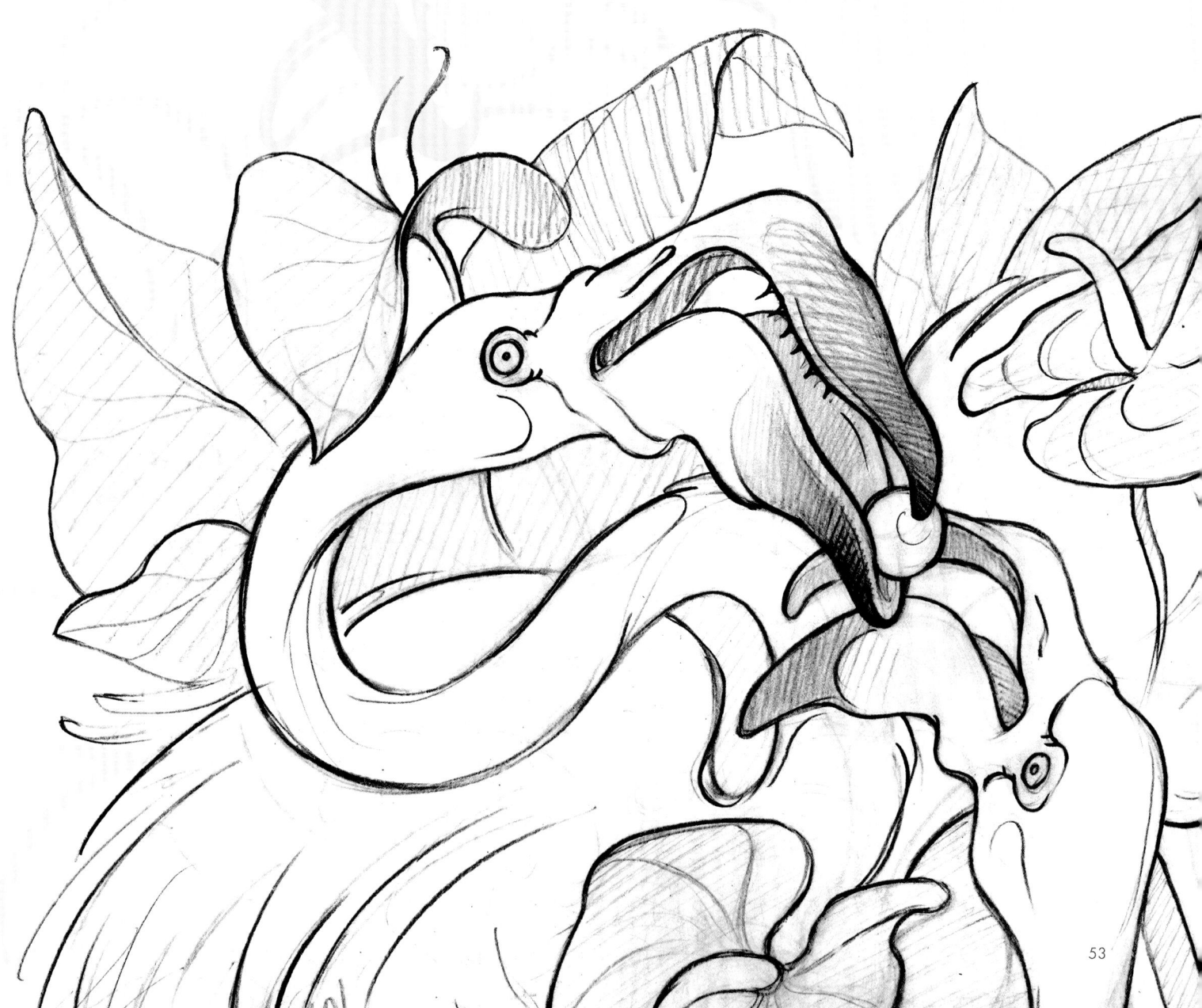

FROM REFERENCES TO SKETCHES

References are powerful tools that help me achieve specific goals in my work. However, it's also a skill that must be developed to avoid simply copying. It's a cumulative process.

Initially, I had difficulty going beyond the image in front of me. But the more I studied and analysed different styles and compositional approaches, the more freedom I felt using references with my work. Over time, it became easier to change poses and proportions, varying colour schemes and combining images.

That being said, it's important not to rely too heavily on references and avoid getting too comfortable with them. I always consider why and when I will use them. If I already have an idea, I challenge myself to first visualize it, letting my imagination capture a fragment, pose, emotion, or composition. I consider a work successful when the final image does not resemble the reference at all.

You can also misuse references. One of the biggest mistakes is using references from other people's paintings. Analyse them, but don't copy them! This can impose limitations on your work and stifle your own imagination. Additionally, be careful not to overestimate others' abilities. An artwork may seem perfect, but there is a risk of copying mistakes, such as incorrect perspective or anatomy. It's better to learn from your own work.

I usually start with a few quick sketches to warm up before moving on to more detailed ones. In college and at the art academy, we practised quick sketches of objects and worked with models who changed their poses every five to ten minutes. This is how we learned to perceive movement, capture character, and work intuitively. Today, I use this skill to analyse and look for different ways to visualize an image.

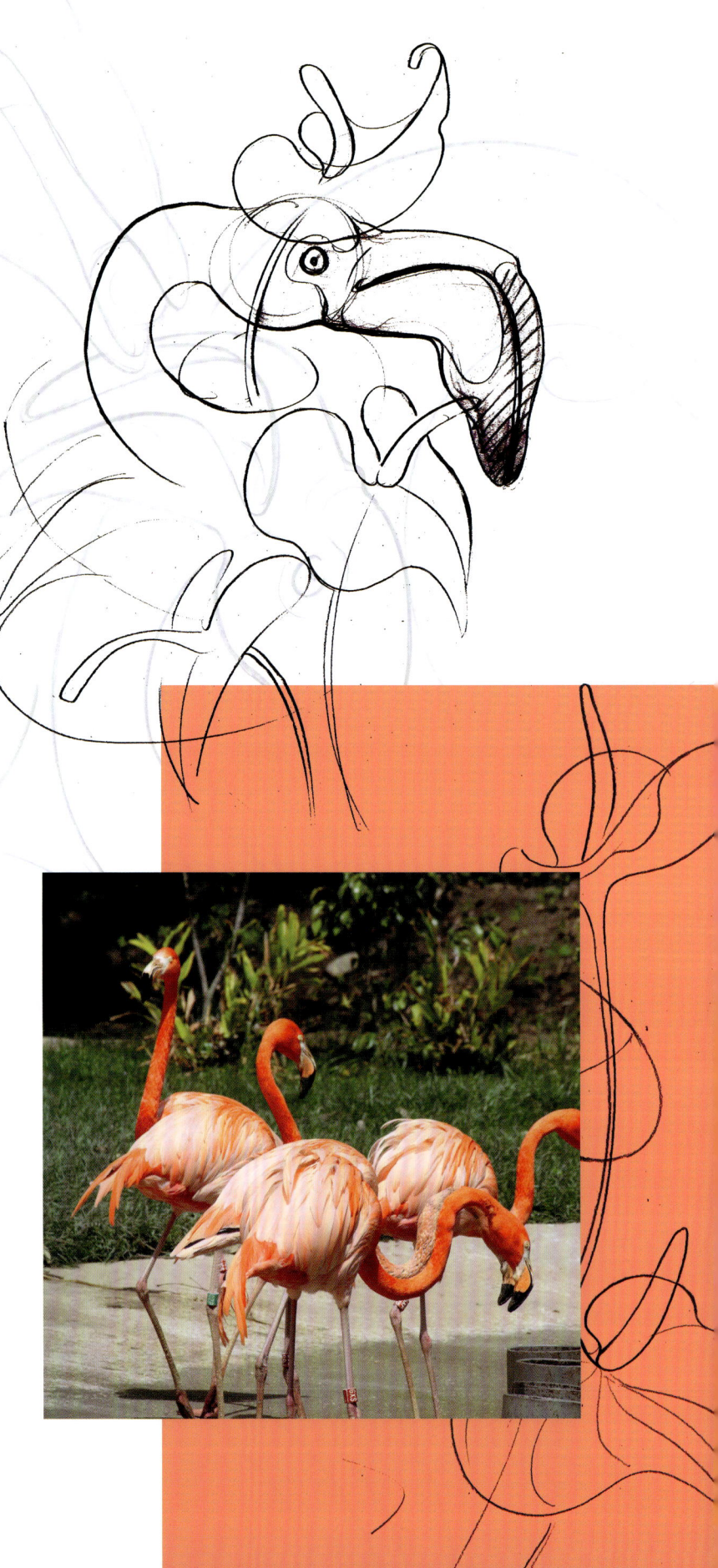

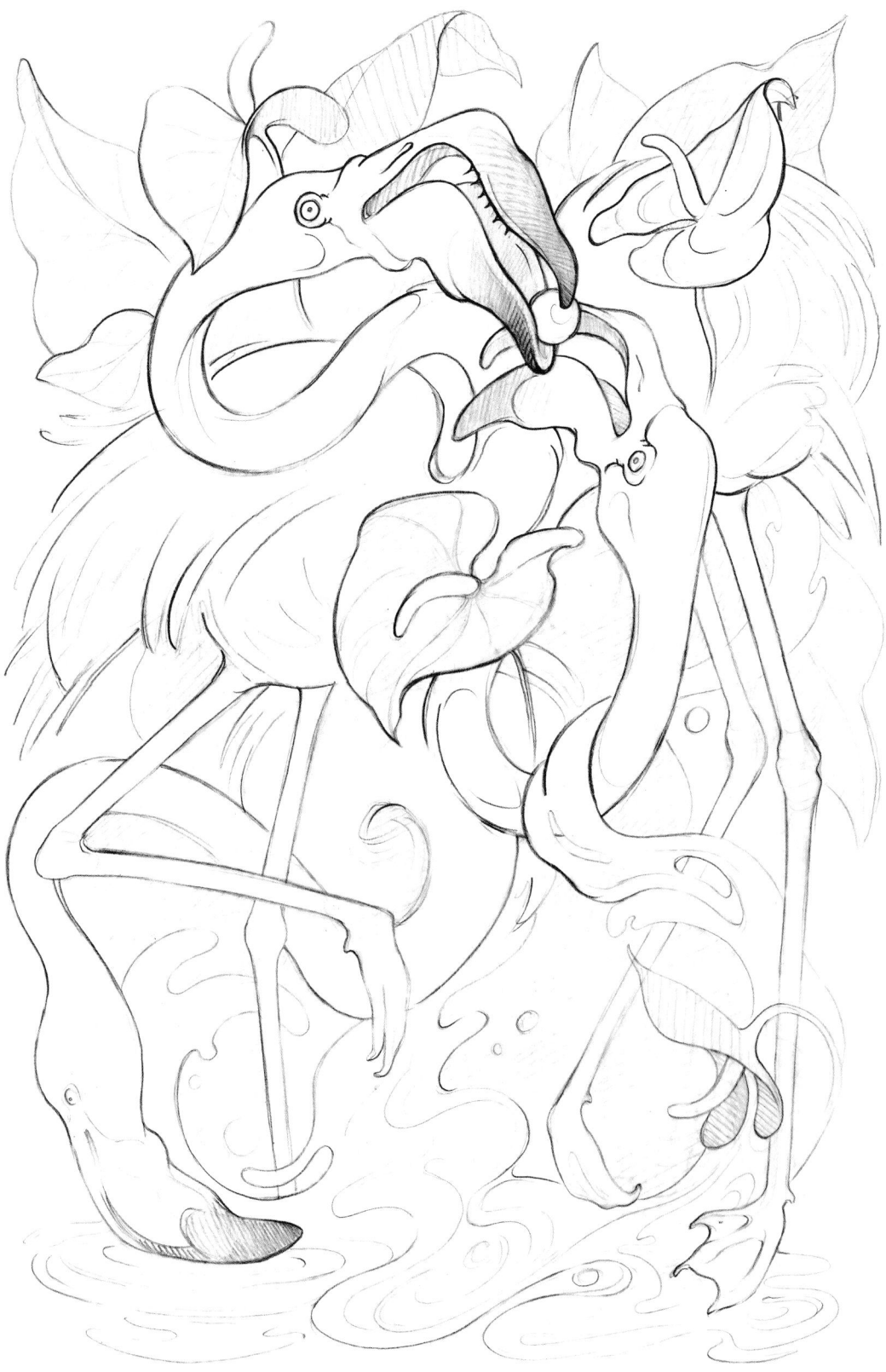

In this work, the tops of the flamingos' heads are emphasized the most. This is for several reasons: first, the heads are located in the upper-third area of the image and intersect, creating a point of tension. Their arrangement forms a triangle that naturally attracts the eye. The open beaks and curved necks add dynamics, making this area more active. As for the pearl: according to the principle of isolation, if one element is unique, the eye is drawn to it.

At first, my sketches often looked as if they had been through a real battle. Gradually, the simple, initial lines evolved into something more refined, but a lot of erasing would be involved. Over time, I noticed that the sketches became overloaded and overworked, so I began keeping fresh sheets of paper nearby to continue the work. During breaks, I would compare all the sketches and select the best pieces of each one, combining them all to make one new drawing. And that's still how I work today!

COLOUR & DETAIL

People often ask me how I choose colours for my work. Before I start working with colour, I have a kind of ritual: I put a sketch in front of me and mentally 'complete' it. I envision the sequence of paint application, the tonal solution, and the approximate colour palette. Sometimes this process takes half an hour, sometimes several hours, and sometimes I don't feel ready until the next day. In this section I'll explain more about colour and how I choose my palettes.

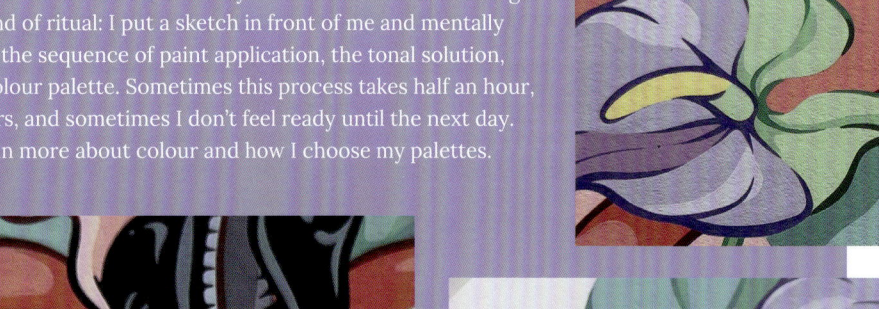

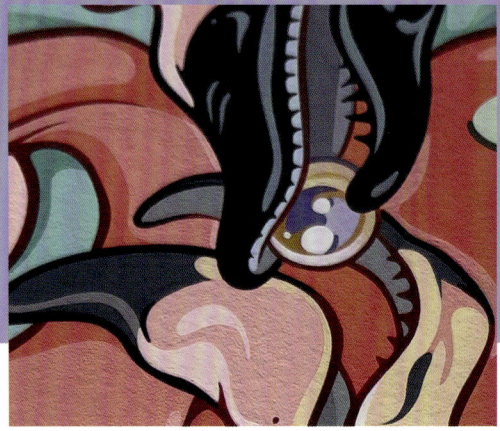

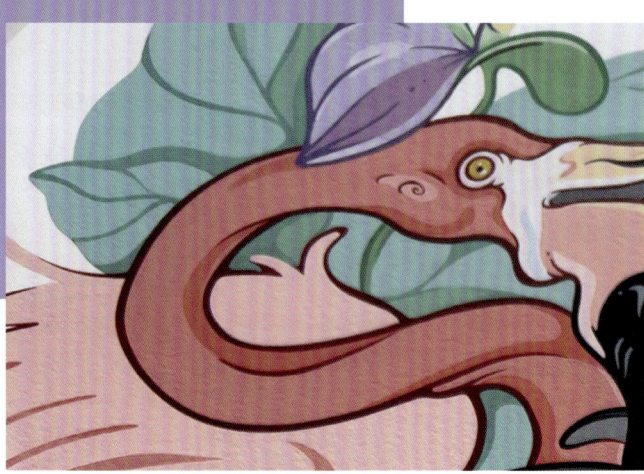

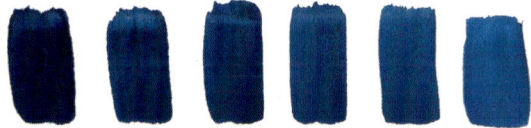

Cerulean blue + phthalocyanine blue = shade.
(Phthalocyanine blue can be replaced with ultramarine, cobalt, or any other paint with a dark blue pigment)

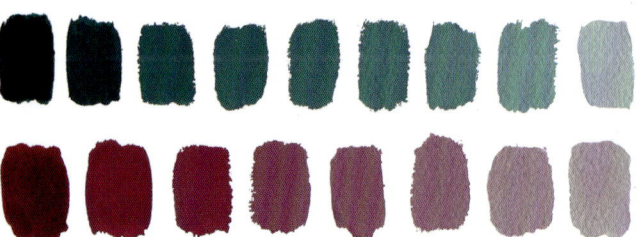

Colour + white = tint. Tint is formed by mixing a colour with white, which increases its lightness

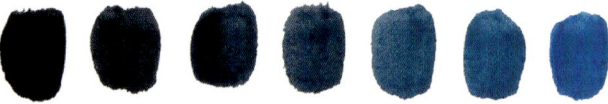

Colour + black = shade. It's formed by mixing a colour with black, which increases its darkness. I don't always use black because it can make the mixed hues appear 'gloomy' or 'dirty'. Instead, I replace it with a darker shade. In the next image you'll find an example

VALUE

Value is the lightness or darkness of a colour. In the initial stages, I prioritize understanding the overall tonal value over determining the colours right away. That's why I don't always create a separate colour sketch. However, I always add tonal accents to a black-and-white sketch by hatching areas where dark colours will be added later.

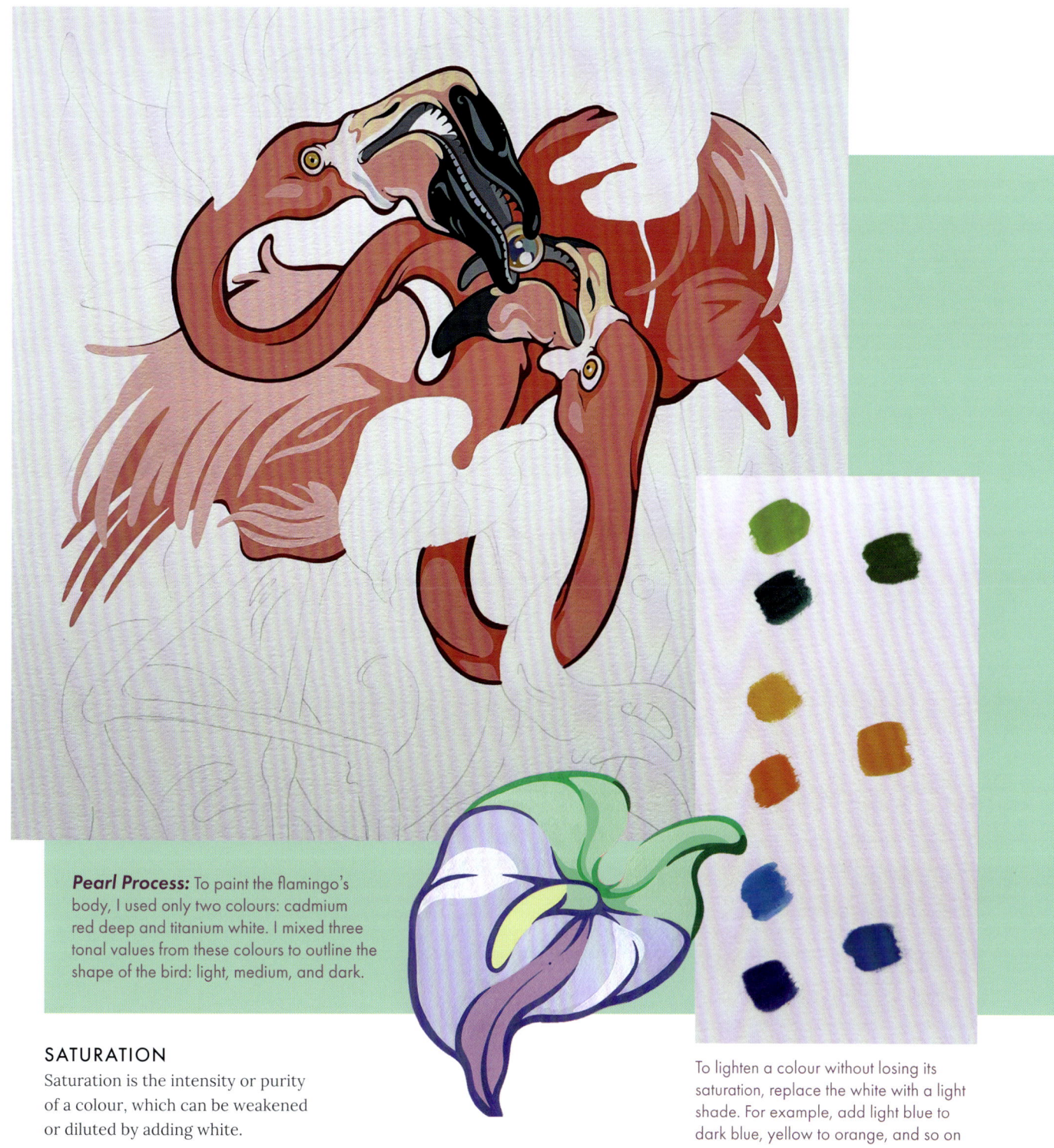

Pearl Process: To paint the flamingo's body, I used only two colours: cadmium red deep and titanium white. I mixed three tonal values from these colours to outline the shape of the bird: light, medium, and dark.

SATURATION

Saturation is the intensity or purity of a colour, which can be weakened or diluted by adding white.

To lighten a colour without losing its saturation, replace the white with a light shade. For example, add light blue to dark blue, yellow to orange, and so on

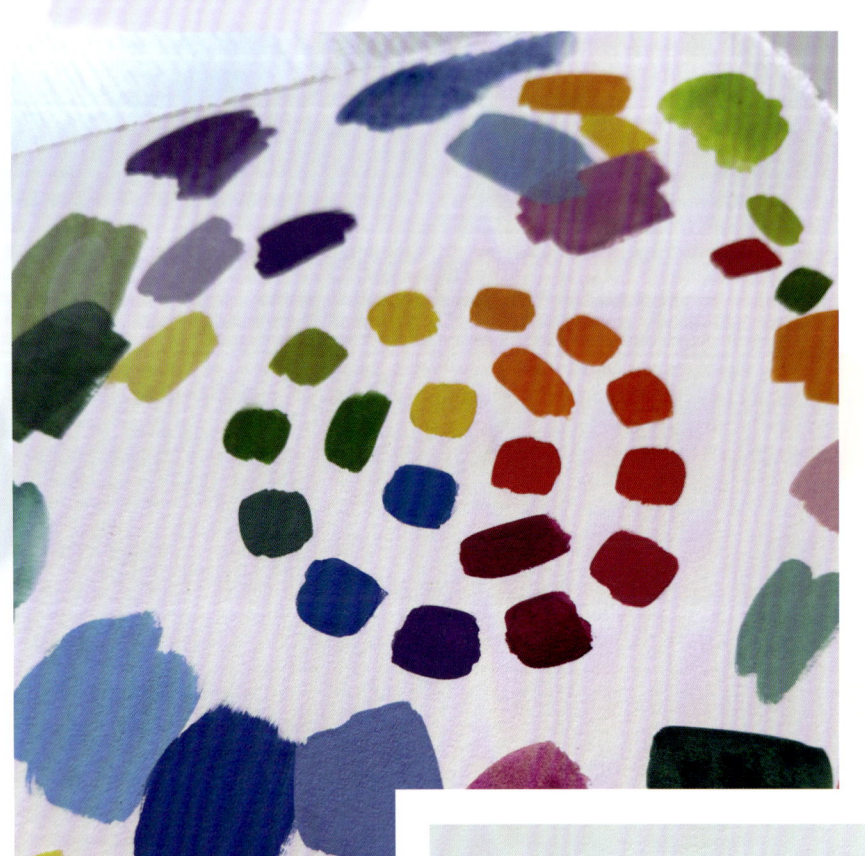

COLOUR COMBINATIONS
Though I work with colour intuitively, my approach is still based on a fundamental understanding of the Itten colour-wheel system and its harmonious combinations.

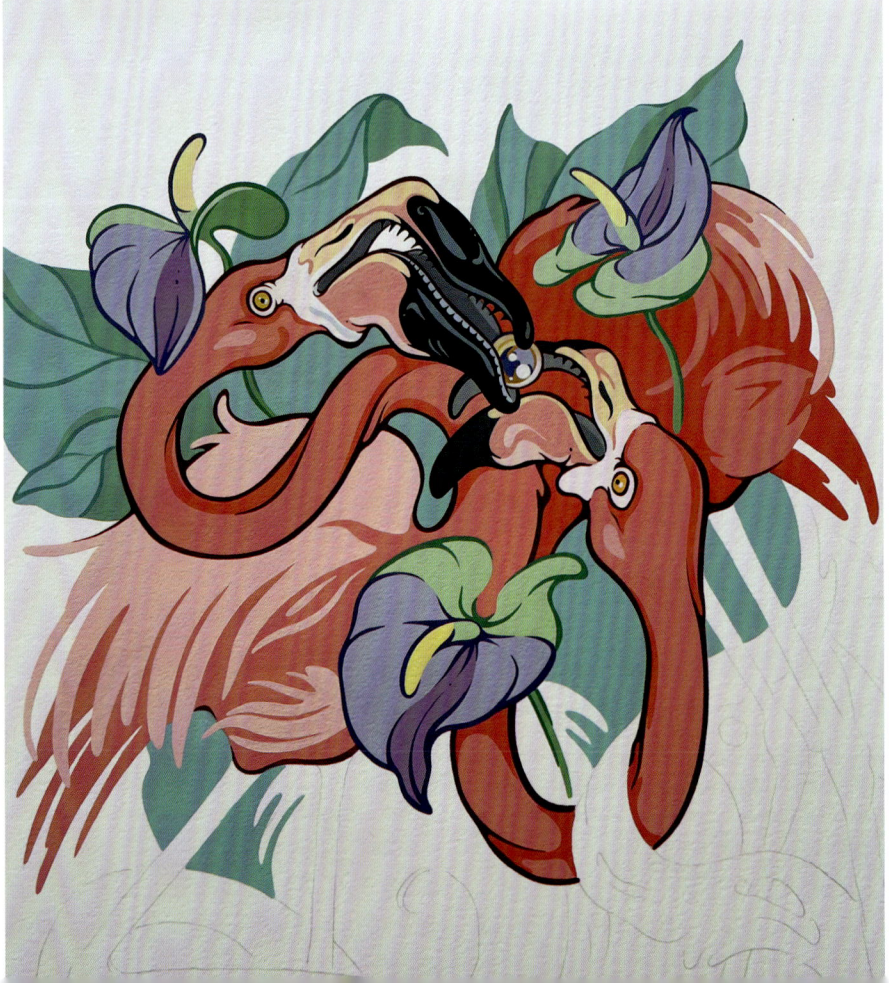

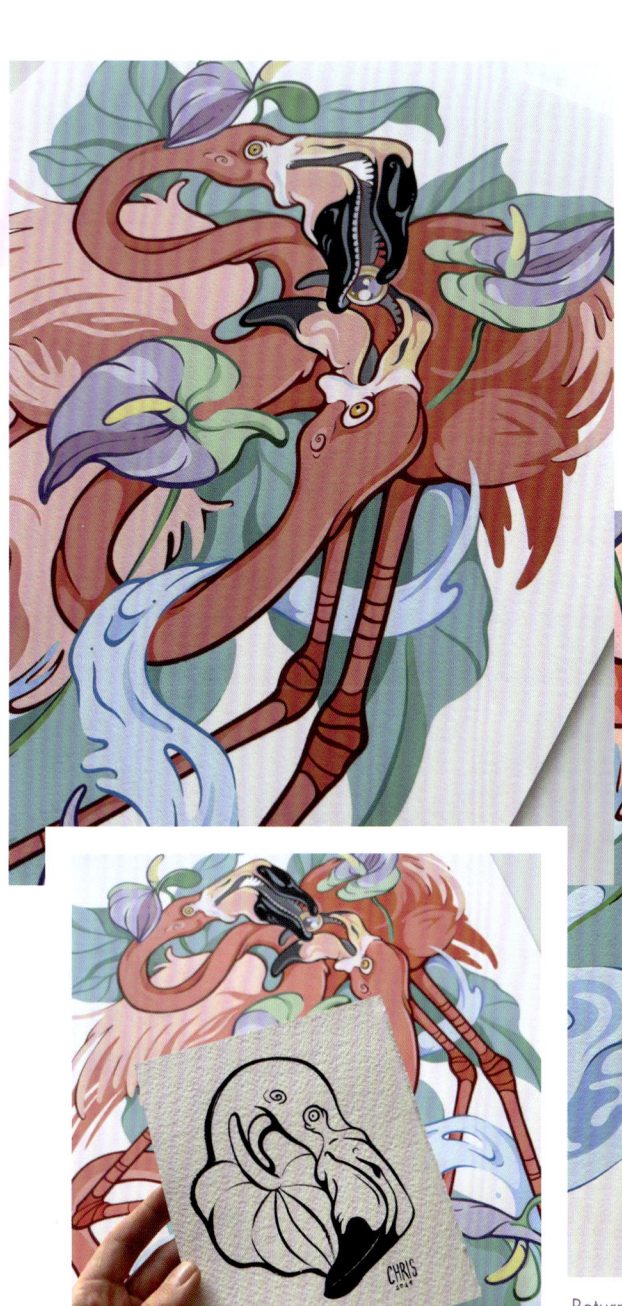

To create contrast, I use combinations of primary, secondary, and achromatic colours. Primary colours are yellow, blue, and red. Secondary colours are green, purple, and orange. Achromatic colours are black and white.

In general, working with other paintings follows the same scheme, just with a different number of paired colours, tones, and saturation.

Returning to the same work, the palette is quite restrained here. Warm pink and cool green, which are opposite each other on the colour wheel, is a complementary combination. As additional accents, I introduced purple and yellow. The blue supports the green range (an analogous colour), and I also used an achromatic colour: deep black, a neutral colour. Due to this property and its deep saturation, it enhances the perception of the surrounding colours and makes the flamingo beaks more expressive

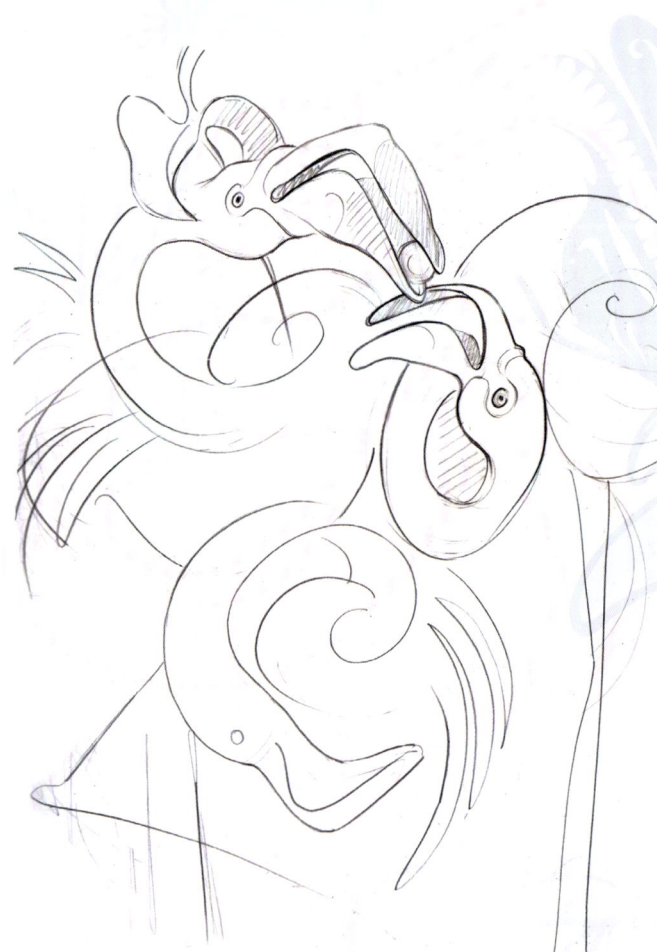

LINE WORK

Line work has always played an important role in my work. To me, it is a guide that directs the eye and emphasizes movement and form, and as you can see, much of the line work differs in colour. Sometimes it serves as an accent, sometimes as a shadow, and other times as a rhythm.

ATMOSPHERE

When I mix colours, I rely on my feelings. The bright, rich shades that often appear in my work evoke joy and warmth. This seems to stem from my childhood when I used to draw with coloured pencils and try to squeeze every bit of brightness out of them. My favourite movies, illustrations, and cartoons were vibrant, lively, and filled with light.

When I use dark colours, they usually symbolize depression; a state I want to escape. That's why I add bright colours to make the picture 'shine' with light and warmth. This is currently my interpretation of colour, but I am sure it will change and take on new meanings.

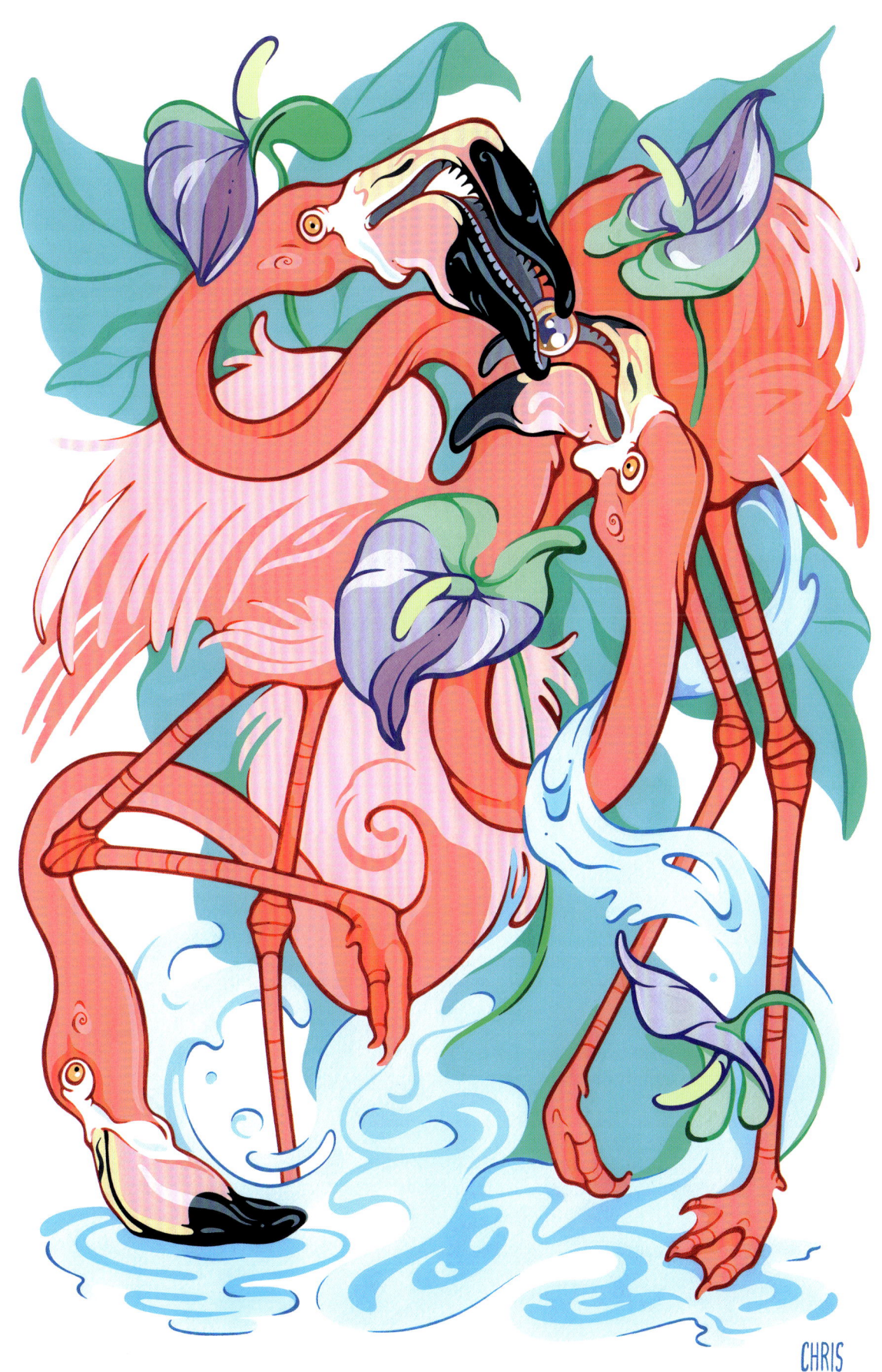

UNFURL:
HOW THE COVER
CAME TO BE

This was my first time creating an illustration for a book cover, and I'm glad it was for such a special project. From the beginning, I felt a great sense of responsibility because the cover image often shapes the first impression readers have when choosing a book. However, if I had focused too much on that, I would have lost my creative freedom. Once I let go of external and internal expectations, a clear idea came to me.

I chose to paint a newt because it is a little jewel of the Carpathian Mountains just beyond my hometown, and in many cultures it symbolizes transformation. There comes a day when they make the transition from water to land, which made me think of when I started sharing my artwork with the wider world and my style evolved into something new.

The second, but no less important, symbol on this cover is the fern frond. After all, it is what prompted the book's title. The word 'unfurl' may appear simple, but it carries a heavier weight for me. I drew parallels between the way a fern unfurls from a tightly coiled state and my own personal history of growth, development, and self-discovery.

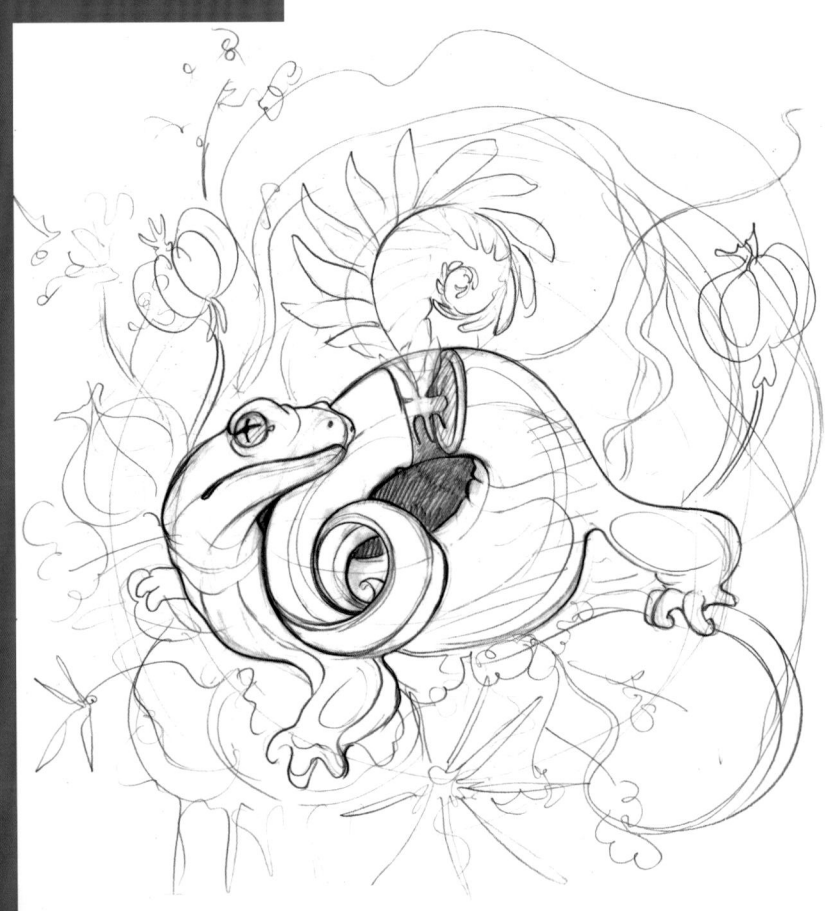

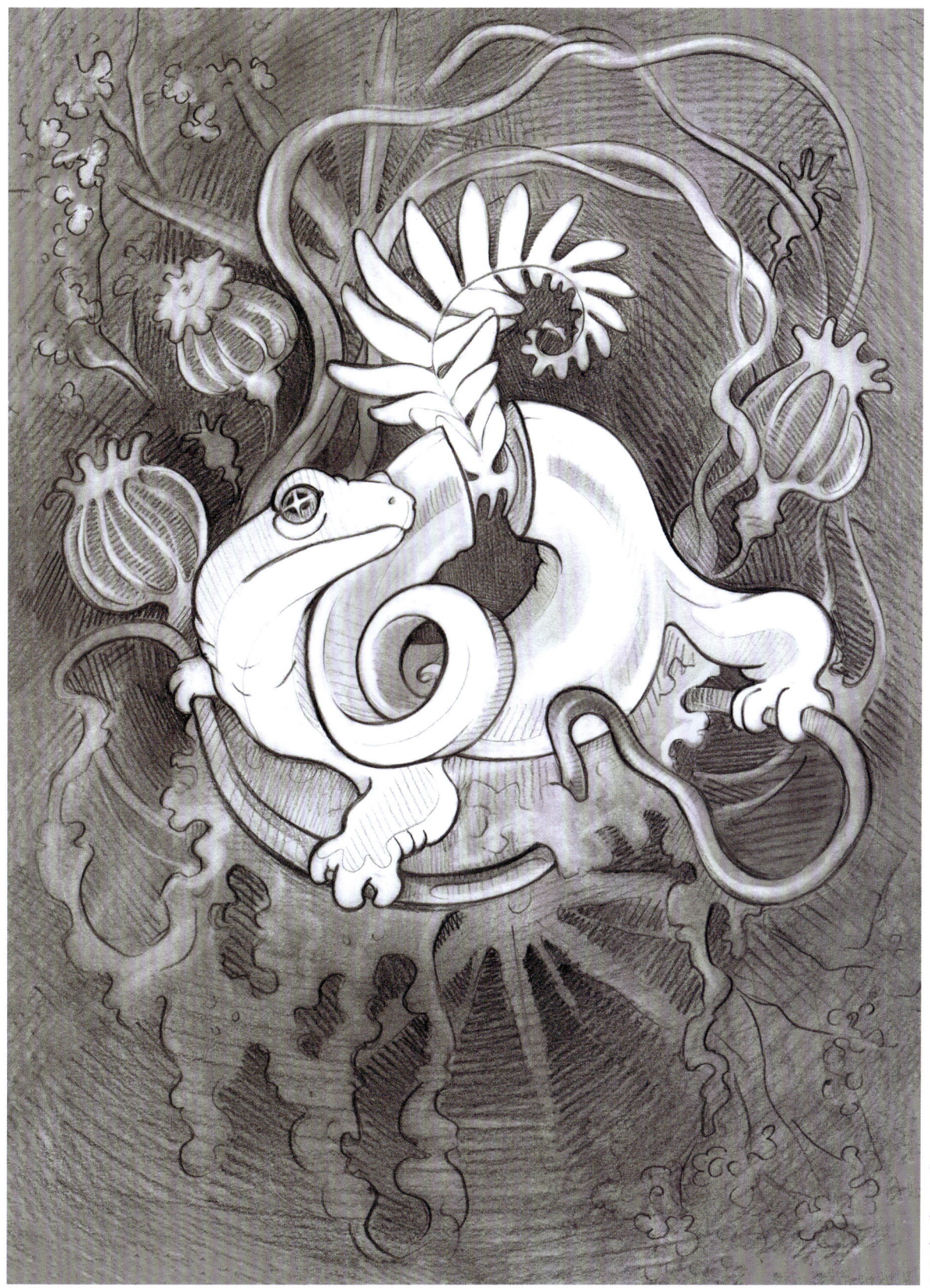

A traditional sketch using a simple pencil

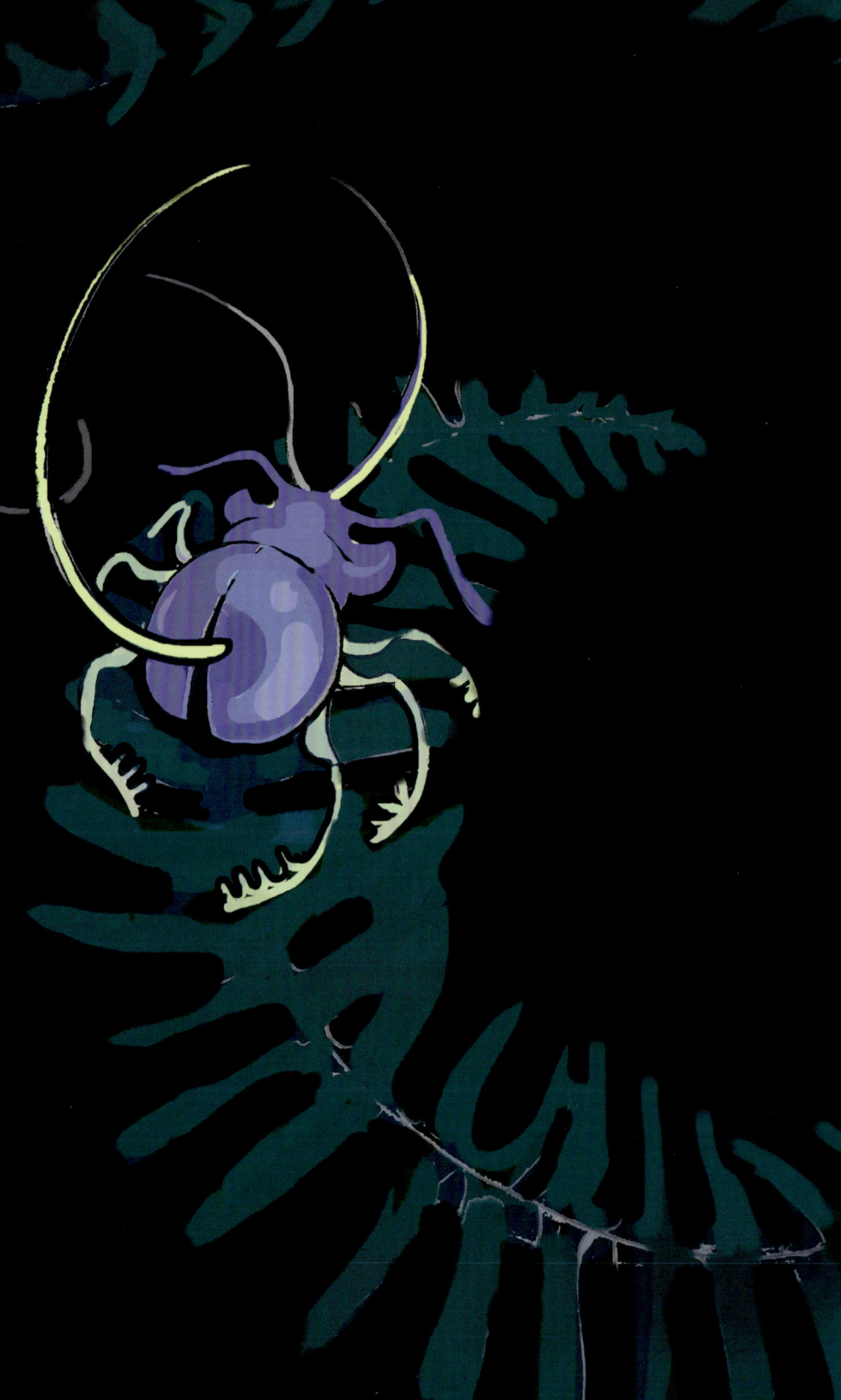

'You are
a beetle'

Without a colour sketch, it would
have been impossible to present my
idea to the 3dtotal team and confirm
that it could work. I scanned my sketch
and tried to approximate the colour
scheme in Photoshop. I really feel like
a dinosaur when it comes to computer
programs! I decided the newt should be
the brightest, so I chose warm colours –
primary yellow, ochre, and orange – and
added muted cool tones around it to
create depth and contrast.

As for the beetle on the back cover,
my Ukrainian surname, Tyzhuk, literally
translates to 'you are a beetle'. My years
in high school would not have been
complete without my classmates' jokes
about it. Today, when I think back to
those times, I realize the jokes weren't too
harsh. At the time, though, they offended
me. But of course, the more I worried
about it, the more attention it received.

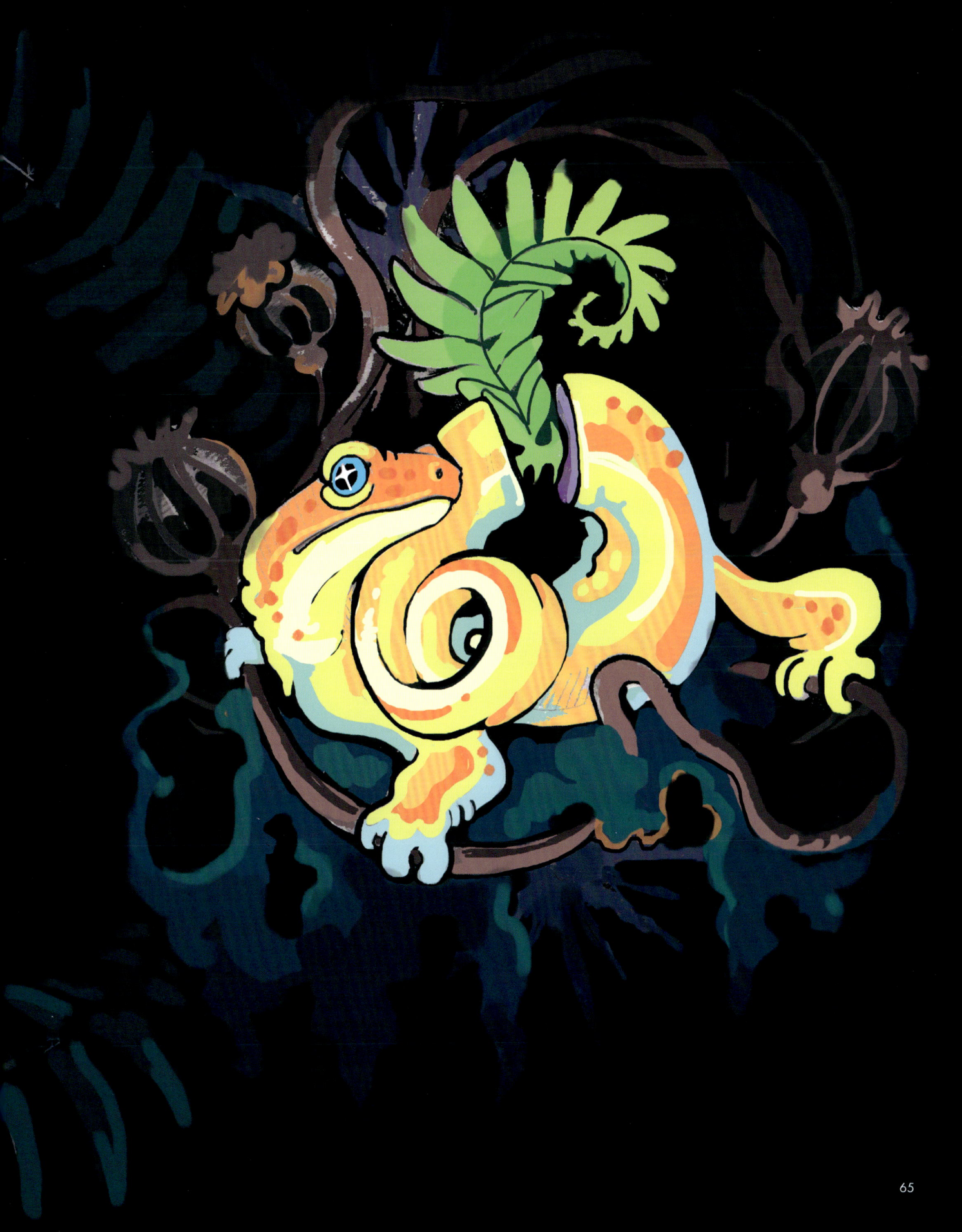

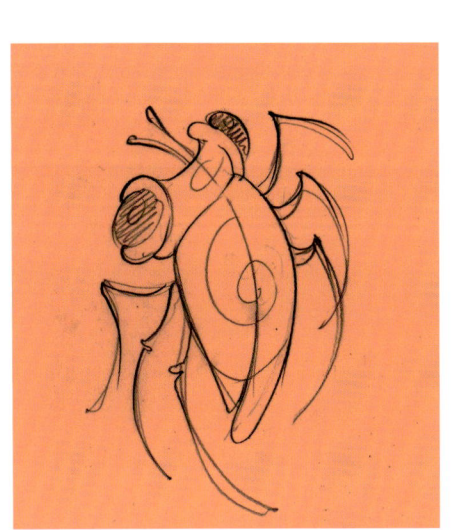

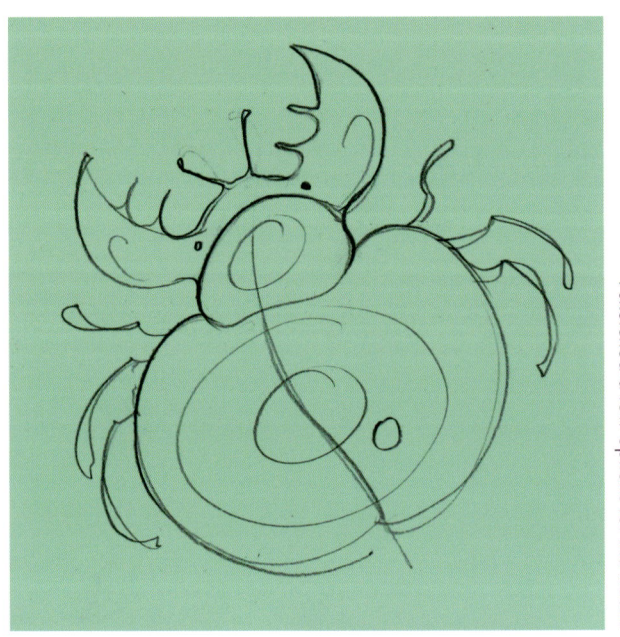

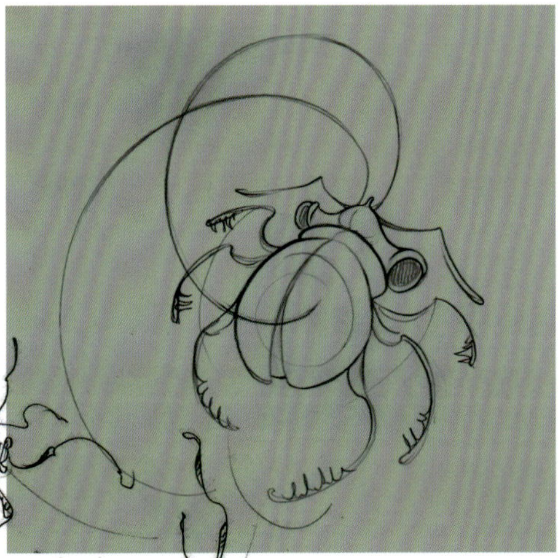

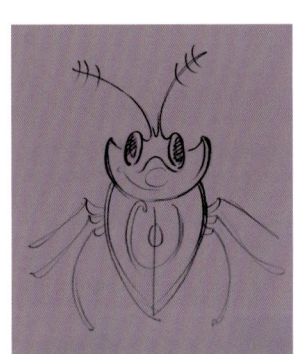

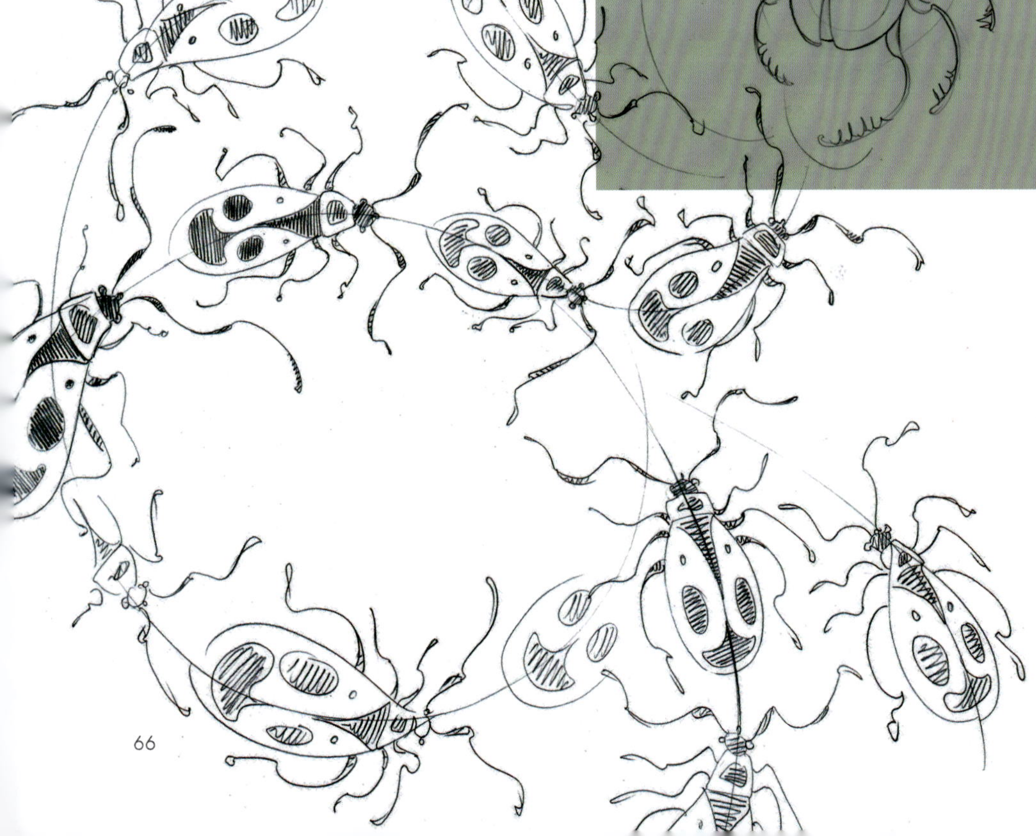

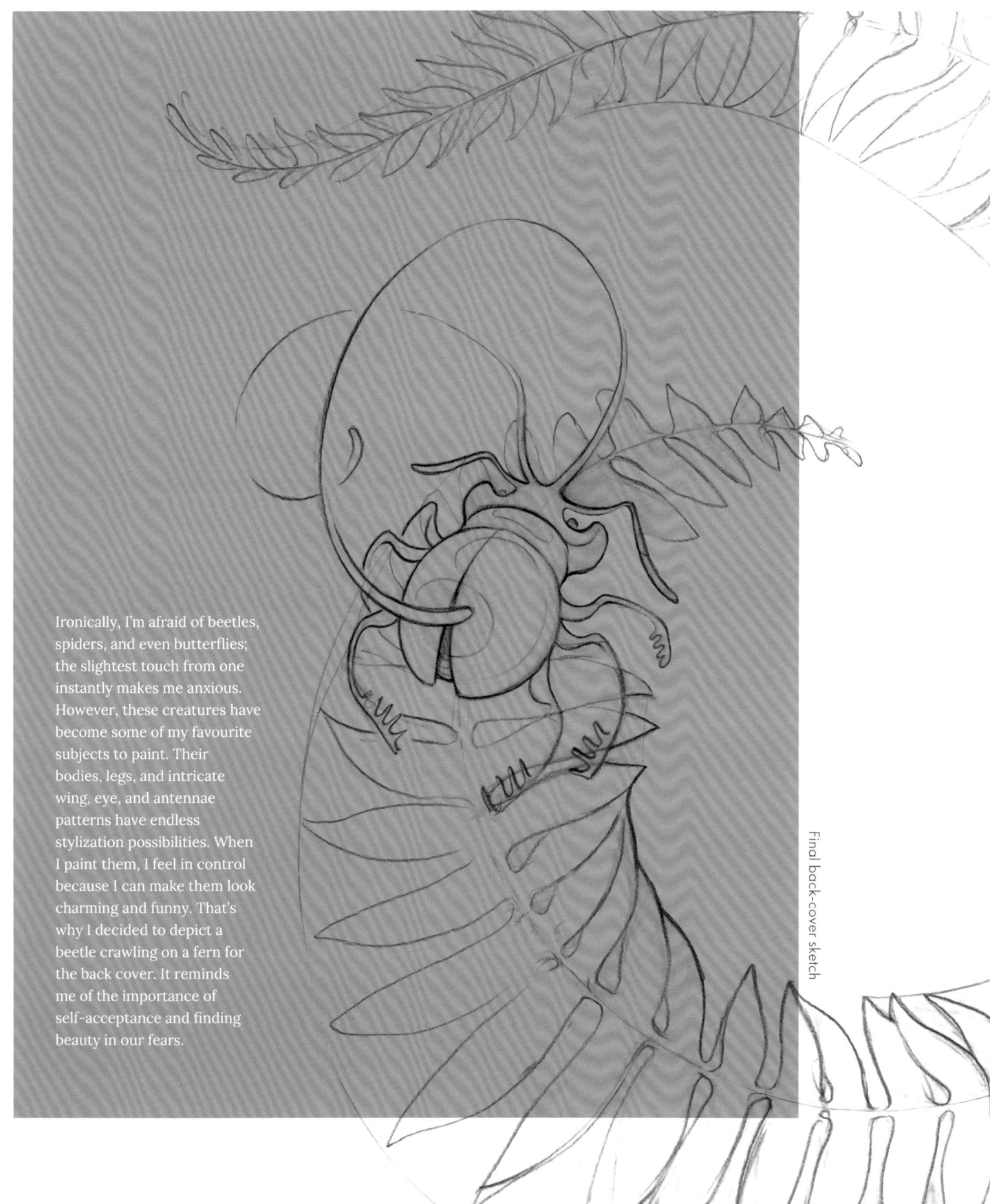

Ironically, I'm afraid of beetles, spiders, and even butterflies; the slightest touch from one instantly makes me anxious. However, these creatures have become some of my favourite subjects to paint. Their bodies, legs, and intricate wing, eye, and antennae patterns have endless stylization possibilities. When I paint them, I feel in control because I can make them look charming and funny. That's why I decided to depict a beetle crawling on a fern for the back cover. It reminds me of the importance of self-acceptance and finding beauty in our fears.

Final back-cover sketch

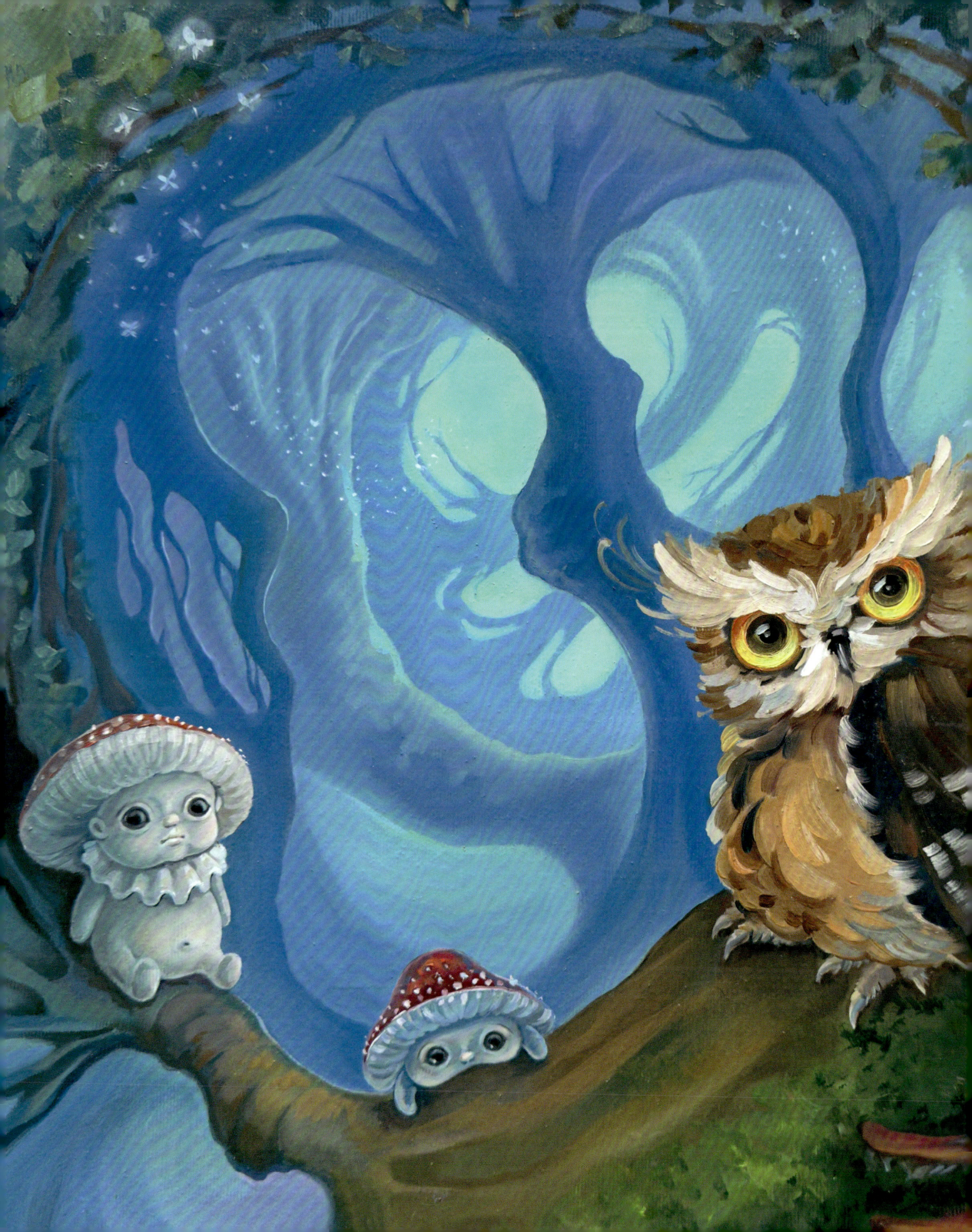

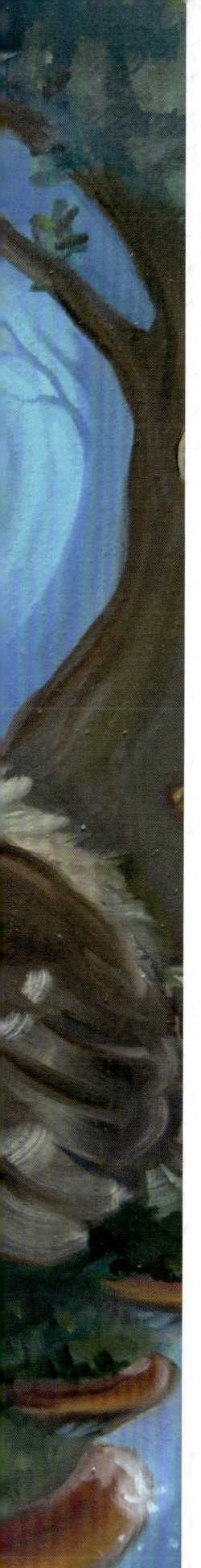

Gallery
Oil paintings
& Sketchbooks

OIL PAINTINGS

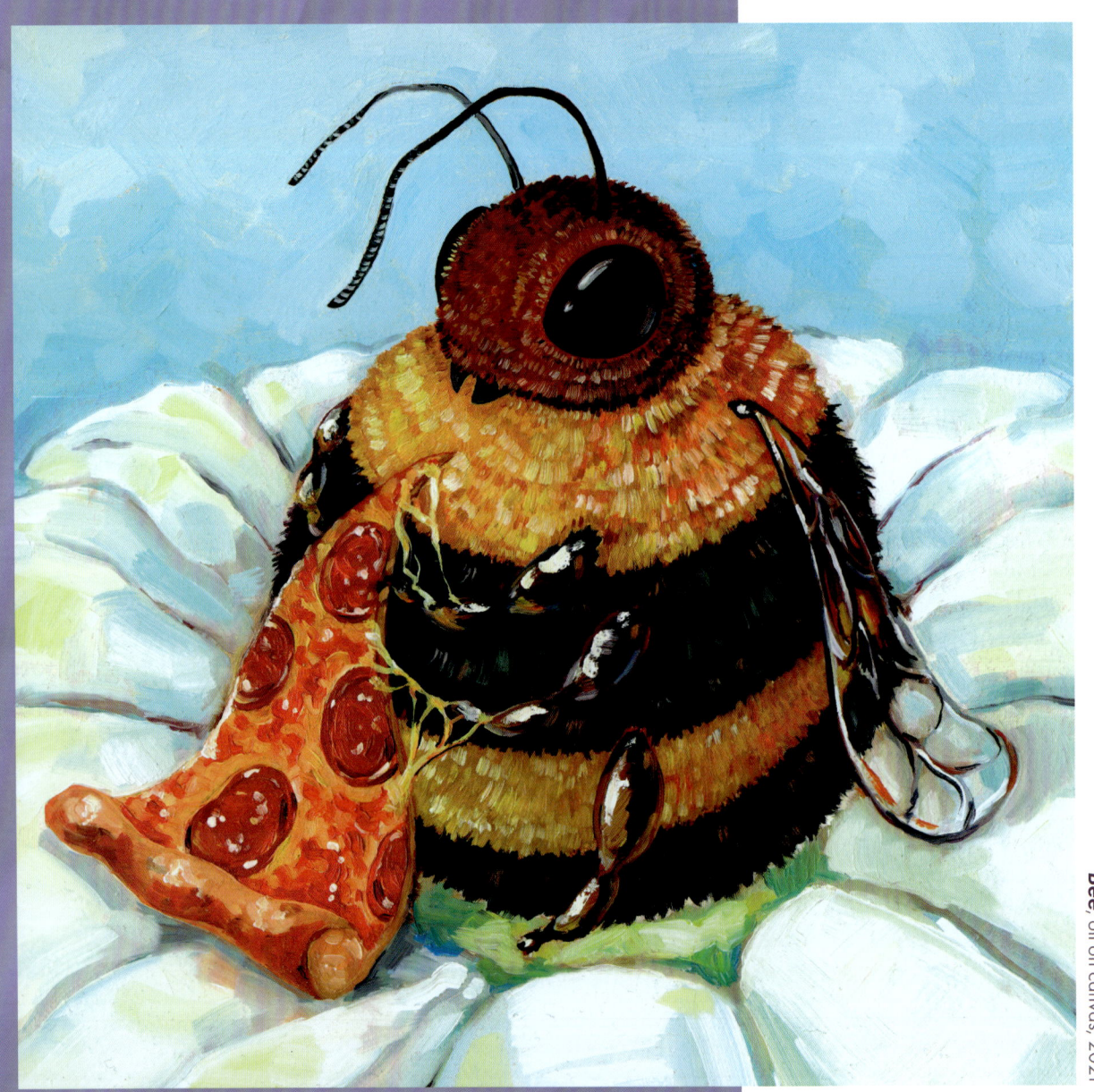

Bee, oil on canvas, 2021

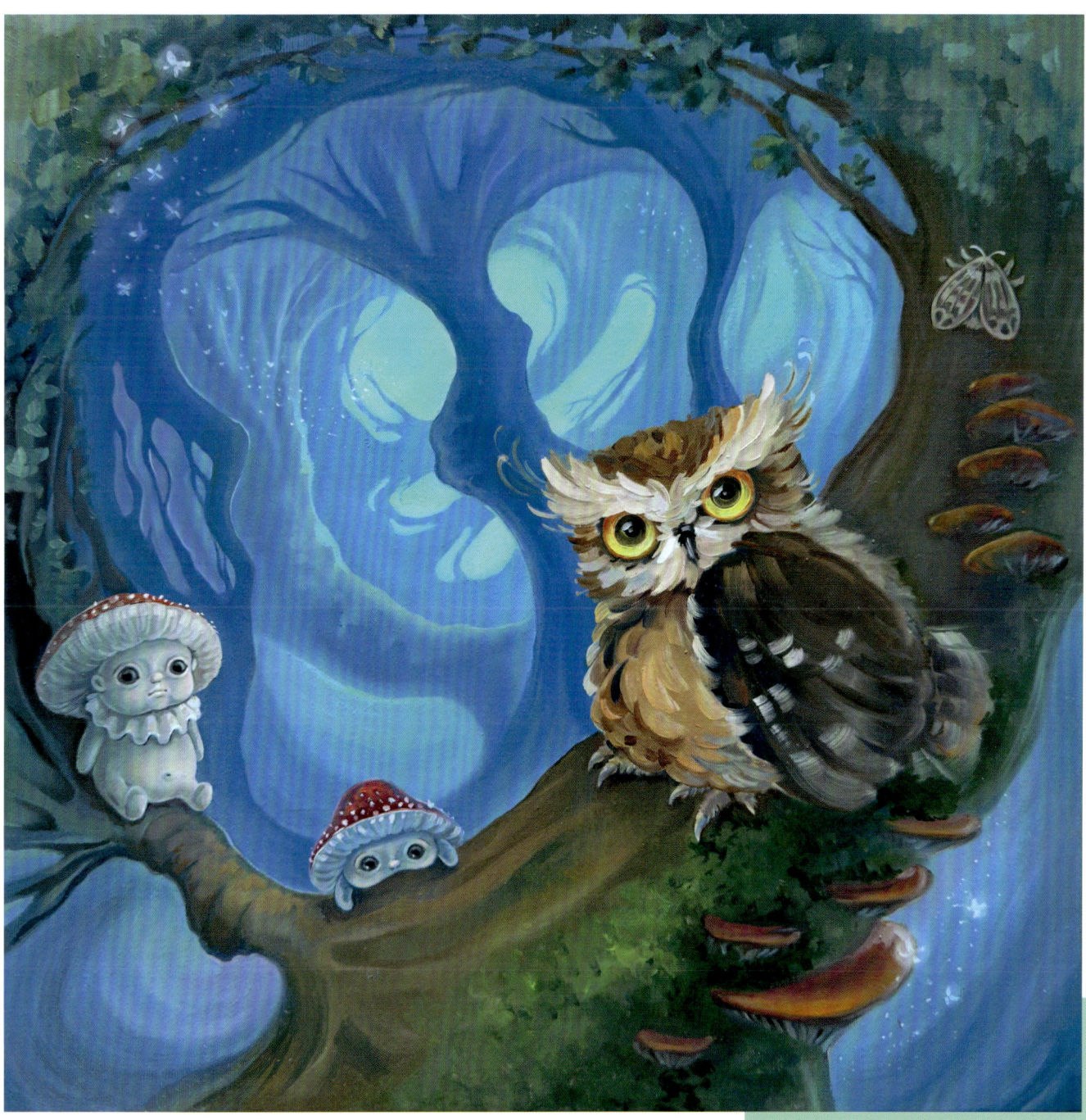

Mysterious Forest, oil on canvas, 2021

I wanted to break away from realistic art and escape into a world of dreams and fantasies. That's how my first surrealist paintings appeared. I like that this technique offers many ways to express myself, from translucent layers to thick, pasty strokes that create texture, colour depth, smooth transitions, and rich shades. This period of my work was short-lived, giving way to other techniques. However, I think it was just an introduction. Working with oil has left its mark, and one day I will return to it to see how it responds with new ideas and fresh feelings.

‘Working with oil has left its mark, and one day I will return to it’

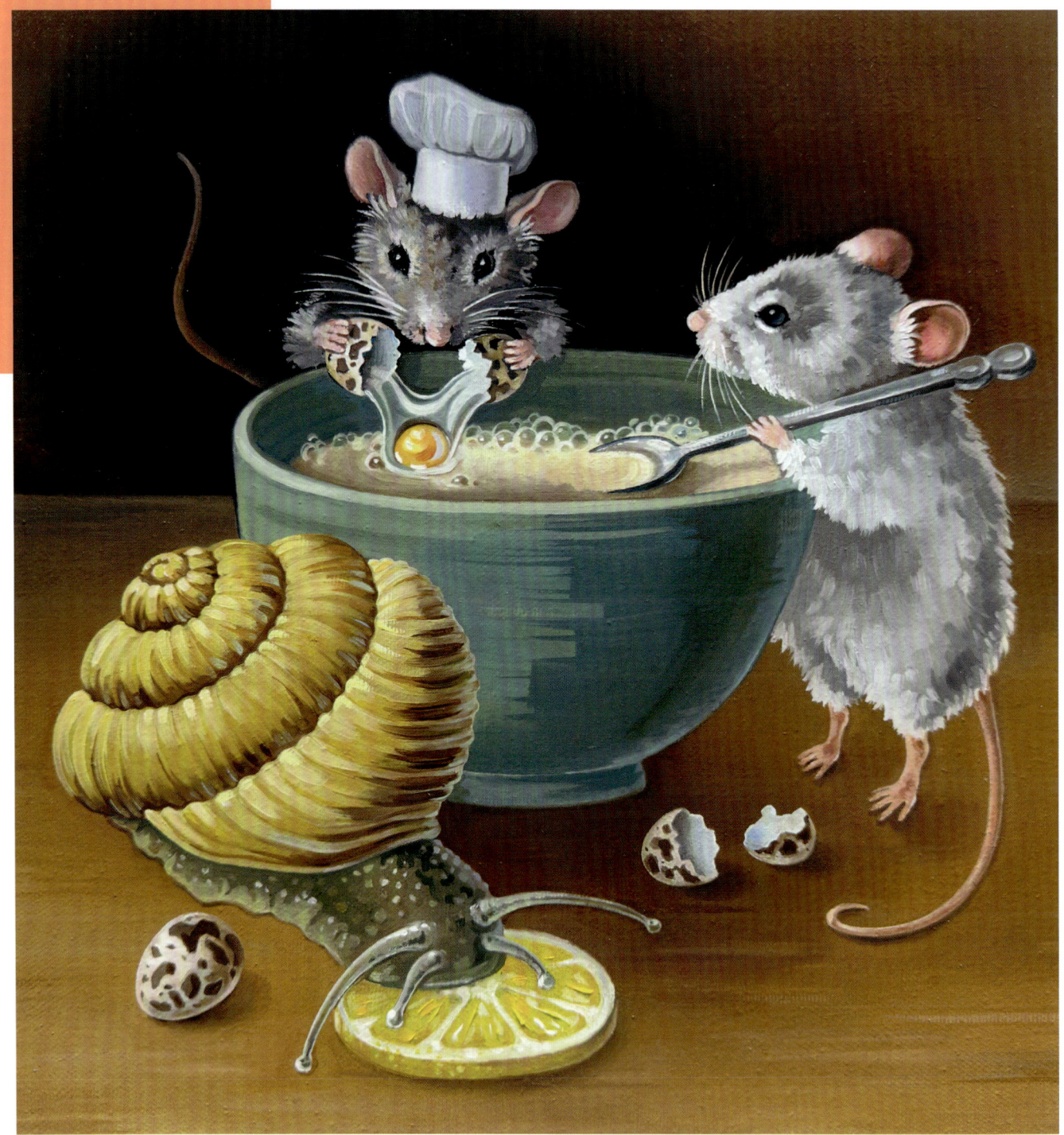

Kitchen Still Life, oil on canvas, 2021

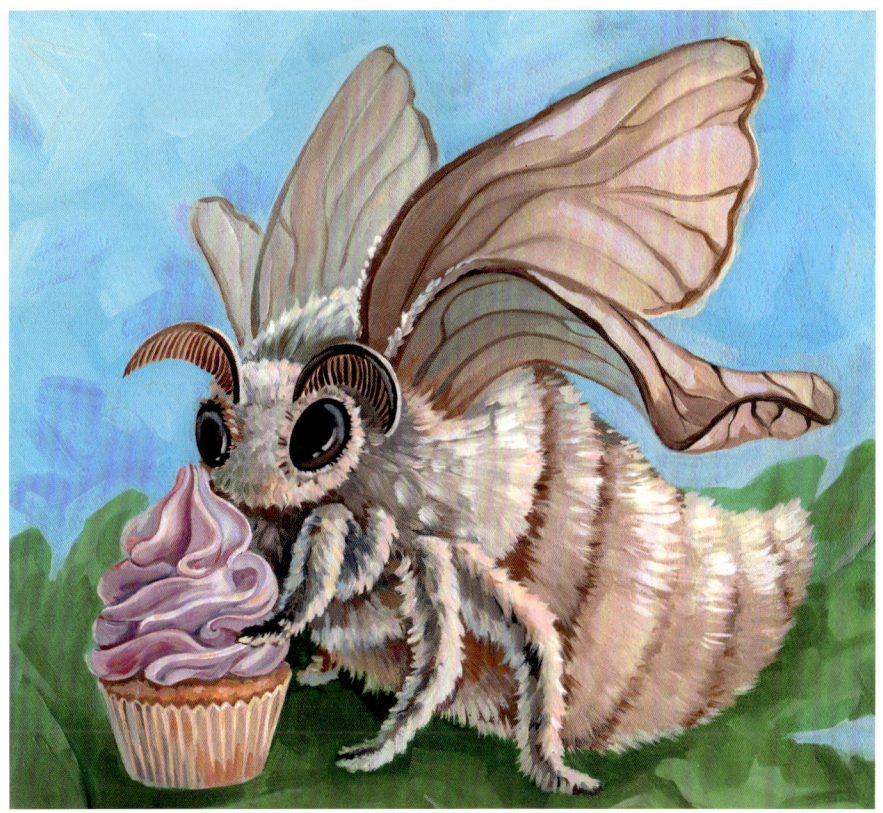

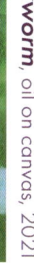

Silkworm, oil on canvas, 2021

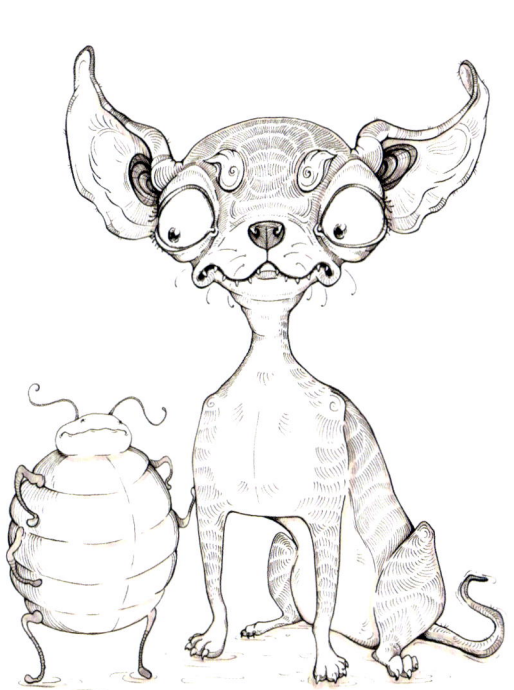

Mini sketches, fineliners, 2022

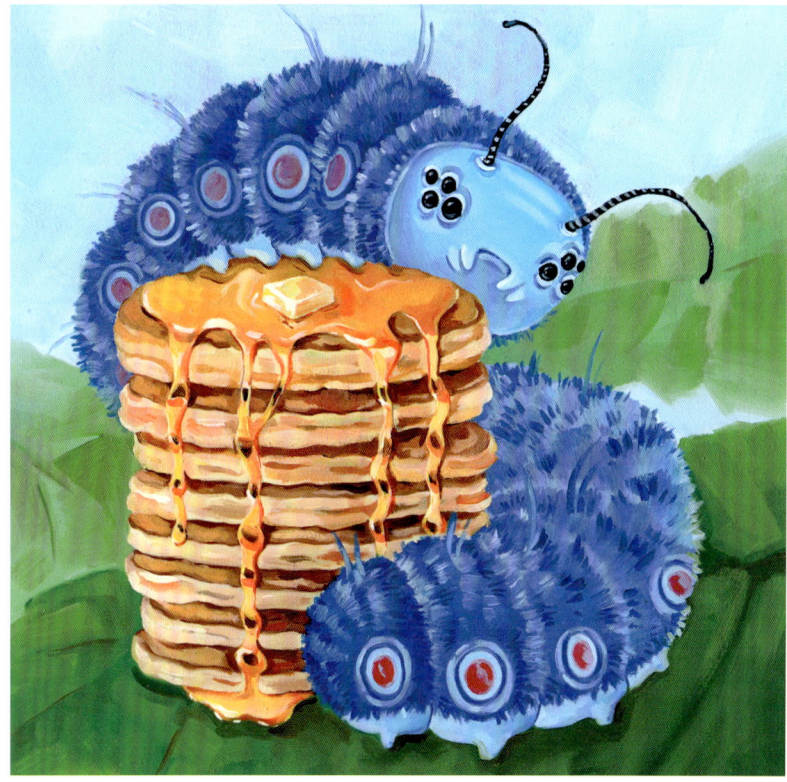

Caterpillar, oil on canvas, 2021

SKETCHBOOKS

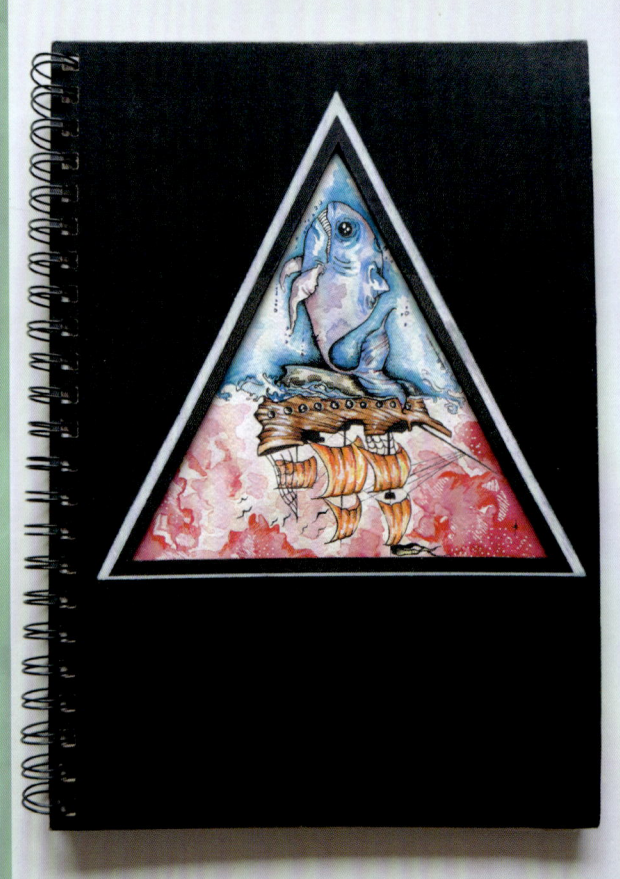

My first sketchbook, 2017

I have never owned many sketchbooks, but I treat each one specially, starting with the cover. I designed my first one when I was fourteen, and a few years later, I started creating a unique look for each new sketchbook.

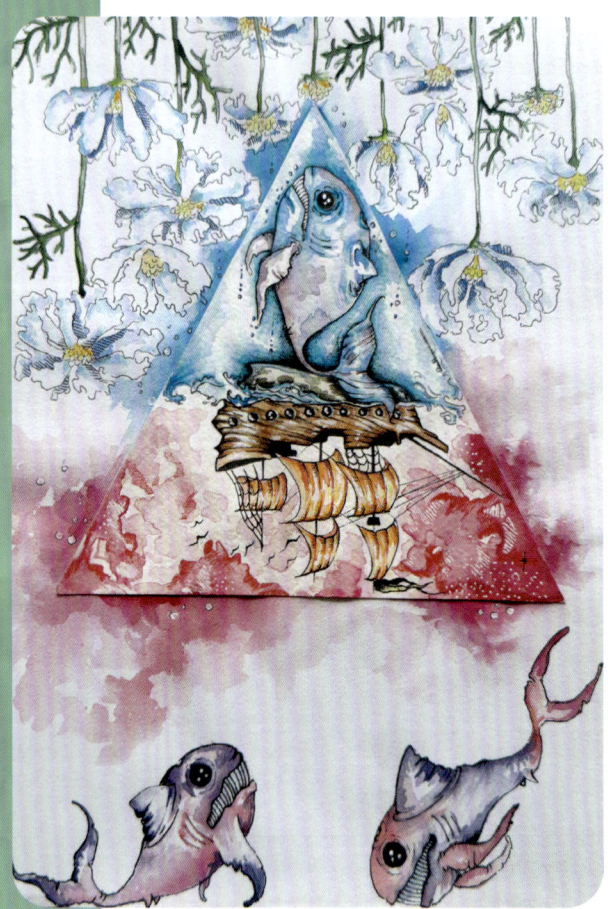

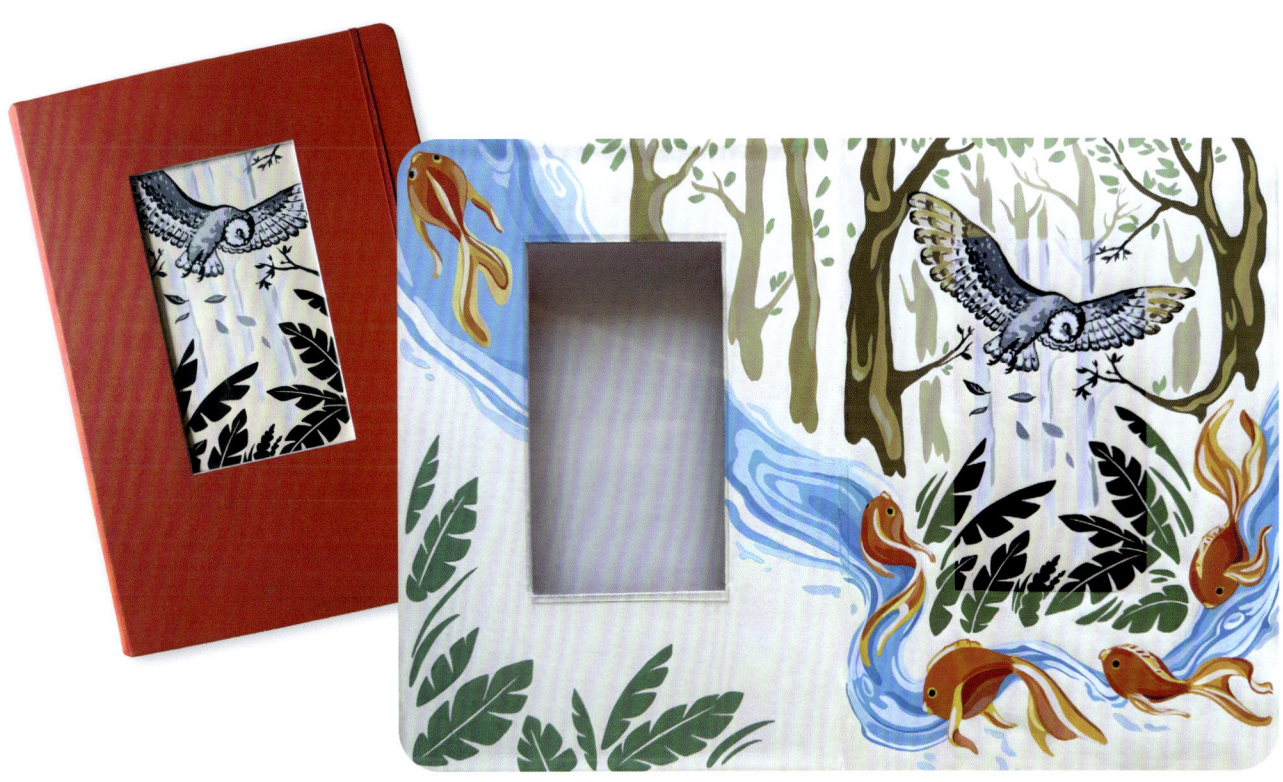

My second sketchbook, 2022

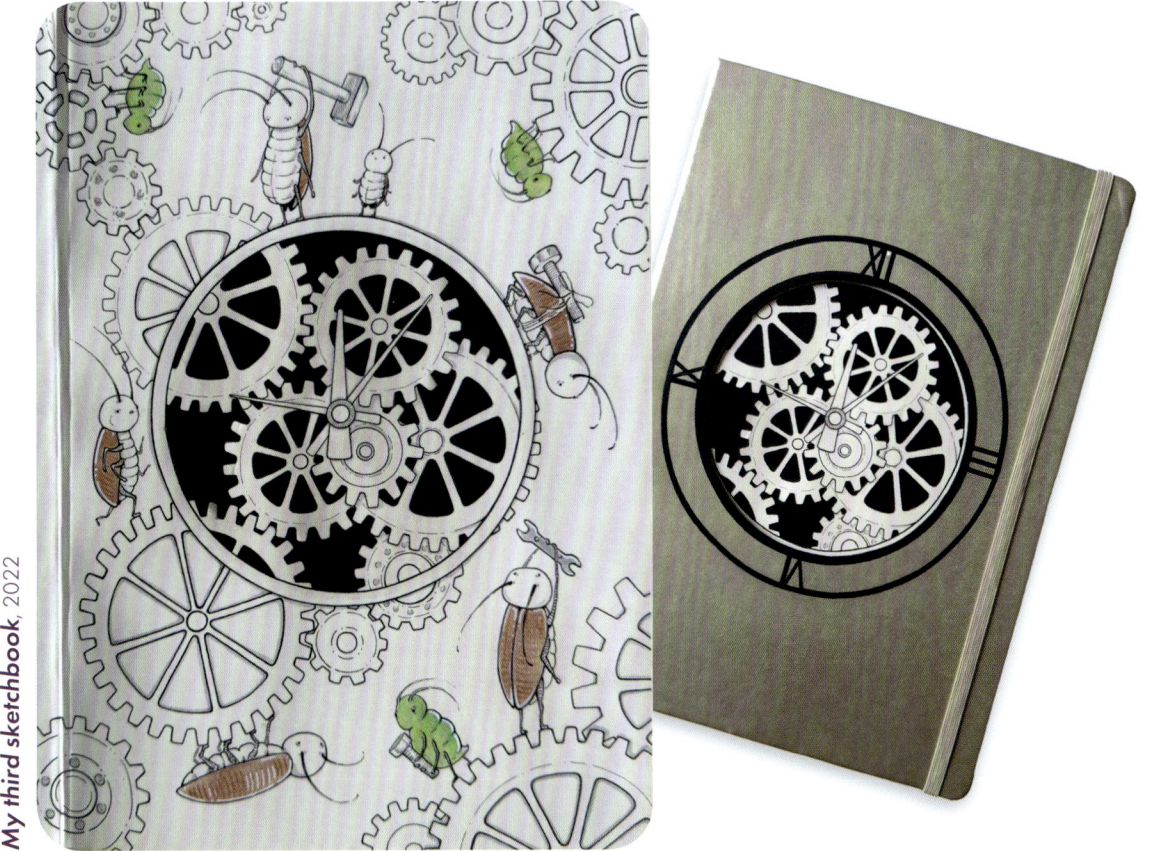

My third sketchbook, 2022

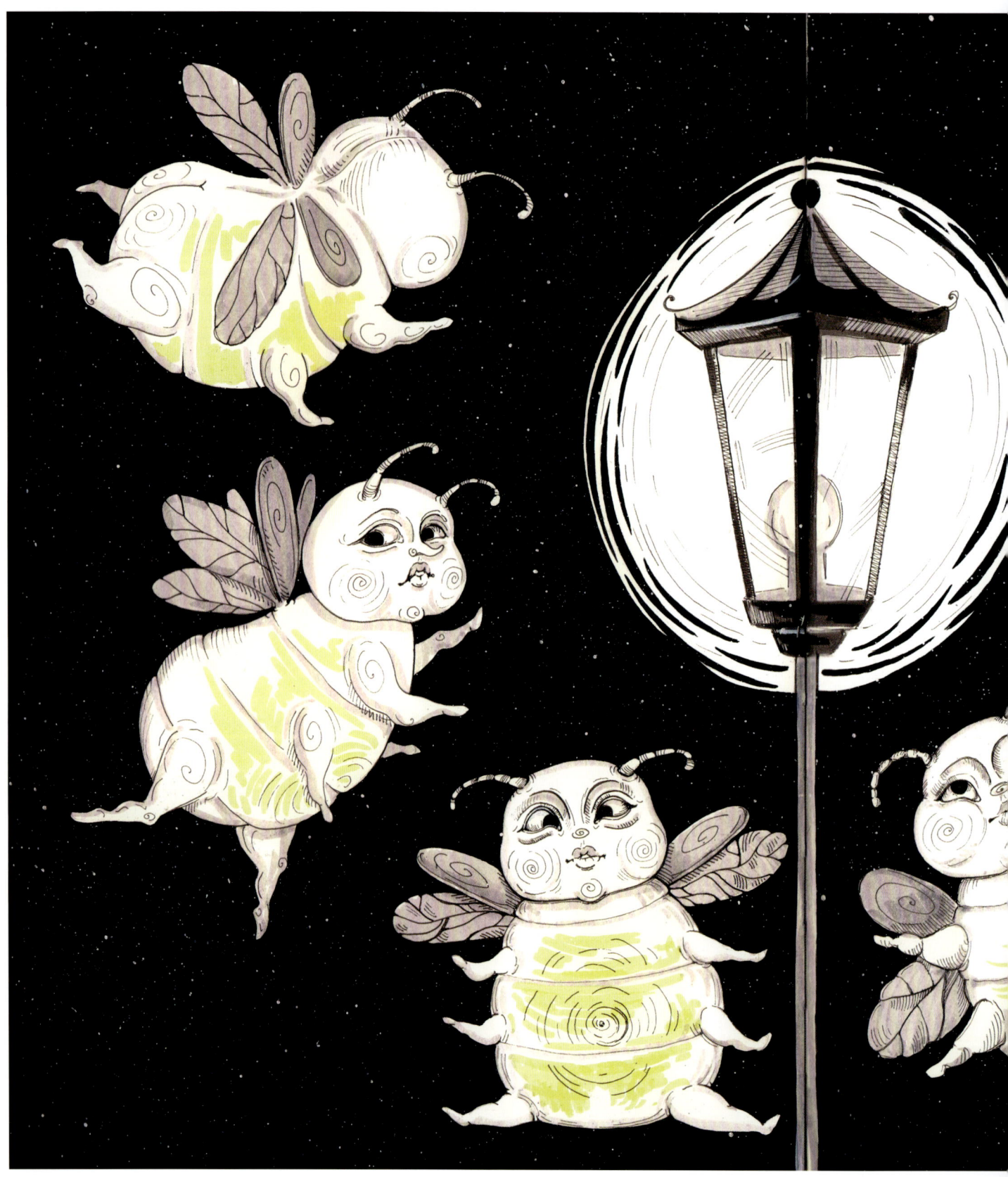

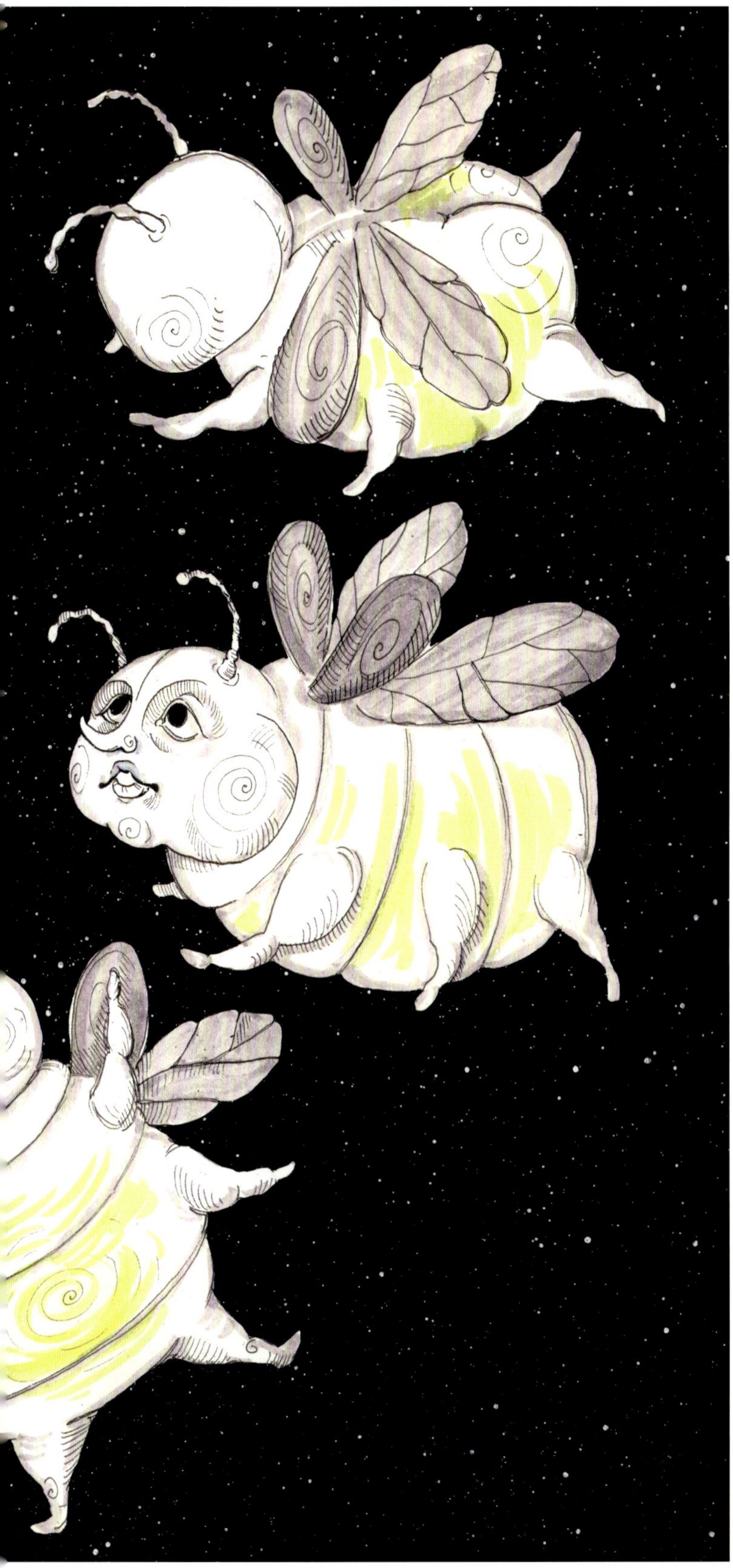

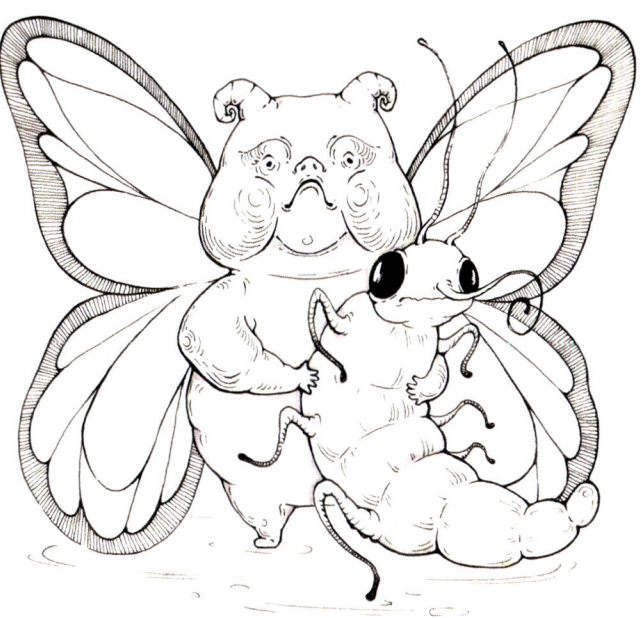

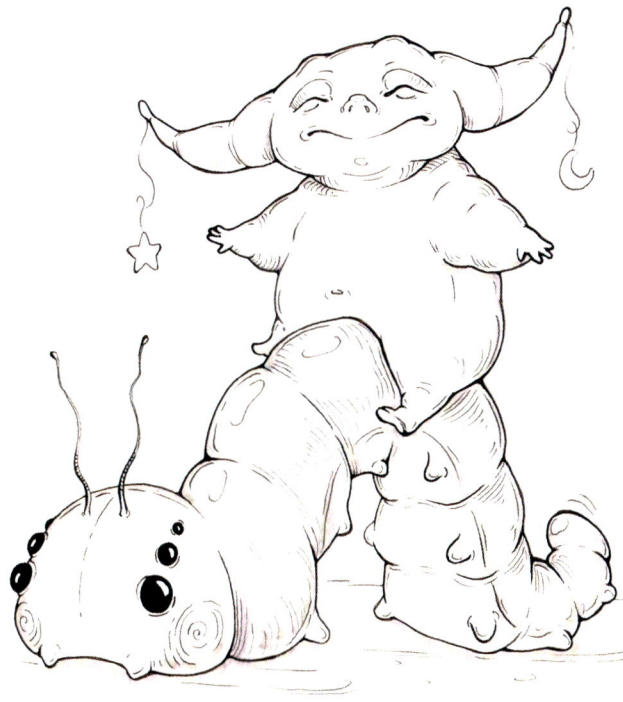

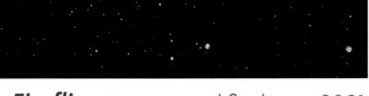

Fireflies, tempera and fineliners, 2021

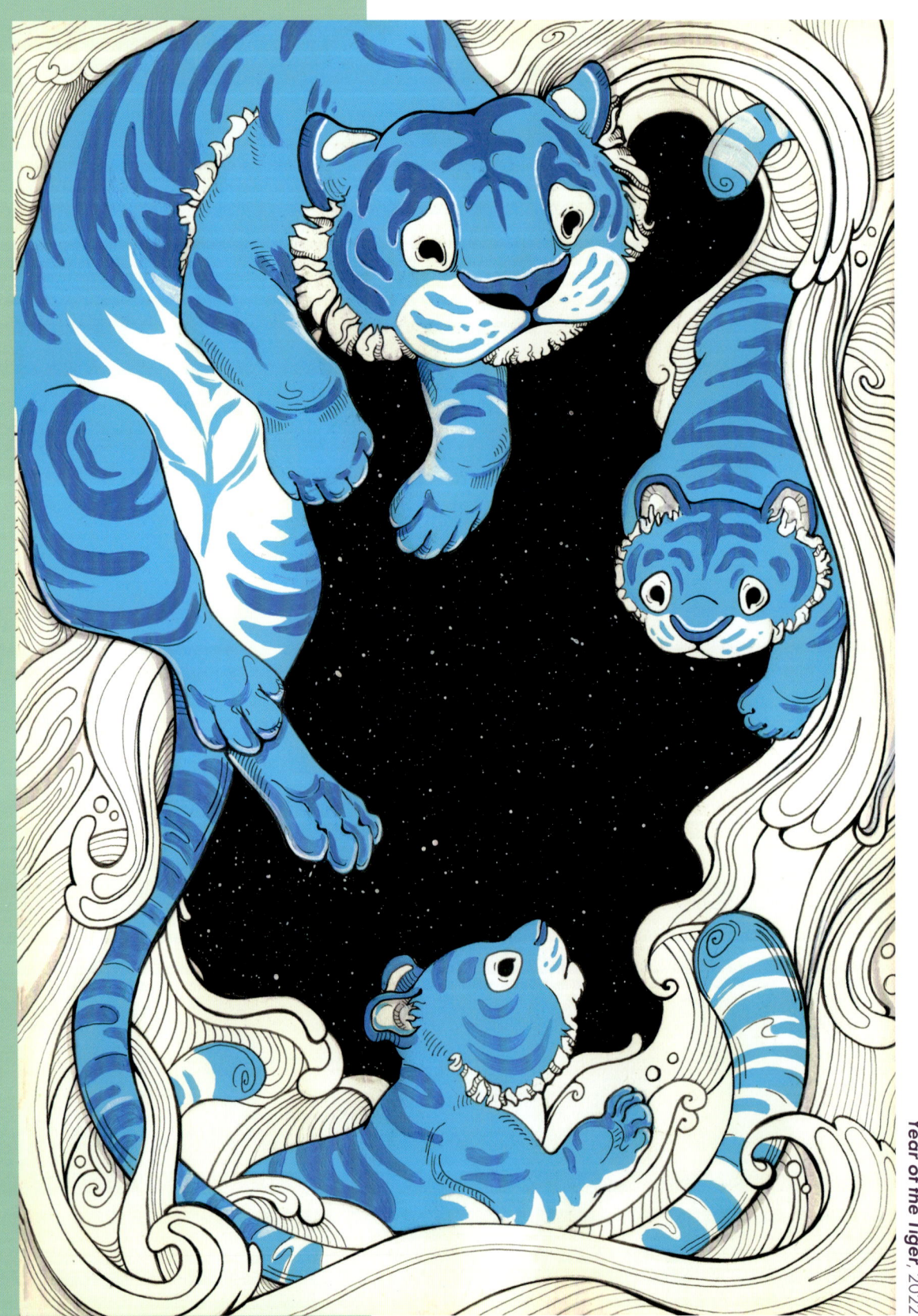

Year of the Tiger, 2022

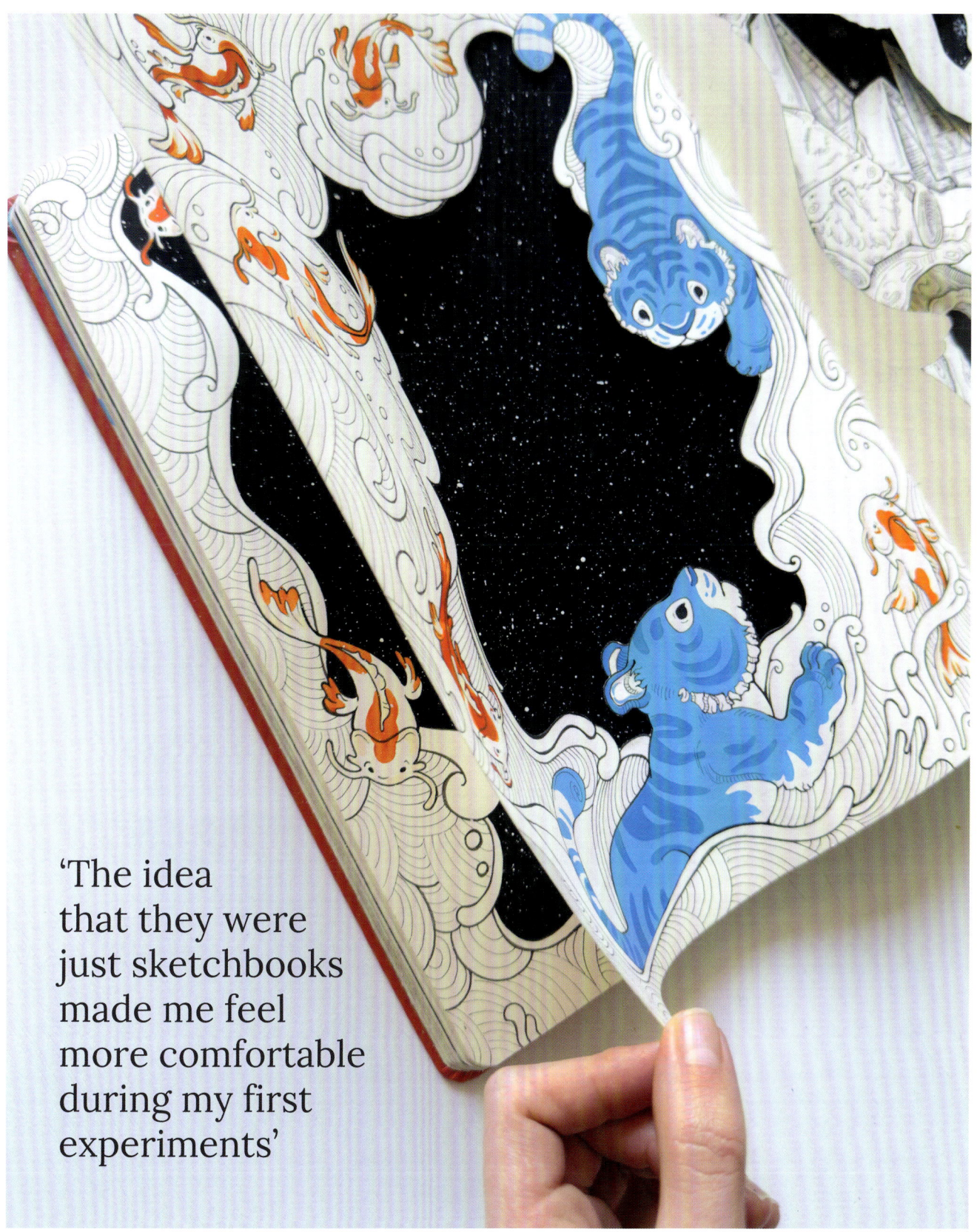

'The idea
that they were
just sketchbooks
made me feel
more comfortable
during my first
experiments'

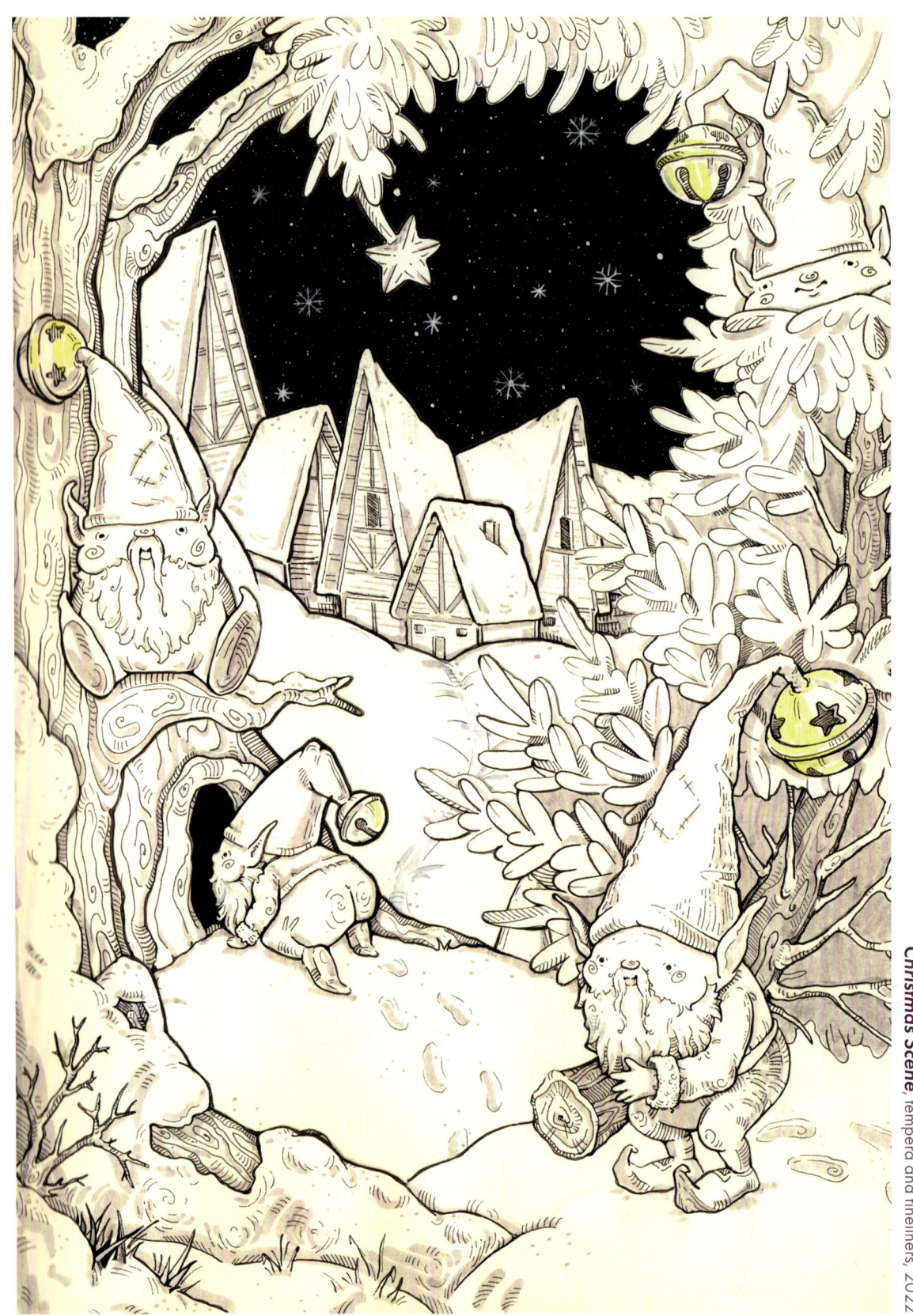

Christmas Scene, tempera and fineliners, 2022

'I started creating a unique look for each new sketchbook'

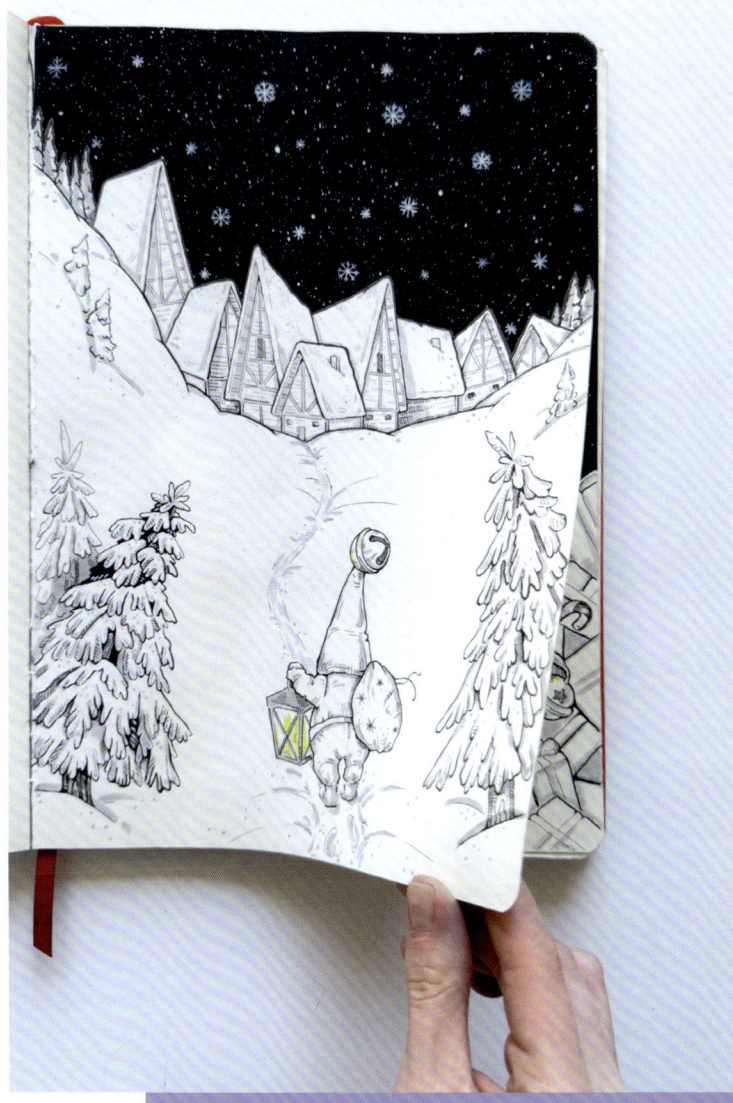

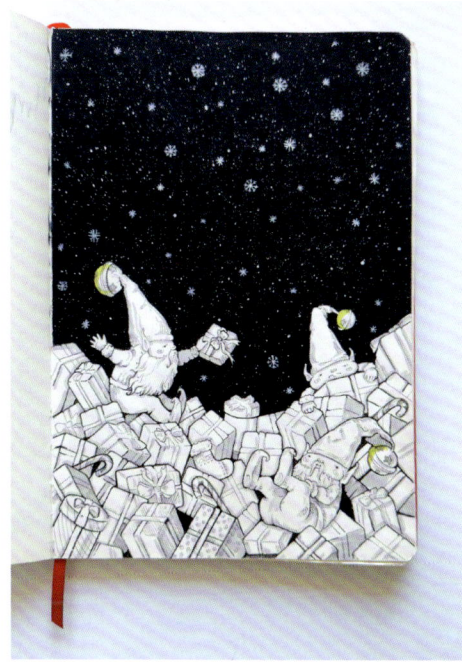

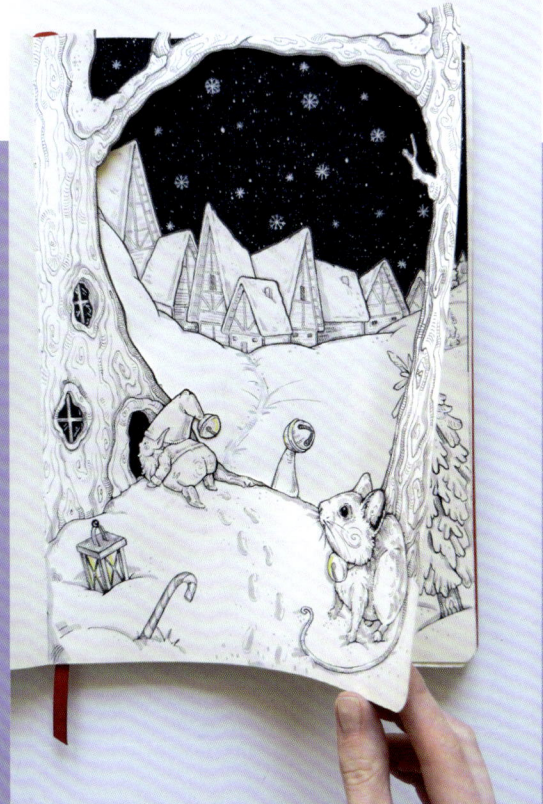

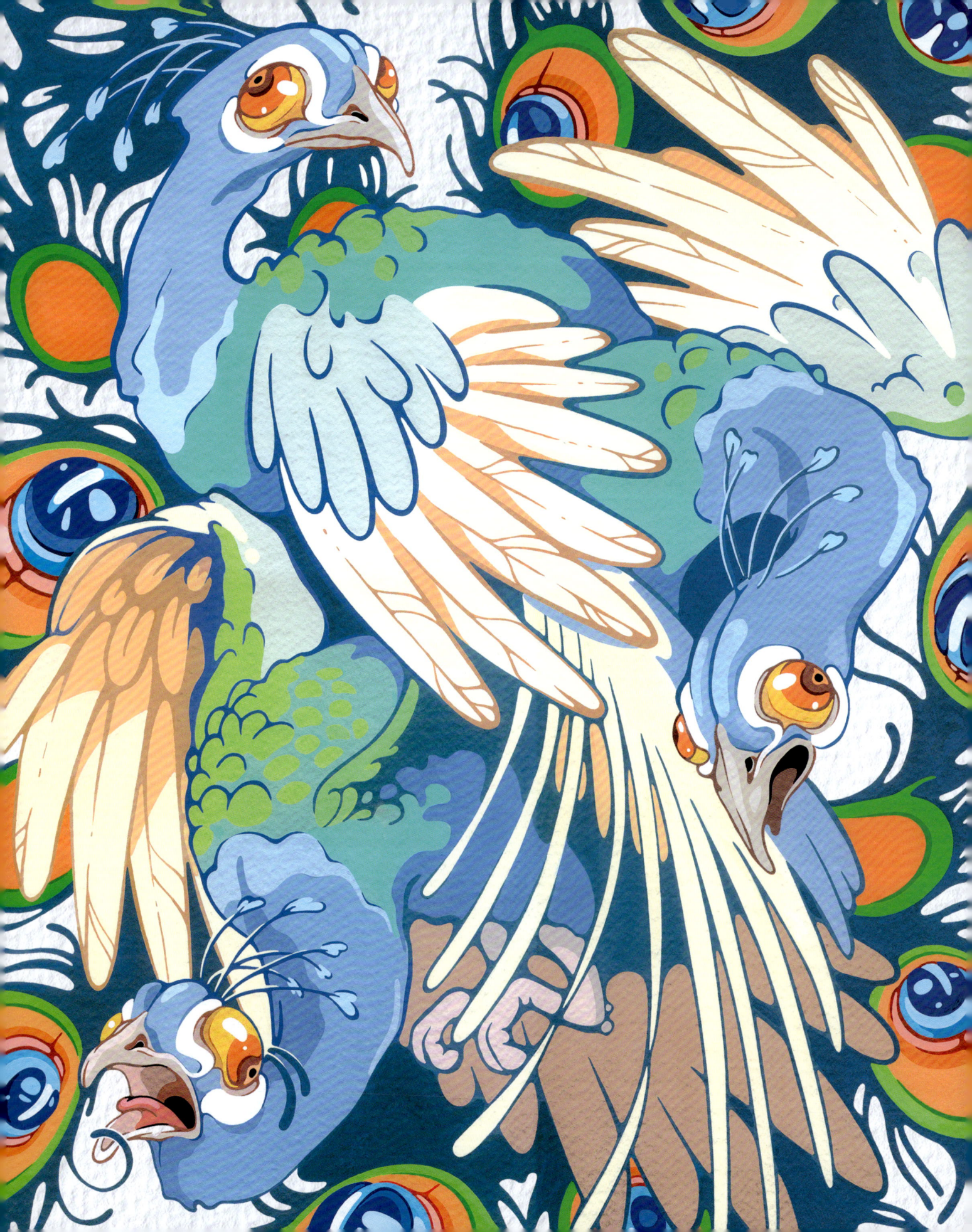

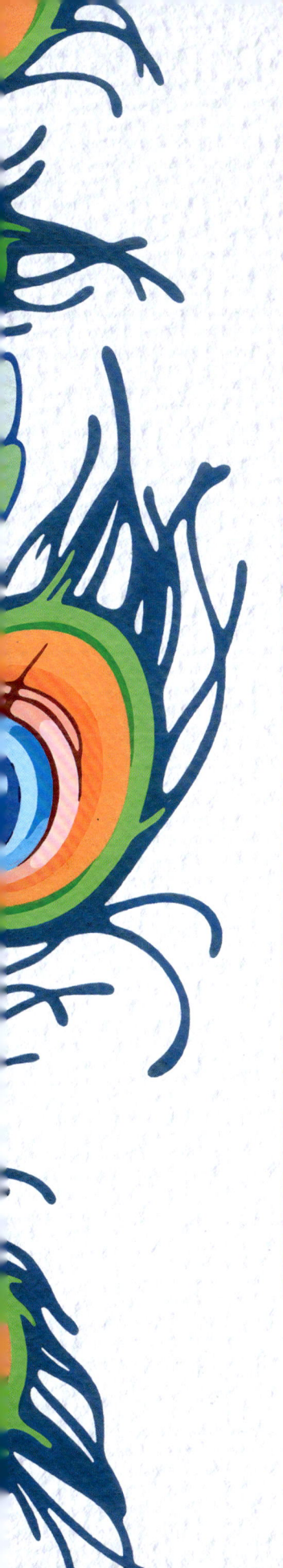

Self-reflection

INNER & OUTER CRITIC

When a student made a mistake in our art class, our teacher would jokingly say, 'May you be kicked by a duck!', a Ukrainian expression used to express dissatisfaction. Although her voice would sound harsh, she was actually very kind and provided an atmosphere that made people feel comfortable and enthusiastic about creating. I always thought it was a skill to maintain a balance between seriousness and lightness.

In college, it was a different story. Performance evaluations were not always pleasant, but they were fair. There were times when I felt angry, disappointed, or afraid that I would fail again. However, failure is an integral part of learning, and you must find the strength to move on time and time again. Every action, even a mistake, leads to growth. Fortunately for me, I had the opportunity to ask my creative parents for advice, and was so grateful for it. It's special to have someone around who will support you no matter what, and it's important to have someone whose opinion you value, even if it differs from your own.

Discussions can be interesting and useful if you remember that everyone has their own point of view.

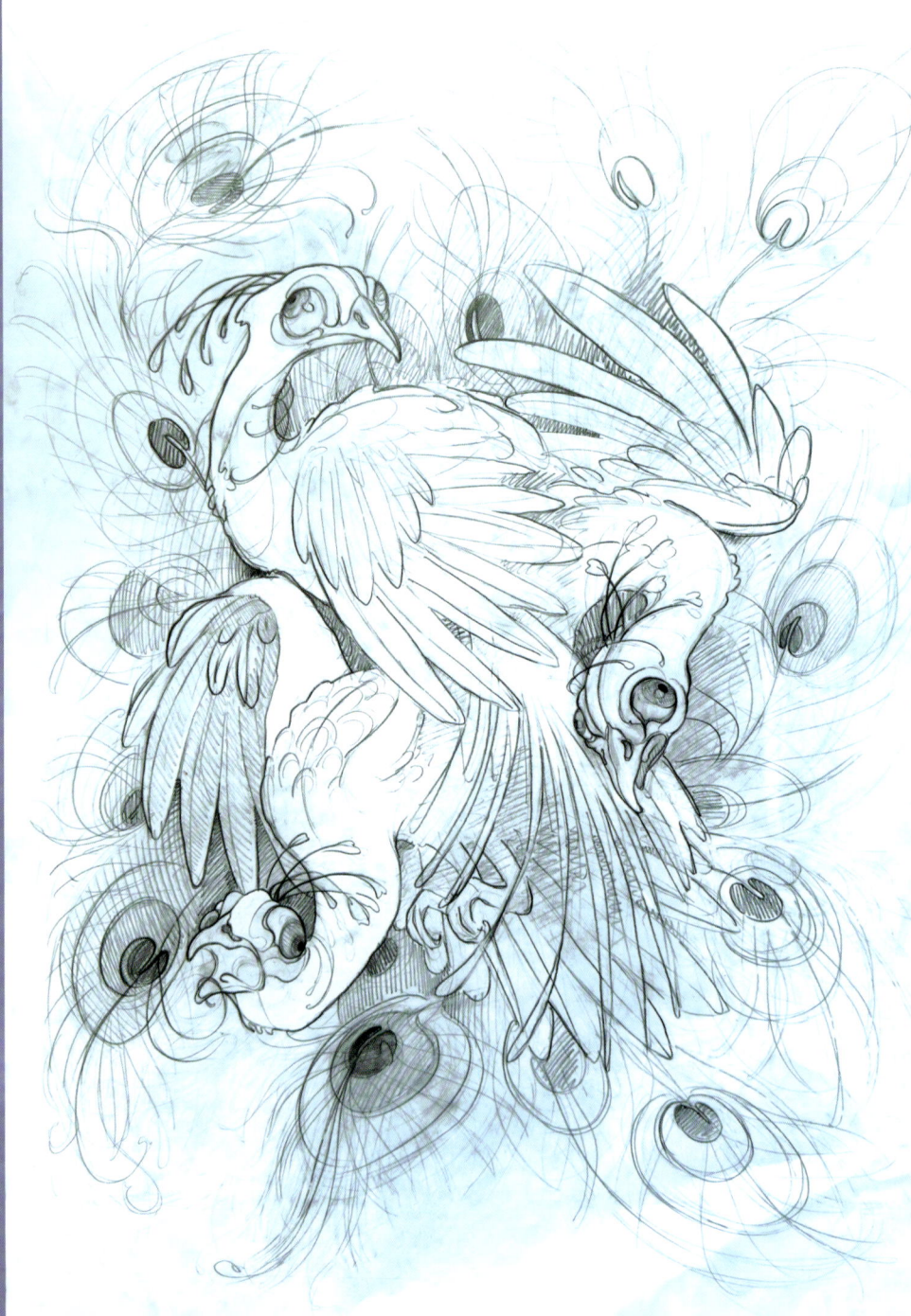

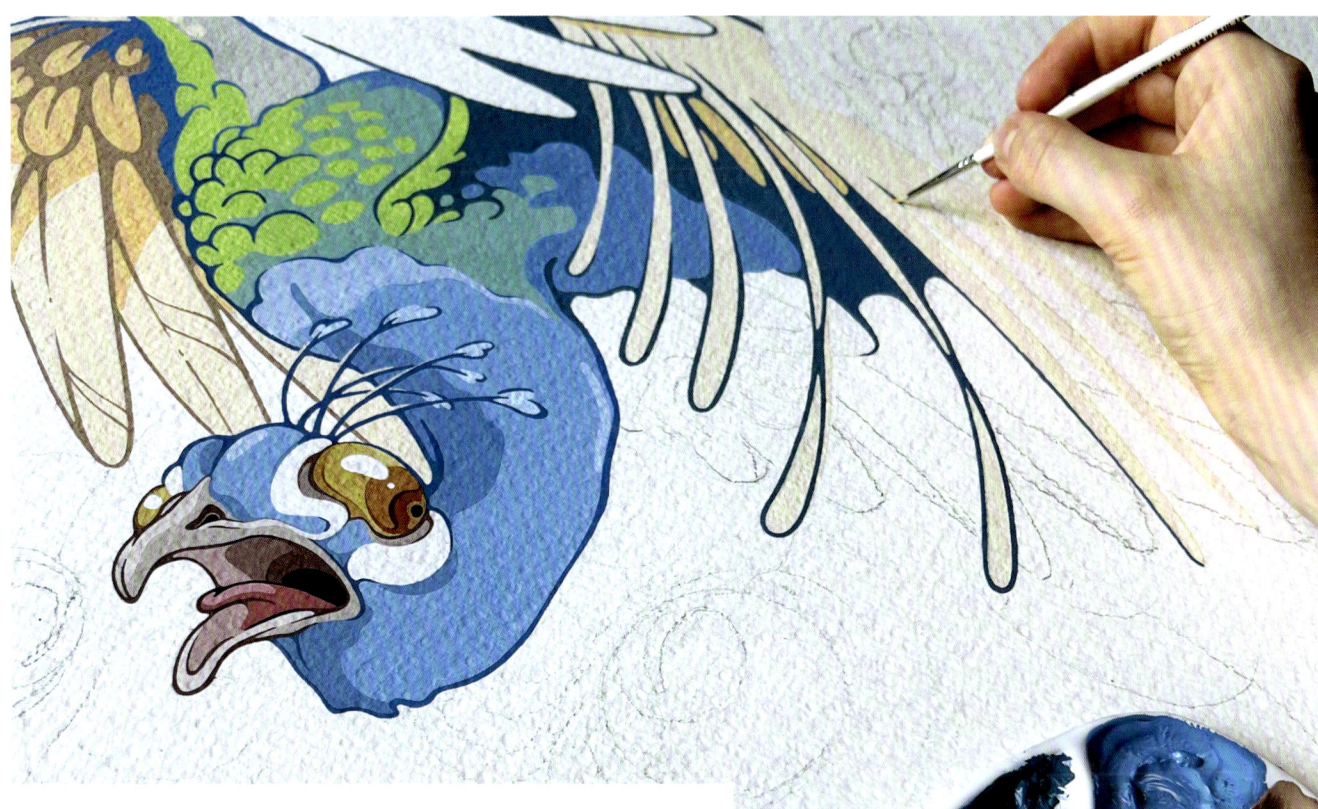

It's important to learn how to respond positively to comments, listening and analysing to determine what can help you and your work. I am not always ready to hear something unpleasant, but this process allows you to expand your perspective. If an artist was constantly told that everything was perfect, what would be the point? Creativity would stop, and there would be no reason to develop.

However, criticism on the internet is significantly different. It's a constant stream of random thoughts and varying interpretations. Feedback from people who care about my art is important to me – their support inspires me and boosts my self-confidence. But while there are usually more positive words, there are also some that can cause doubt. Thanks to my experience with constructive criticism, I now know how to take in what's helpful and disregard the rest. Everyone sees things differently, and I'm not trying to convince anyone of anything. I just want to share my perspective. It's up to everyone else if they want to accept it or not.

That being said, fears and doubts don't just disappear. Your harshest critic lives inside you. This is the voice that appears more often than any other: *You're not good enough. You are too slow. You won't make it.* I used to try to drive these thoughts away. Now, I'm learning how to respond to them correctly. For example, a doubt might happen while working: *I could have come up with something better. The sketch isn't finalized...* But then I remember that I've coped with difficult situations more than once. In the end, I either liked the result or realized what I needed to improve for the next project.

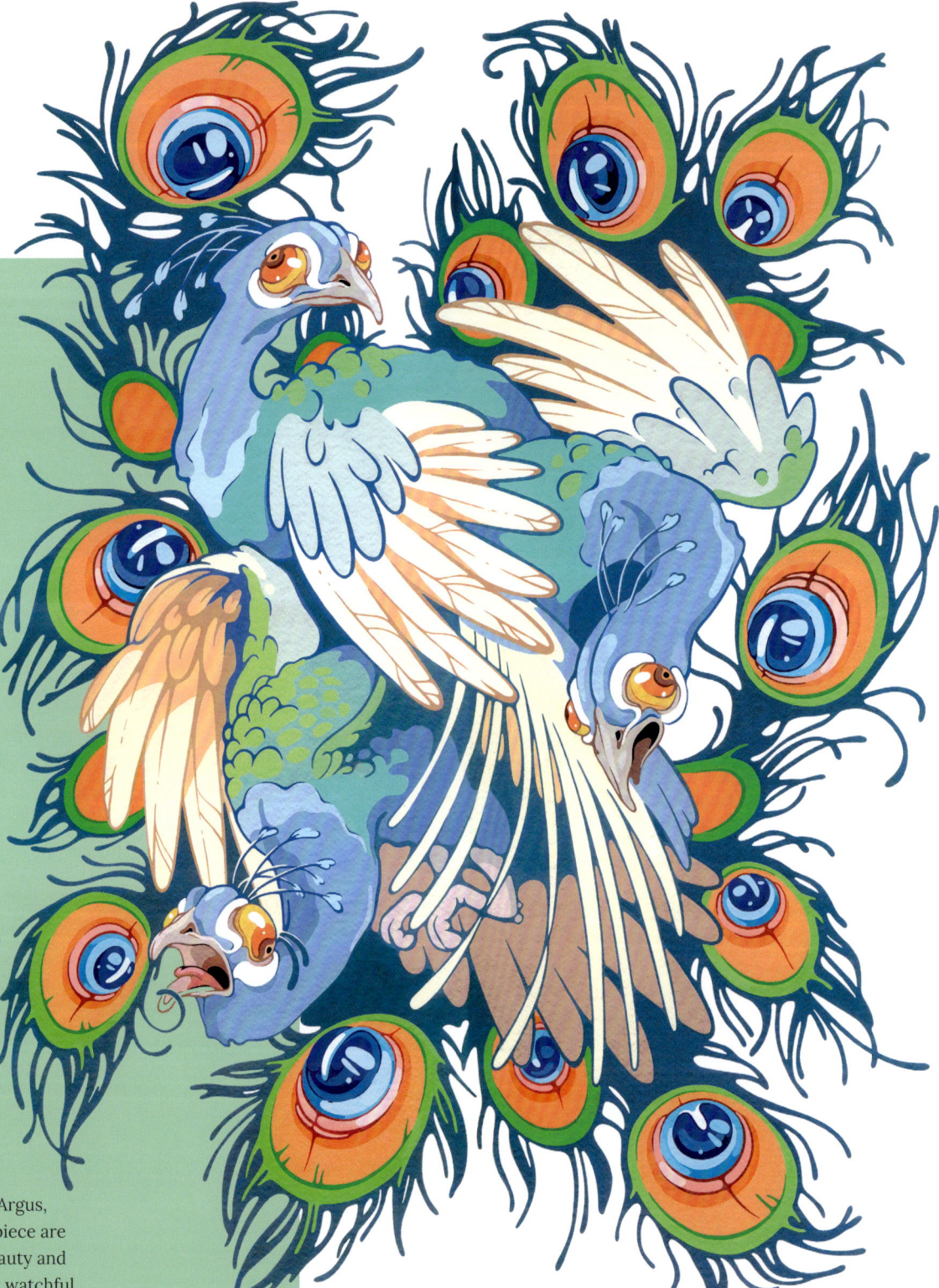

When it comes to dealing with criticism, everyone is stuck in their own web, and every way out of it is different. It may sound simple, but I find comfort in thinking that strength is not an impressive act of heroism, but simply the ability to keep going.

We become our own worst enemies when we criticize ourselves without also acknowledging our beauty. I attempted to visualize this concept in the painting on this page. According to Greek mythology, the 'eyes' appeared on peacock feathers thanks to the goddess Hera, who immortalized her watchful, hundred-eyed bodyguard, Argus, by turning him into her favourite bird. Just like Argus, the feathered 'eyes' in this piece are observing their masters. Beauty and confidence is contrasted by watchful fear and indecision.

Beneath the Beauty, tempera, 2024.

BEING YOURSELF

To be yourself, you have to stay true to yourself. It sounds obvious, but it's easier said than done. What if you're not what others expect? What if they don't like the 'real' you?

I wouldn't say that I was going through a serious creative crisis, but when I graduated from the academy, I felt like I was about to. I had a choice: I could apply for a master's degree as my teachers advised, or I could listen to myself and choose a different path. I usually weigh my decisions for a long time. But back then, I felt that I simply could not continue my studies as expected. I was tired. I lacked the feeling that I was creating art that was true to me.

I want to make it clear that the previous years were not in vain. I gained valuable experience that has made me who I am today. However, continuing my studies would have meant working within a different artistic paradigm, which I did not want to do. So, I followed my intuition. Since then, I have not regretted it.

However, the obstacles have not disappeared. Certain setbacks are part of the process. Sometimes, compositions don't work, even after I spend a long time on them. Other times, the colours don't turn out as planned, and I have to find and fix my mistakes. This whole process is never easy – not like it looks in the videos.

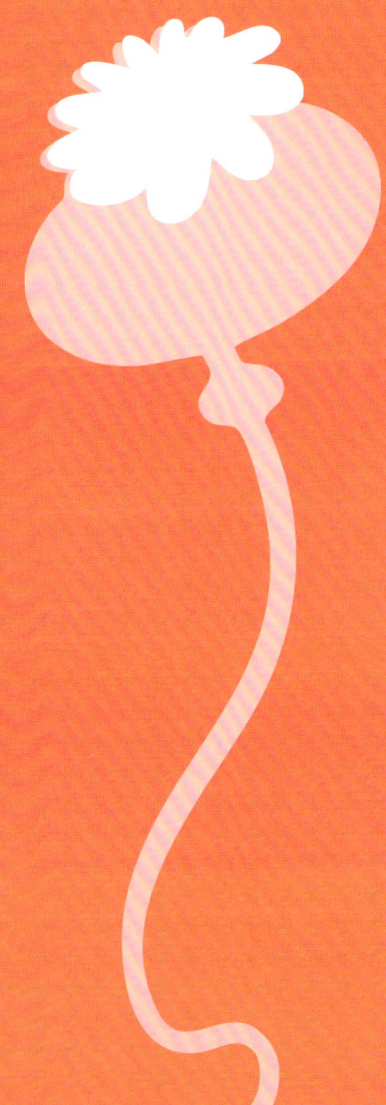

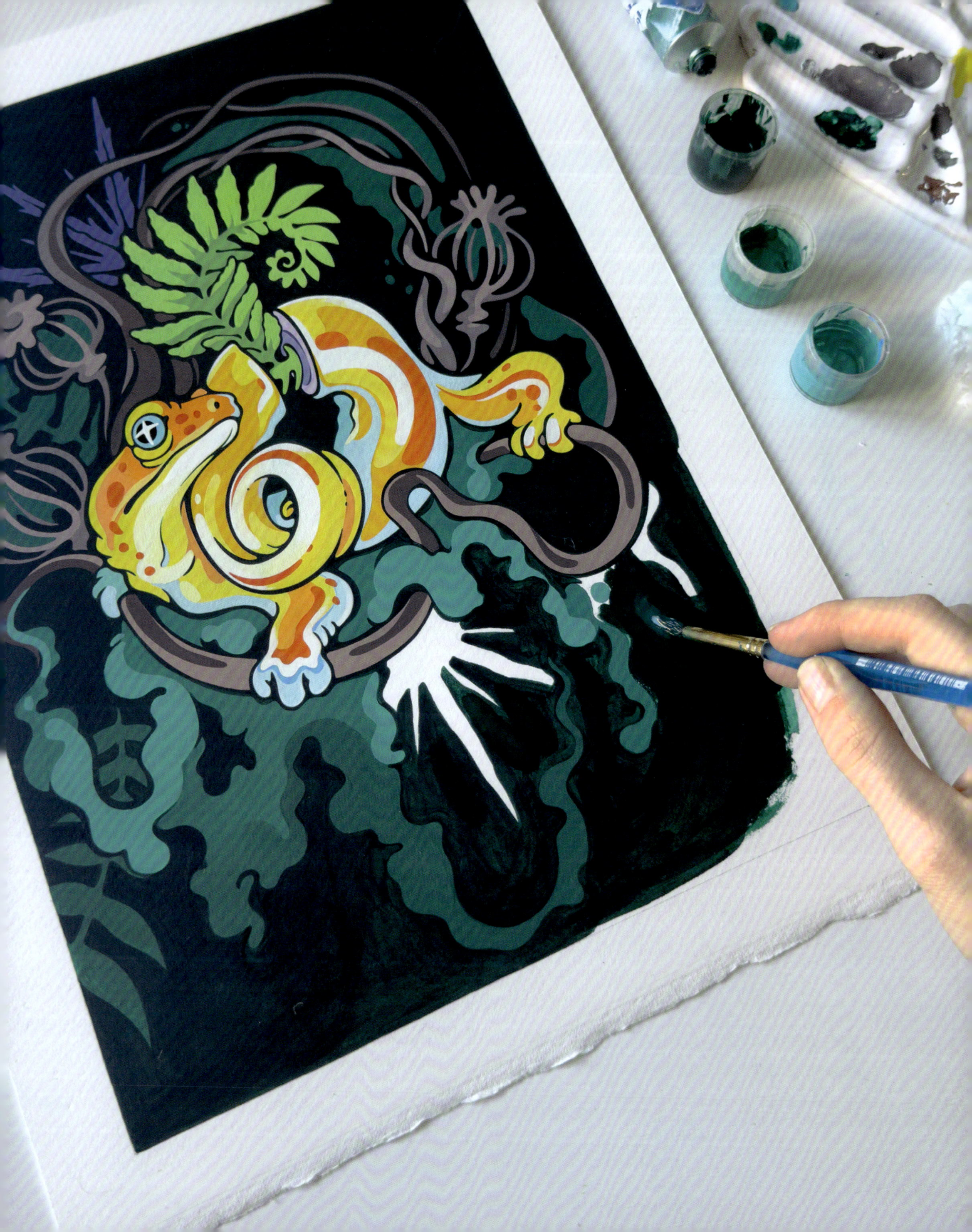

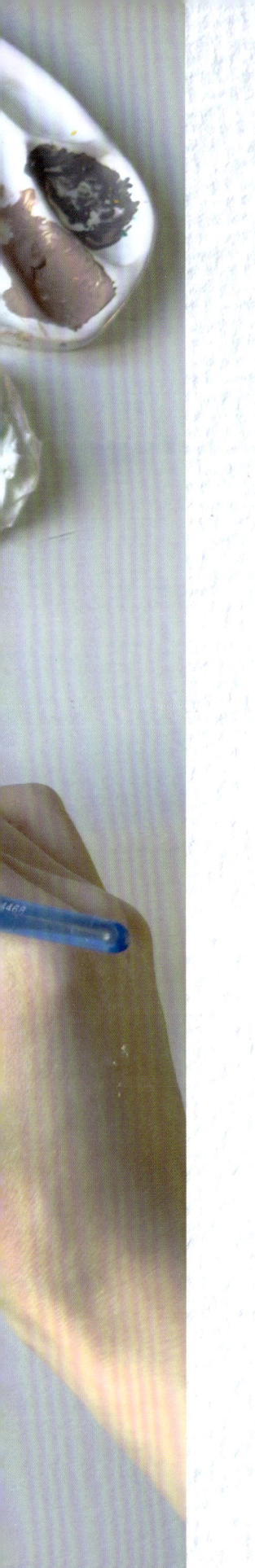

Tutorials

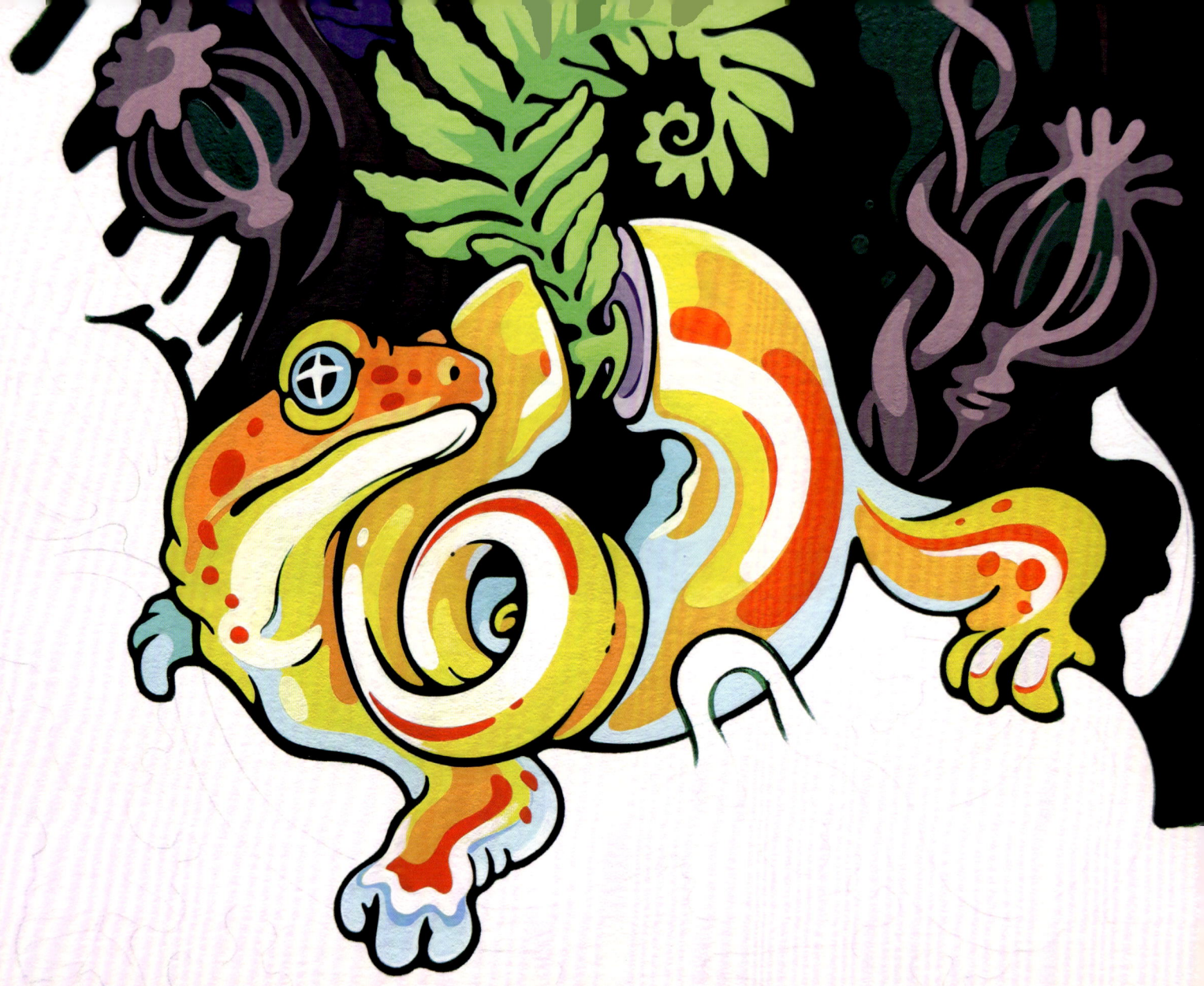

TEMPERA: METHODS & TECHNIQUES

I don't believe in strict rules when it comes to working with paints. Artists can borrow techniques from different styles, combine them, and experiment to find their own ways of bringing ideas to life. Looking back on my years of training, I see that I worked very differently than I do now. However, all that knowledge gave me more room for interpretation, allowing me to use some techniques and abandon others. On the next few pages are the key methods and techniques I've adapted for my current tempera work.

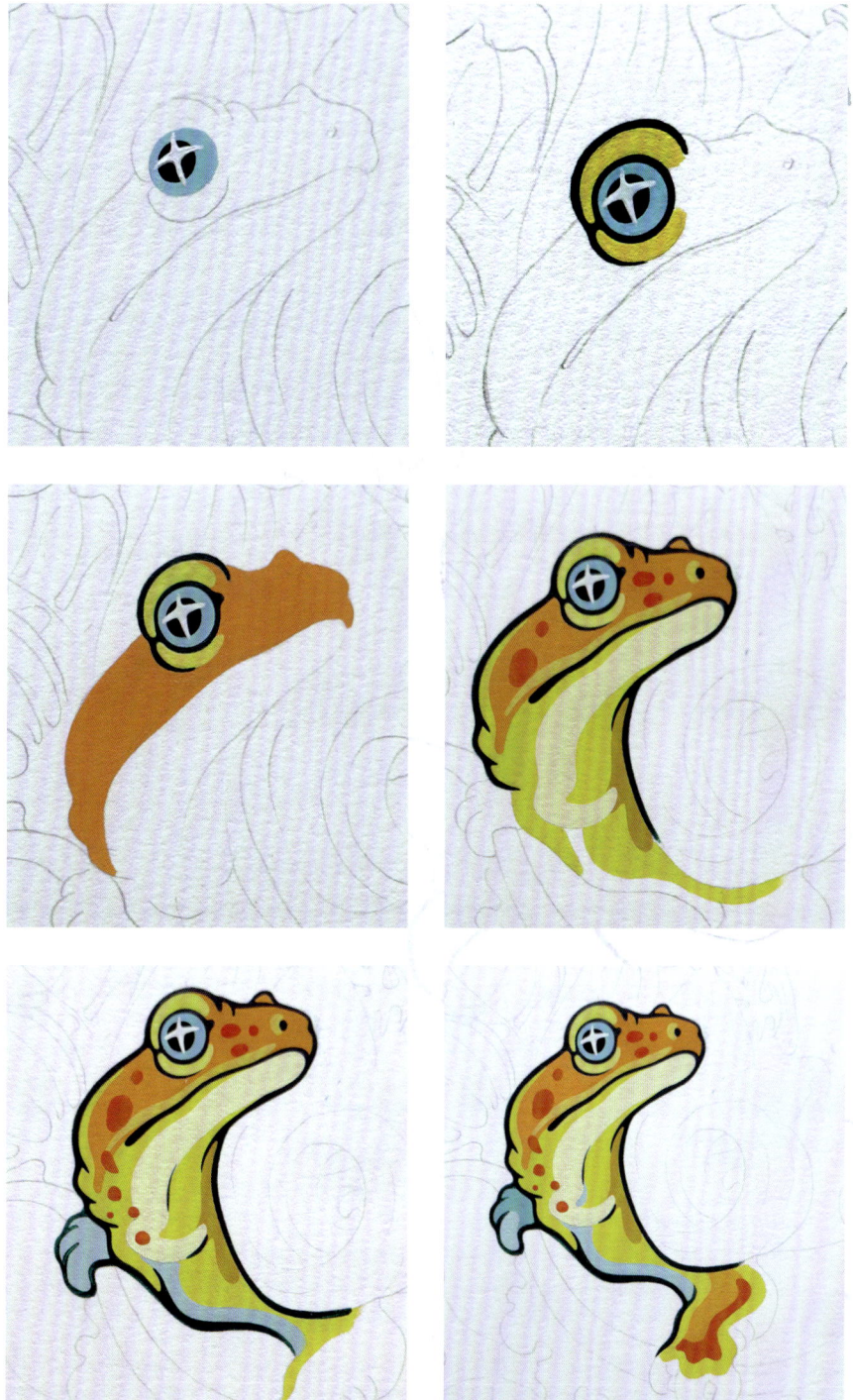

BUILDING FORM WITH COLOUR

I used to work using the 'blocking-in' method, starting with the big picture and working down to the details. Our teachers disapproved of students spending hours drawing the pupil of the eye instead of quick tonal masses. There is a logical explanation for this: when you squint, you see the world as a series of light and dark spots, which allows you to focus on the overall structure of the image.

Now, however, I don't start with the entire canvas at once. Instead, I divide the canvas into fragments of medium-toned colour. Then, I layer lighter and darker accents on top, drawing lines and small details. I only move on to the next fragment after completing the previous one, forming the entire image step by step. This may sound complicated, but this method is important to me because it helps me maintain accuracy in the purity of colours, the evenness of lines, and the smoothness of the paper.

Nevertheless, I sometimes encounter situations where colours don't work as intended. Even the most careful plan can't anticipate every nuance, so I often have to improvise solutions as I go along. In my opinion, this is a good thing because it makes the work process lively and interesting.

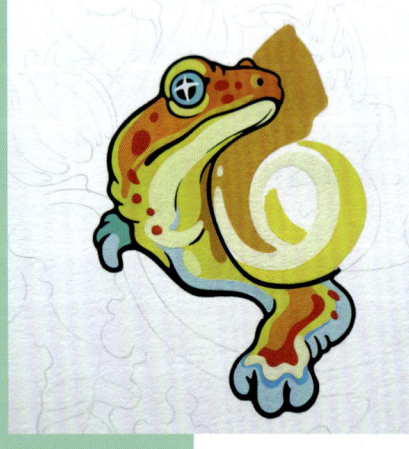
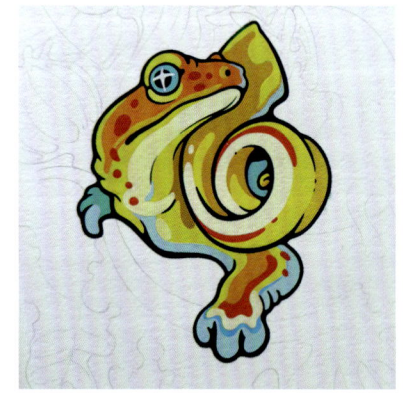
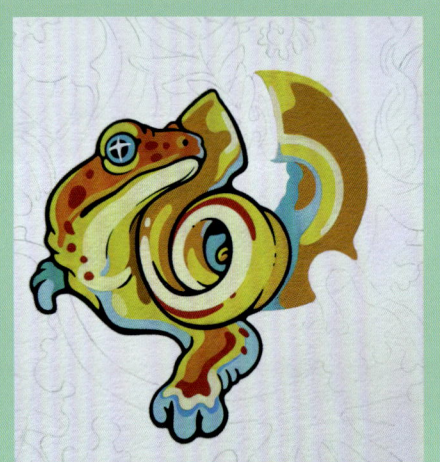
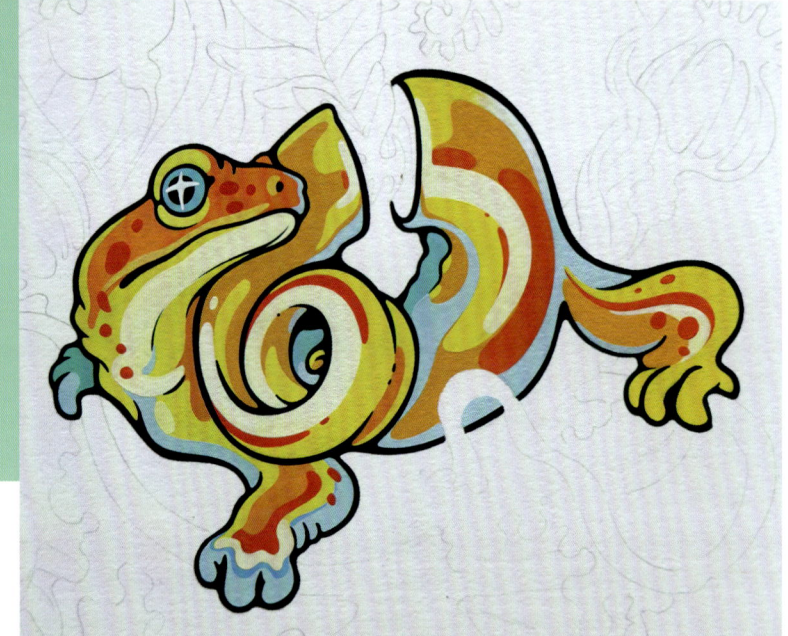

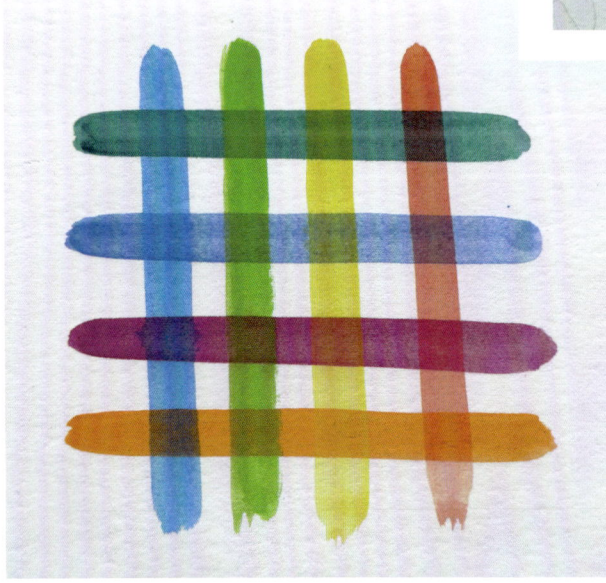

GLAZING

The essence of the glazing technique is to apply thin, translucent layers on top of a dry layer. This deepens the colour, creates shine, and produces soft transitions. This technique is used in traditional tempera painting to create icons, and in oil and watercolour painting to achieve transparent, saturated shades.

CREATING A GRADIENT USING THE GLAZING TECHNIQUE

STEP 01: Apply an opaque colour and wait until it is completely dry.

STEP 02: Mix a new colour that is lighter than the previous one. On the palette, dilute the paint with water to achieve a semi-transparent consistency. Spread the glaze along the transition area, from the edge to the centre. The closer you get to the centre, the more water you should use and the less paint.

STEP 03: Add a little more paint near the edges to make the colour less transparent there.

STEP 04: While the paint is still wet, smooth out any unevenness with a semi-dry brush, if necessary.

STEP 05: Done. Let the paint dry and it will spread evenly.

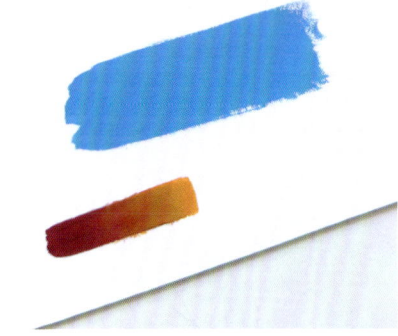
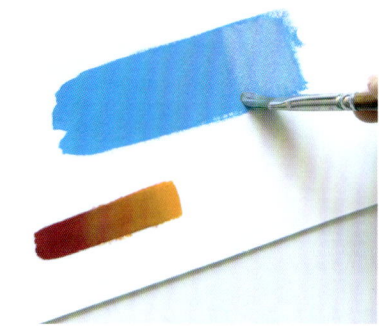
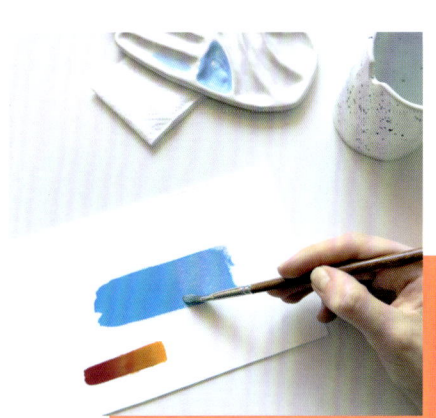
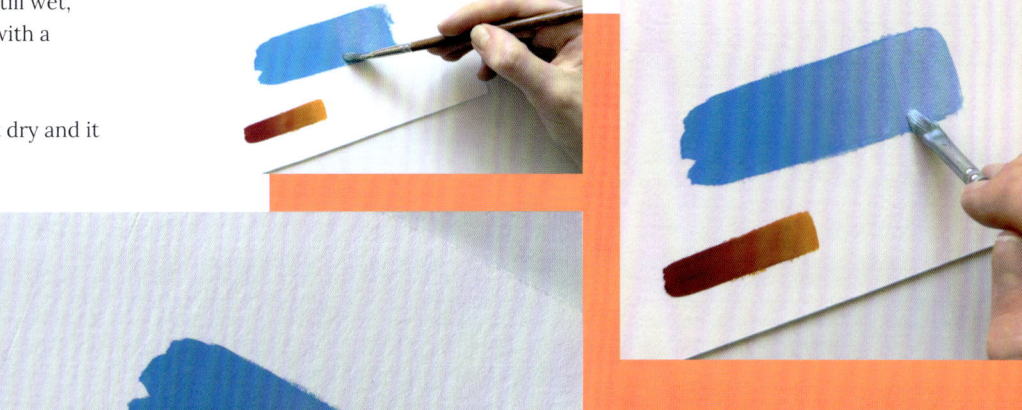

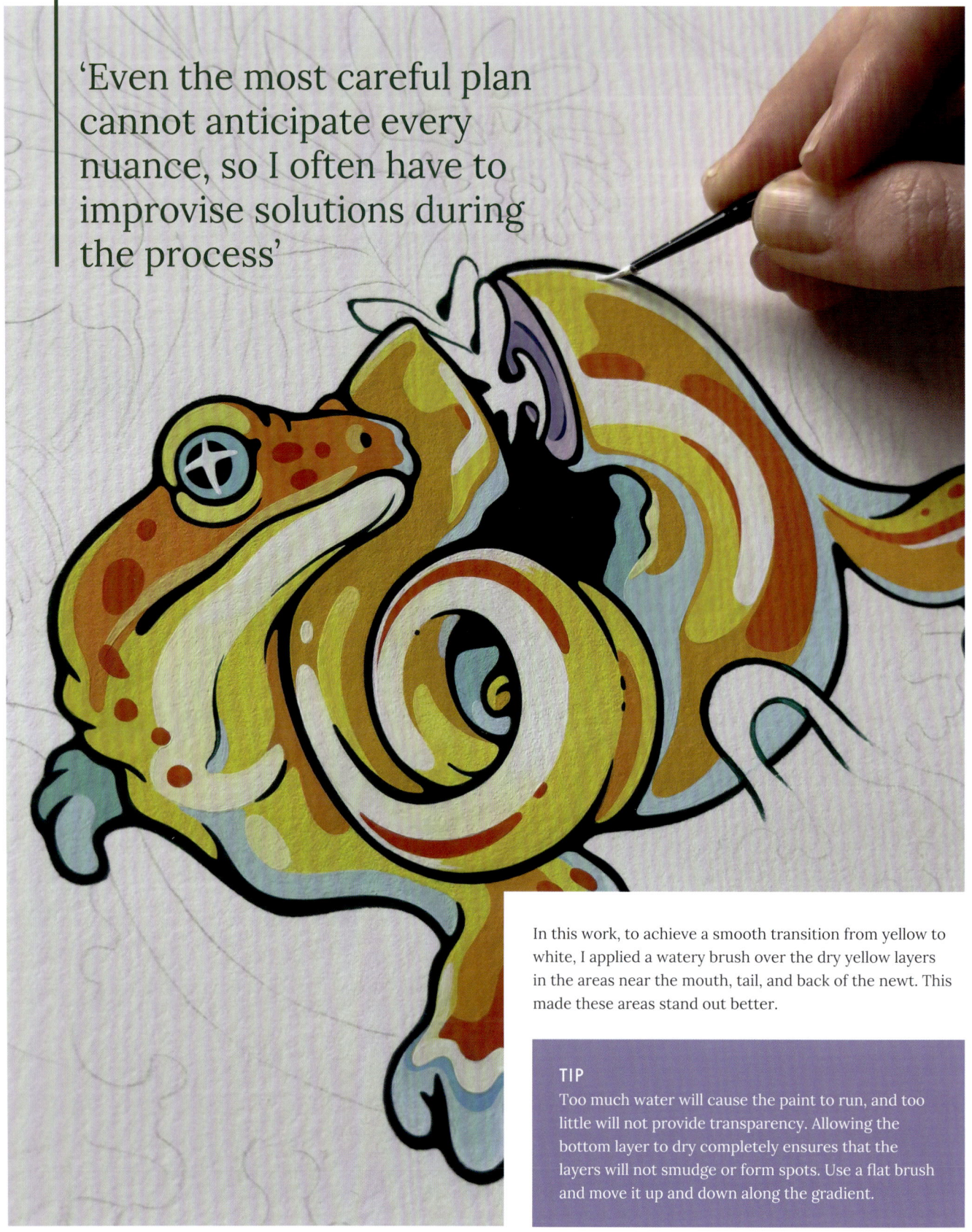

'Even the most careful plan cannot anticipate every nuance, so I often have to improvise solutions during the process'

In this work, to achieve a smooth transition from yellow to white, I applied a watery brush over the dry yellow layers in the areas near the mouth, tail, and back of the newt. This made these areas stand out better.

TIP
Too much water will cause the paint to run, and too little will not provide transparency. Allowing the bottom layer to dry completely ensures that the layers will not smudge or form spots. Use a flat brush and move it up and down along the gradient.

TONAL RENDERING

When working with oil paints, I always start with an underpainting. When it's hard to predict the desired tone, beginning with the darkest areas establishes a solid tonal foundation, makes it easier to create gradations of light and shadow, and reduces 'dirt' in mixtures.

I no longer follow this rule as strictly as I used to, but whenever I am unsure about tonal shades, I still start with the darkest areas first.

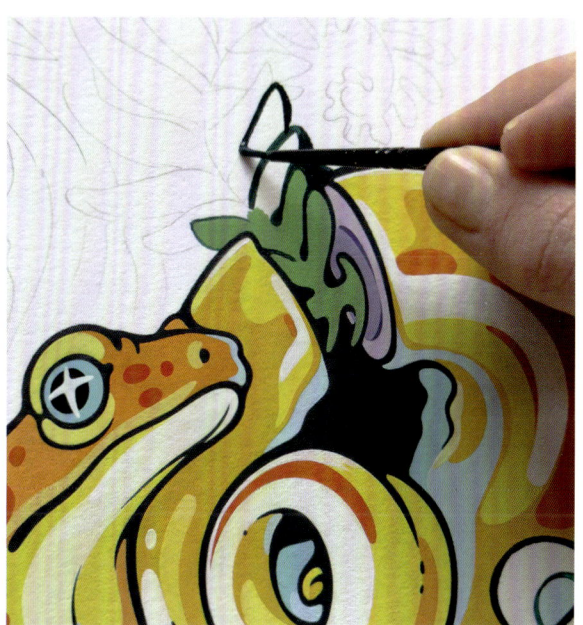

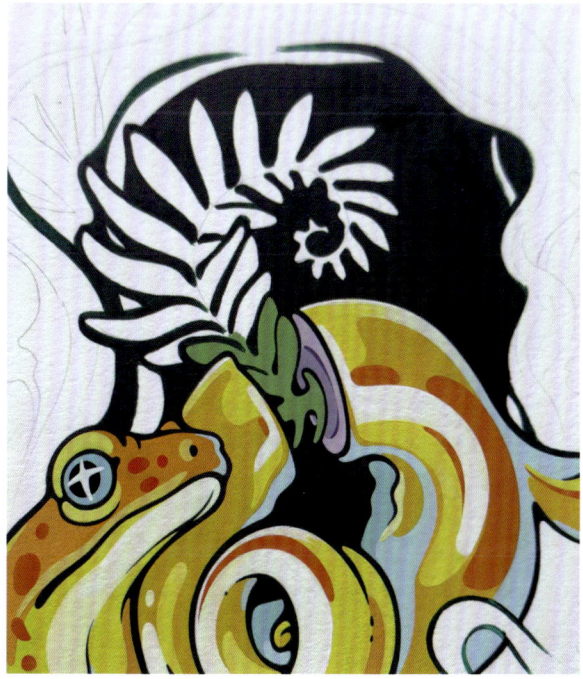

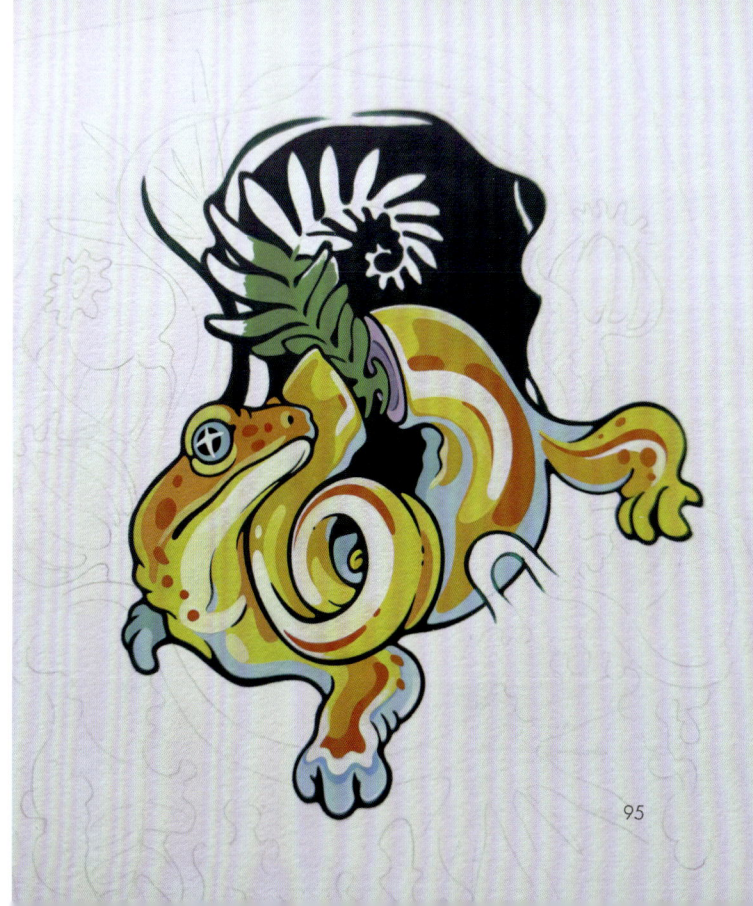

'Beginning with the darkest areas establishes a solid tonal foundation'

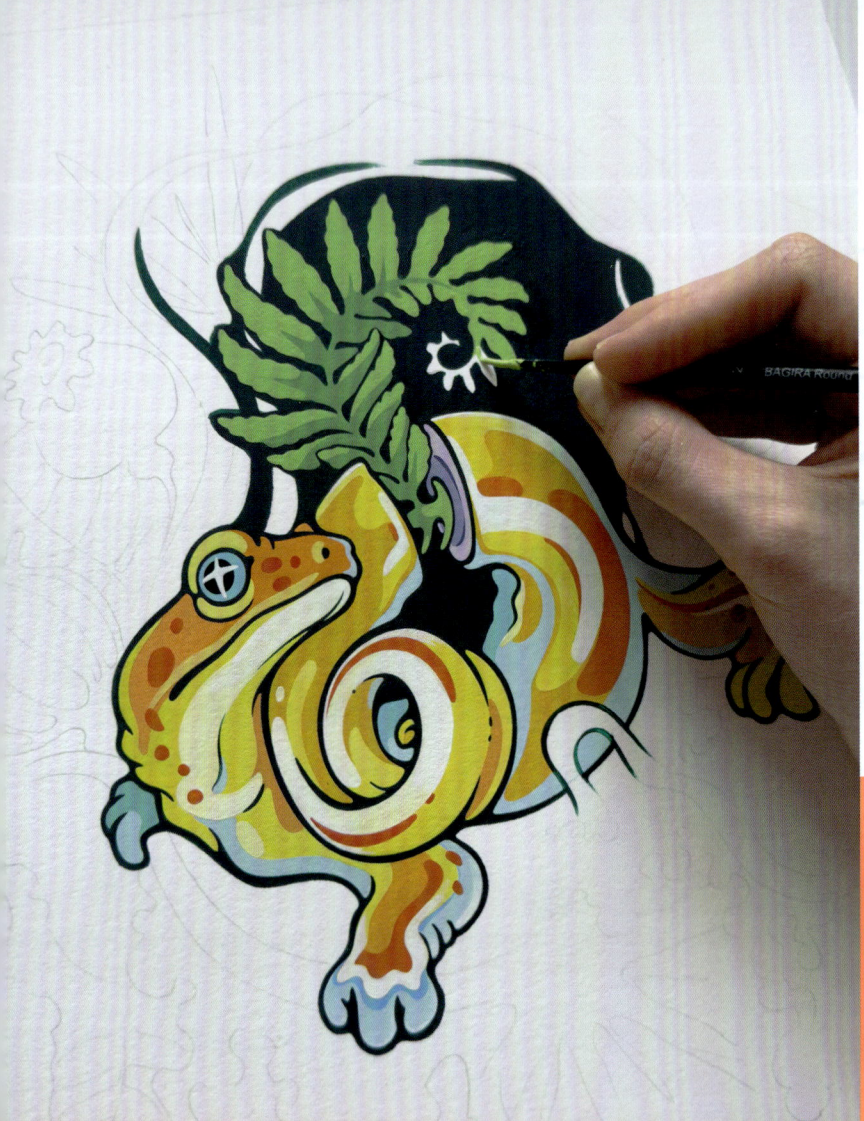

For the background, I chose emerald green, which appears almost black but has a deep, cool tone when dried on the canvas. I filled in the main planes with it and left some areas unpainted. Recognizing the contrast between the darkness and the future medium and light tones, I select individual shades for the ferns in the foreground and the plants in the background.

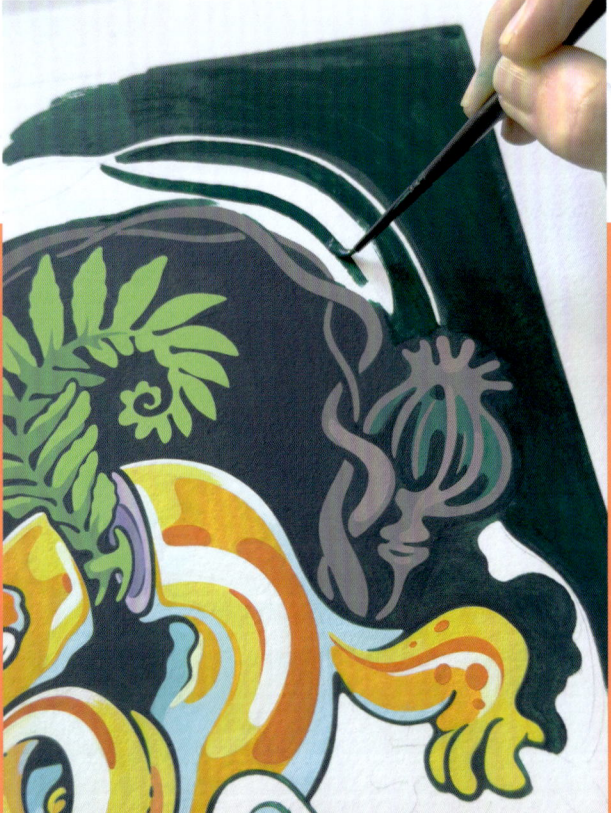

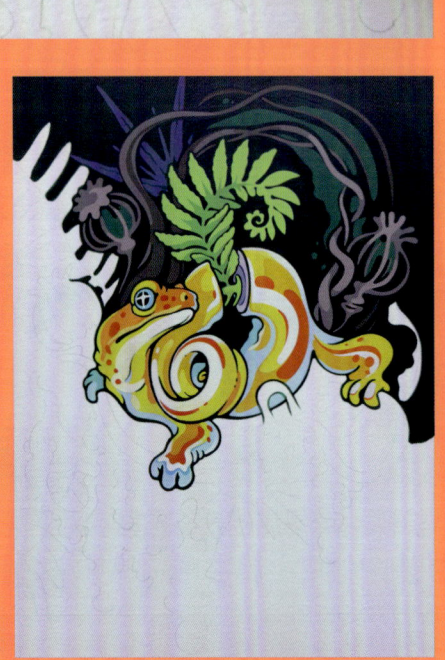

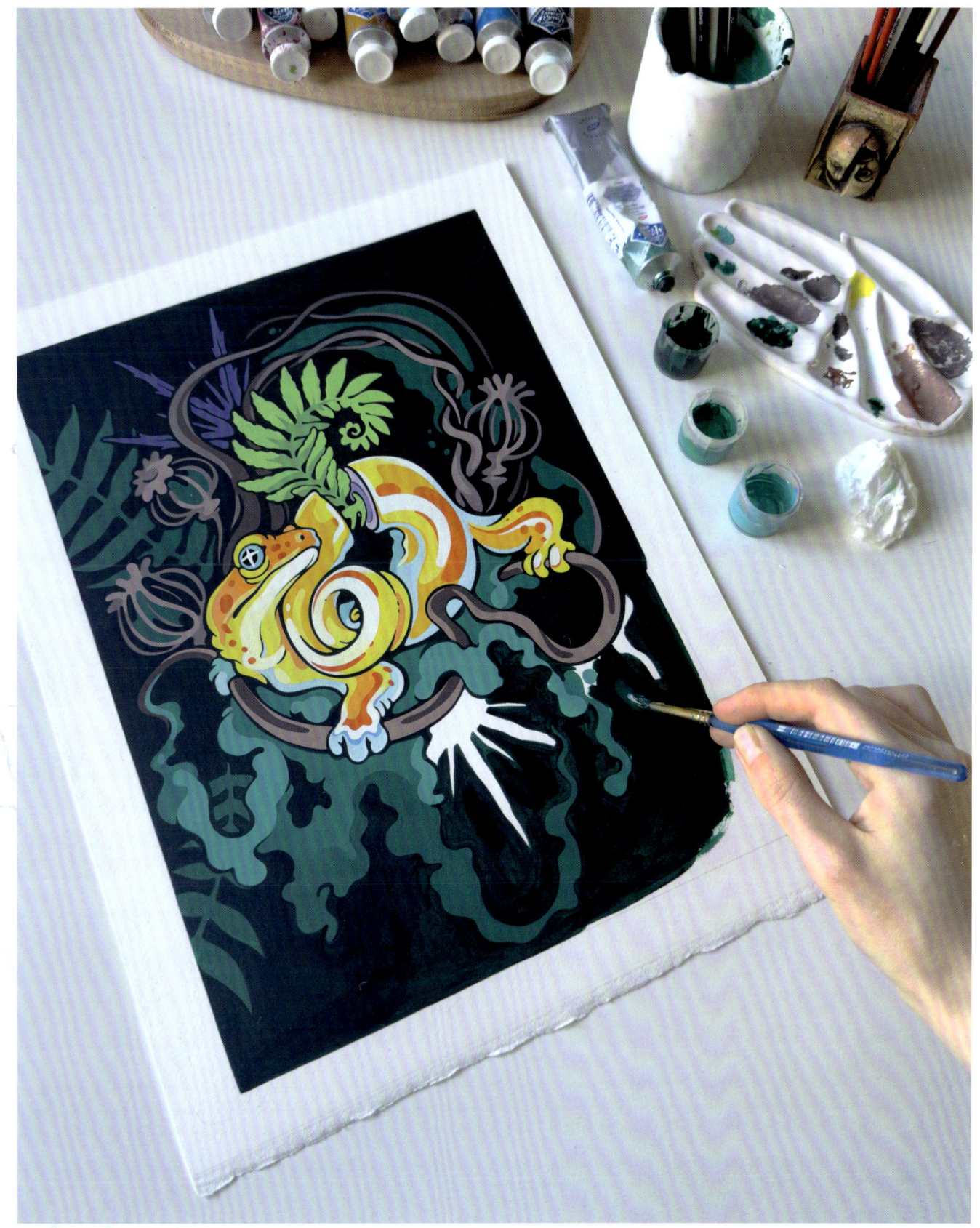

TEMPERA PAINTING: *UNTOUCHABLE*

In this tutorial, I will demonstrate my typical step-by-step tempera painting process. I will create a small illustration centred around one of my favourite themes: insects and plants. The addition of a physalis adds symbolism to the composition, embodying both the fragility and the value of life.

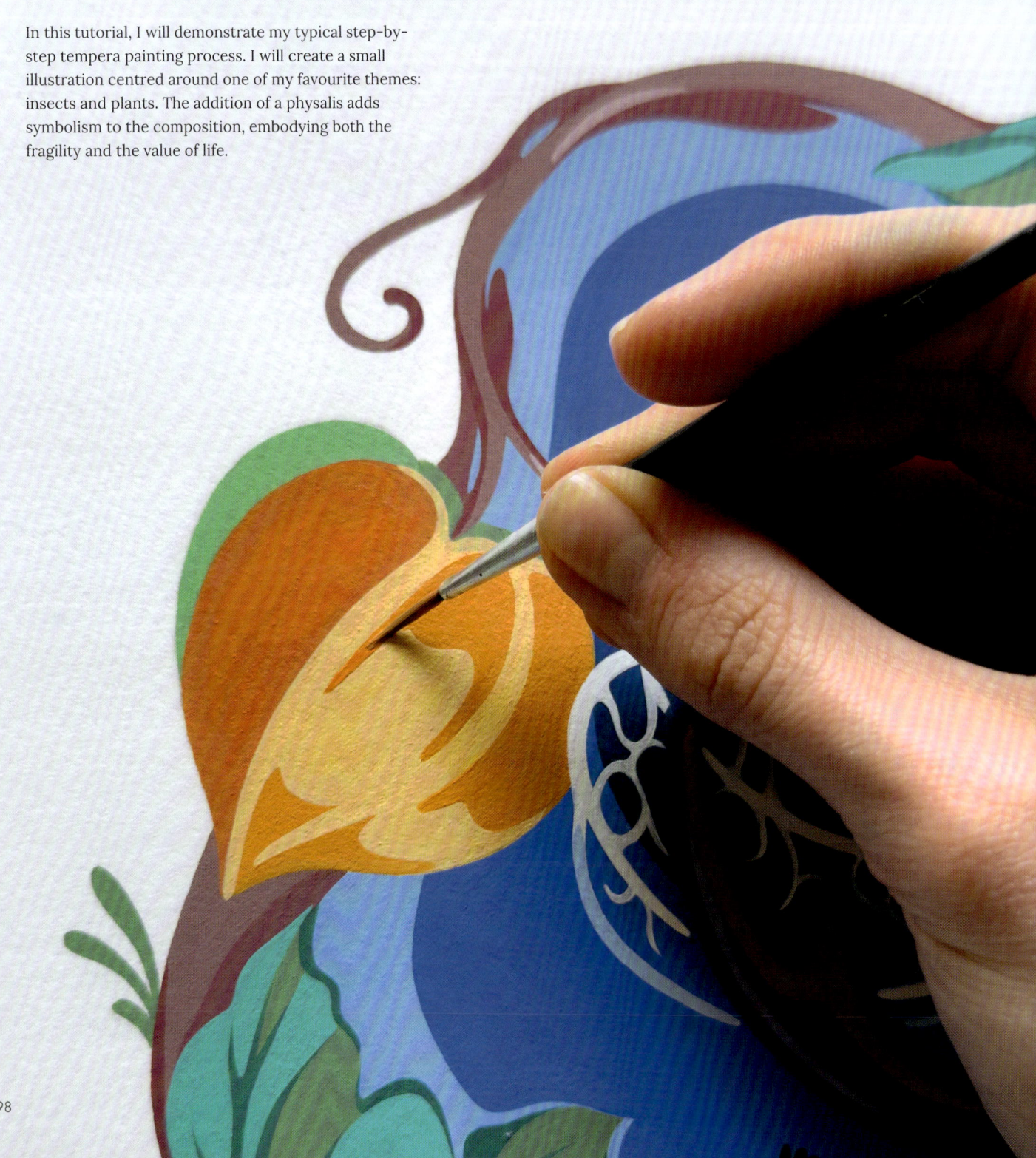

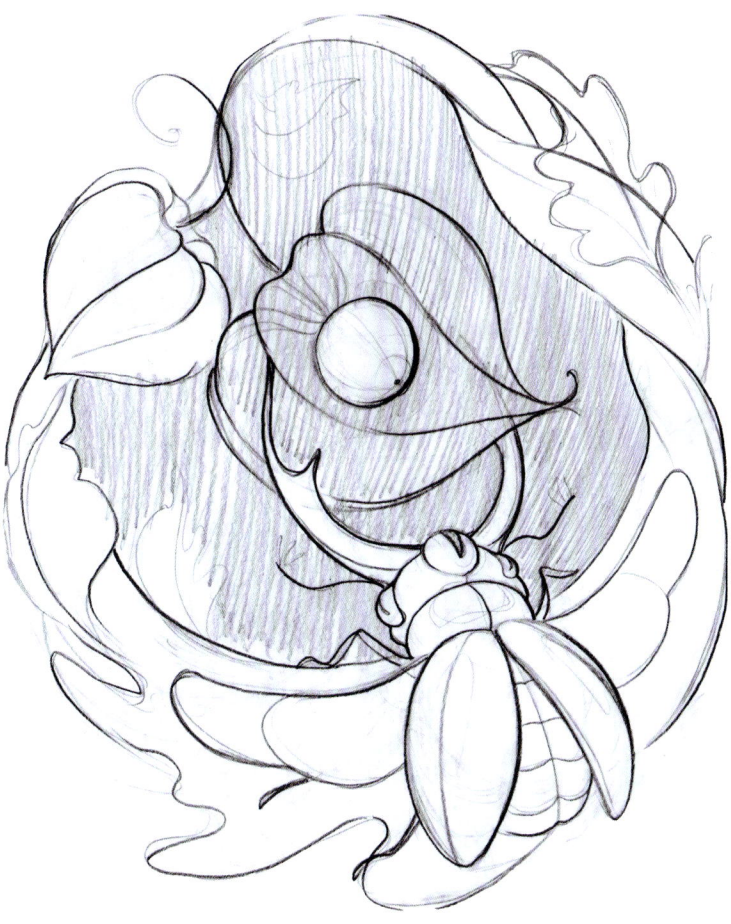

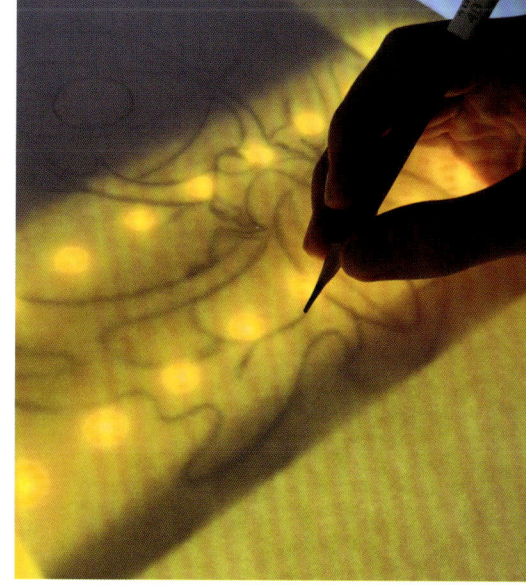

STEP 01: MAKING THE SKETCH

I start by looking for references of beetles. I want the outline to contrast with the thin lines of the physalis, so I decide to use a horned beetle for its unique shape. To make the physalis in the centre stand out, I build the entire composition around it. Since I rarely prepare a colour scheme in advance, I just imagine what colour each element would be and make a mental note to mix the paint as I go along.

STEP 02: CHOOSING PAPER & USING A LIGHTBOX

I choose watercolour paper with a smooth surface to make it easier to draw the details. The density is 640 gsm (I recommend choosing paper with a density of at least 300 gsm so that it doesn't deform when wet). Next, I use the old method of tracing a sketch with a lightbox. To do this, I place the sketch under a sheet of the paper I want to paint on and lightly trace the contours with a pencil. It's important to do this carefully so that I don't have to erase too much later – heavy erasing can damage the texture of the paper and create unevenness.

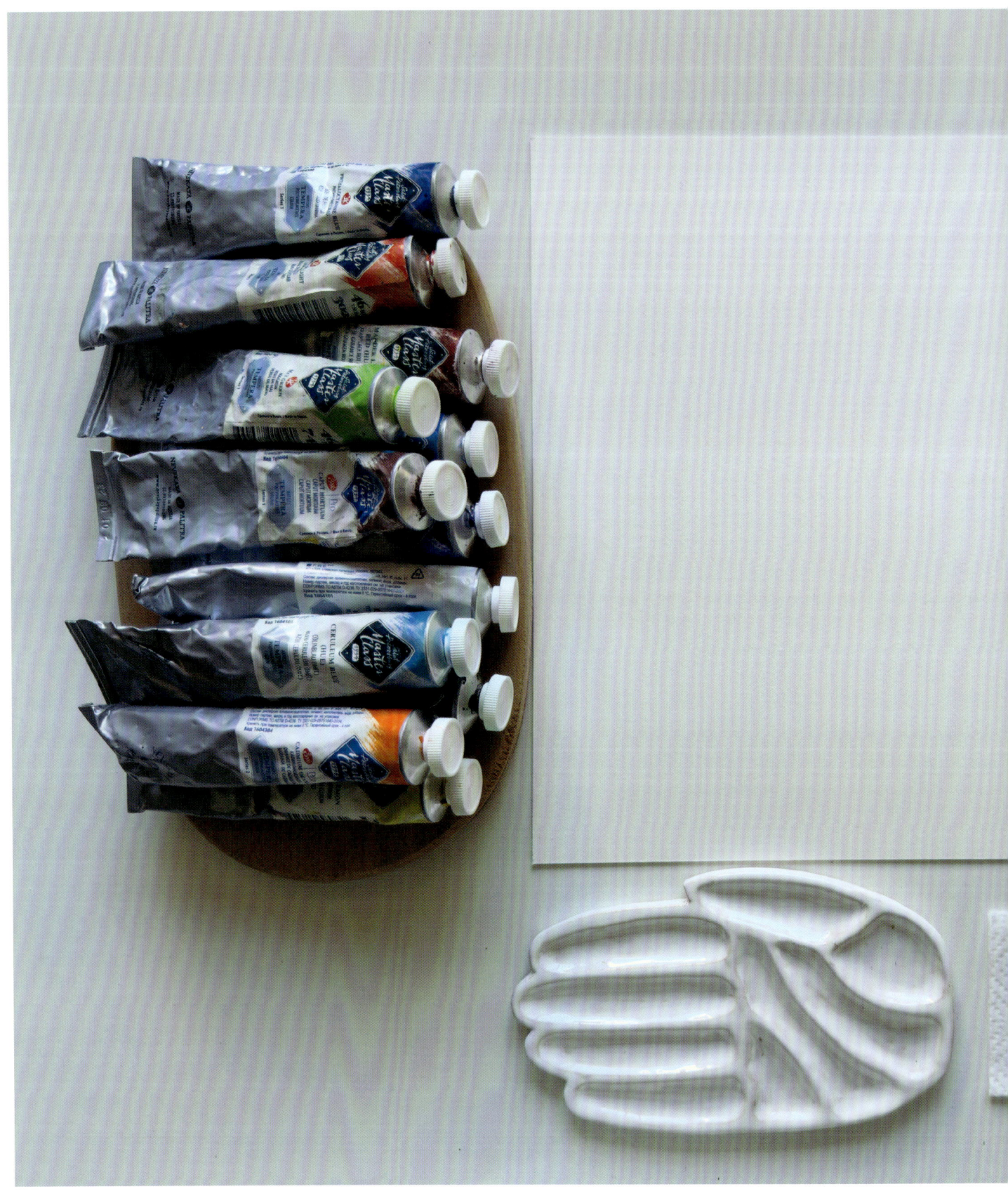

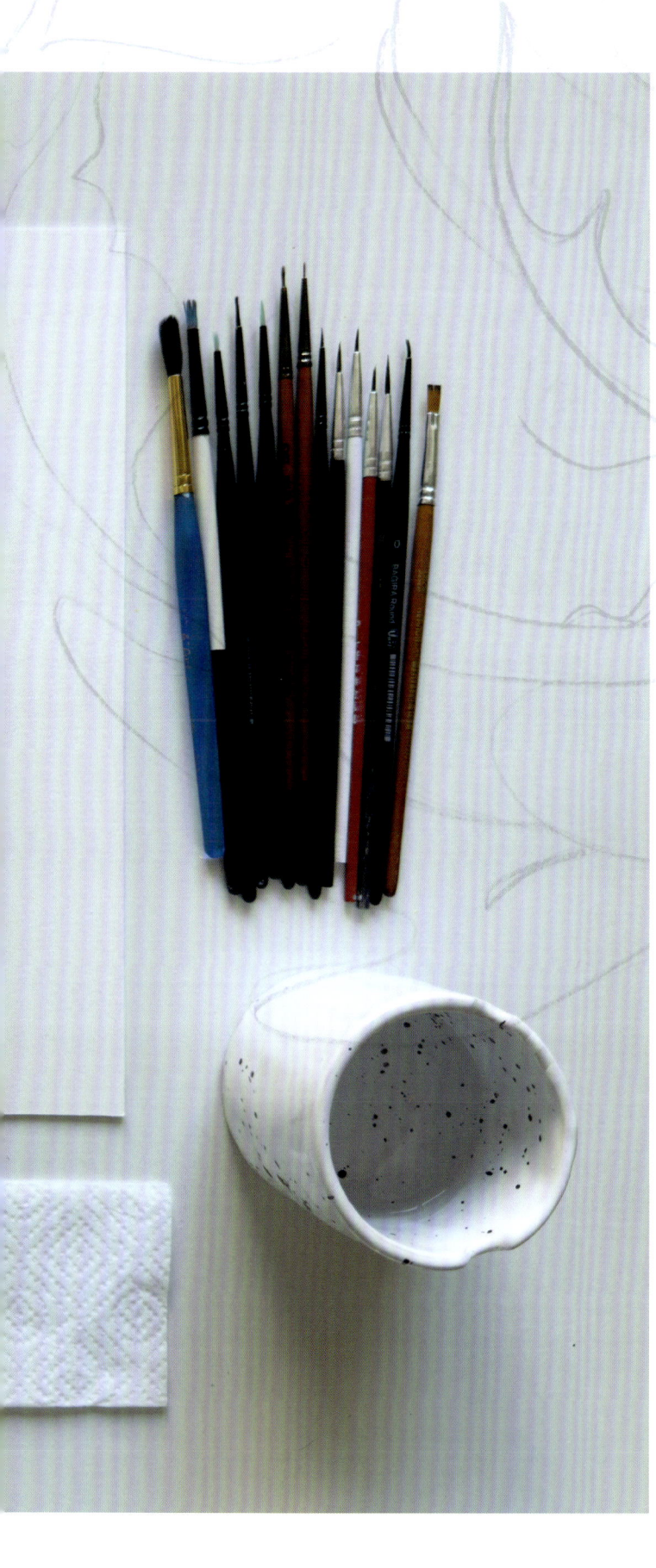

STEP 03: ASSEMBLING MATERIALS

I lay out all the materials I plan to use for this piece, including multiple paint colours, brushes of different sizes, a palette, some tissue, and a pot of water for both diluting the paint and keeping the brushes clean after each use.

TIPS FOR PAINTING WITH TEMPERA

Dilute the paint with water until it has a medium consistency. This allows for better control of the brushstrokes. A mixture that is too watery will form streaks, and a mixture that is too thick will not lie evenly on the surface.

Tempera paints have good covering power, but the density of the coverage depends on the specific colour. Some shades provide rich coverage after one or two coats, while others require three to four thin coats. For best results, allow each coat to dry completely before applying the next one. The same applies to working with gouache and acrylics.

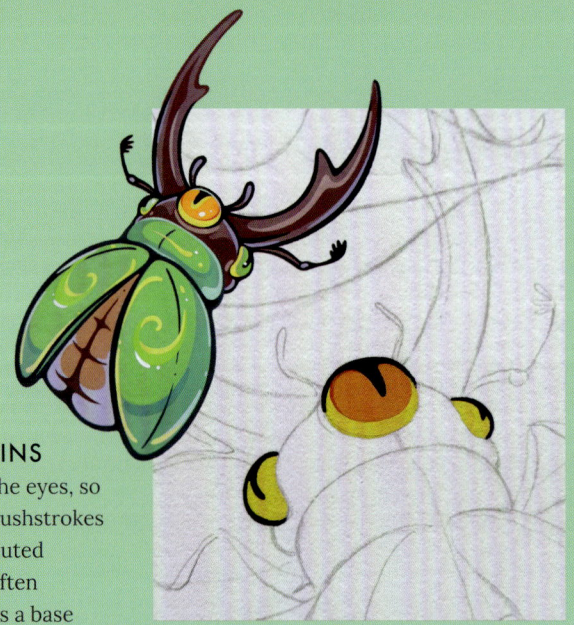

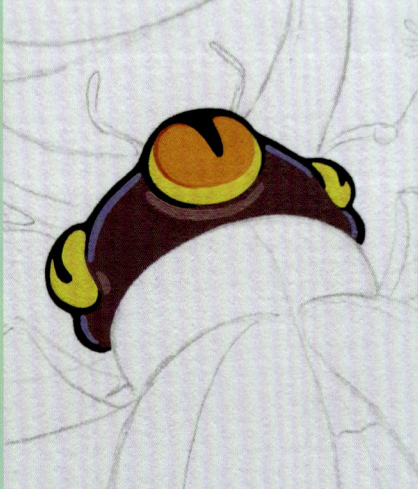

STEP 04: PAINTING BEGINS

I tend to start a painting with the eyes, so this is where I make my first brushstrokes on this image. For this, I use diluted cadmium lemon with white. I often add white to different shades as a base to reduce their saturation. I only use titanium white because it has high opacity (unlike zinc white, which is much more transparent). Once the yellow layer is dry, I paint the iris orange before outlining it in black. I wait for the lower layer to dry completely because if the outline were to smudge, the eye would lose its brightness and clarity.

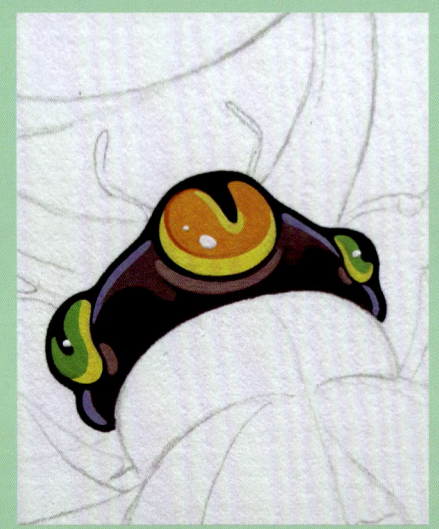

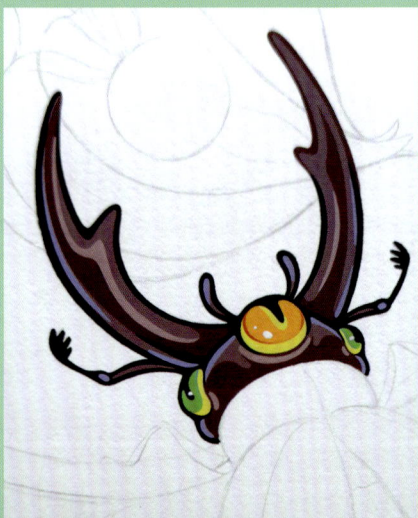

STEP 05: MIXING SHADES

To achieve the colour of the beetle's head, I mix three shades (light, medium, and dark) using two colours: caput mortuum, which has a reddish-brown pigment, and white. I use the medium shade as the base and apply the light and dark shades on top to create volume. At this stage, I also decide to work on the eyes again. I add green irises to the sides of the eyes and small highlights to bring this little creature to life. Next, I move on to the horns, working according to the same pattern. The light purple lines around the edges act as reflections, adding depth. Since I don't have a clear, realistic reference with a specific angle and lighting, I roughly imagine the direction of the light, shadows, and reflections. The important thing is that I strive to stylize, not reflect reality. If I tried to recreate the image from a photo, my stylization would be lost. Finally, I fill in the upper wings with broad strokes of cool green.

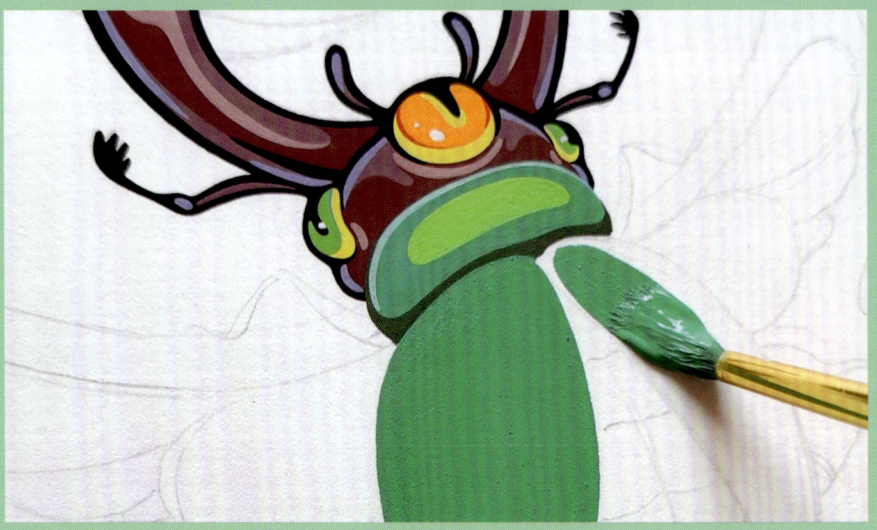

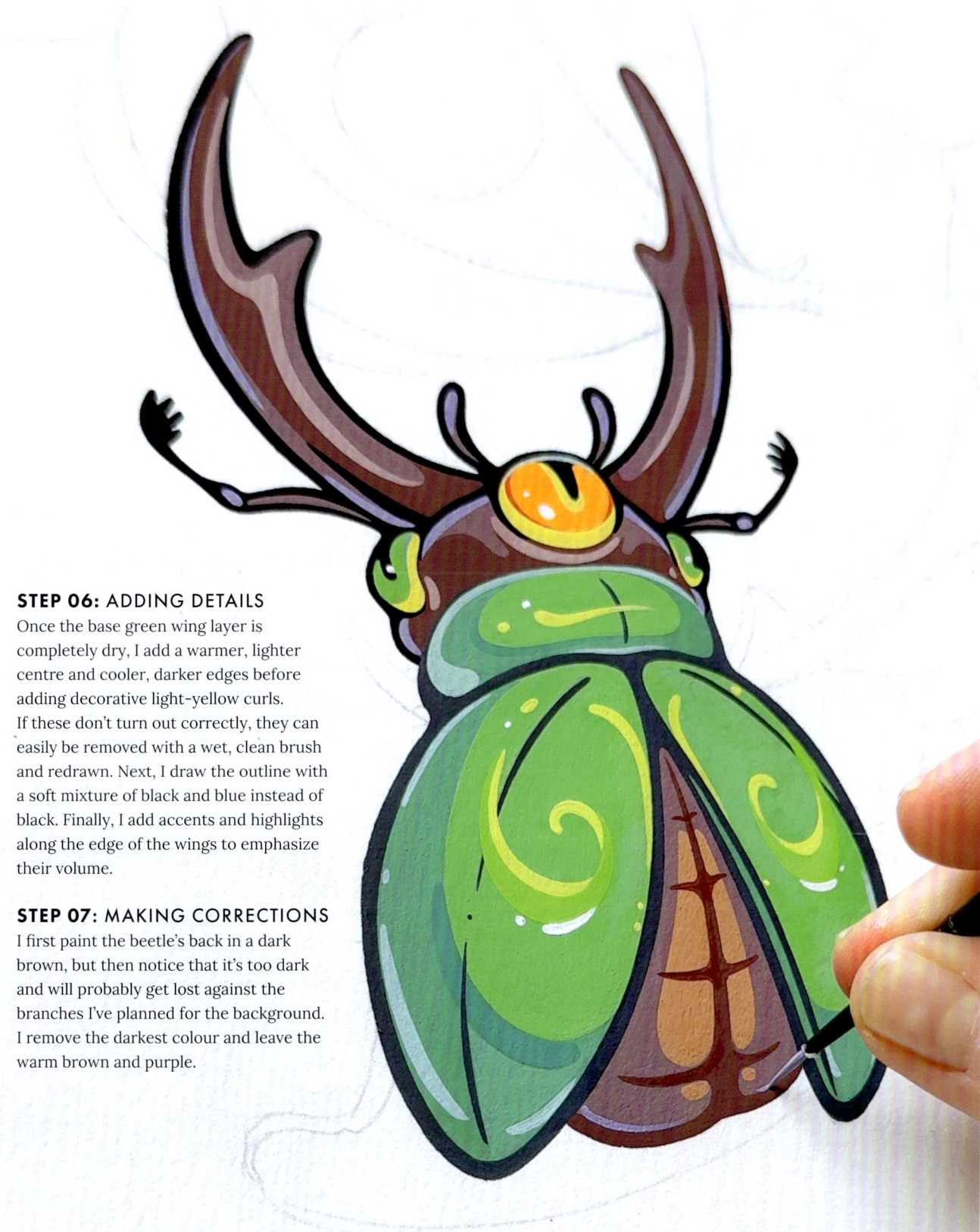

STEP 06: ADDING DETAILS

Once the base green wing layer is completely dry, I add a warmer, lighter centre and cooler, darker edges before adding decorative light-yellow curls. If these don't turn out correctly, they can easily be removed with a wet, clean brush and redrawn. Next, I draw the outline with a soft mixture of black and blue instead of black. Finally, I add accents and highlights along the edge of the wings to emphasize their volume.

STEP 07: MAKING CORRECTIONS

I first paint the beetle's back in a dark brown, but then notice that it's too dark and will probably get lost against the branches I've planned for the background. I remove the darkest colour and leave the warm brown and purple.

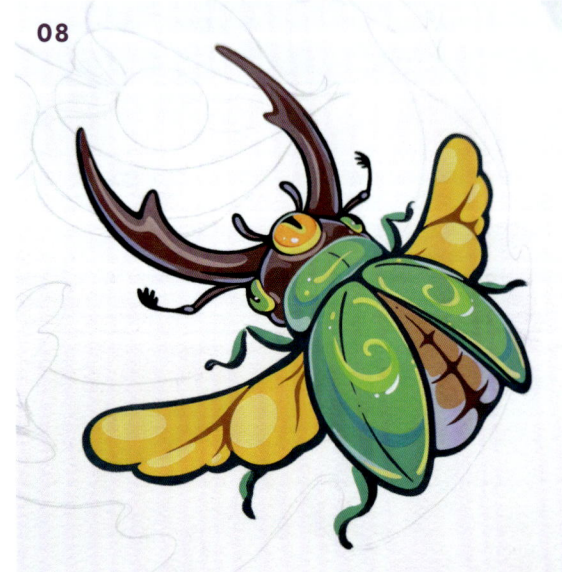

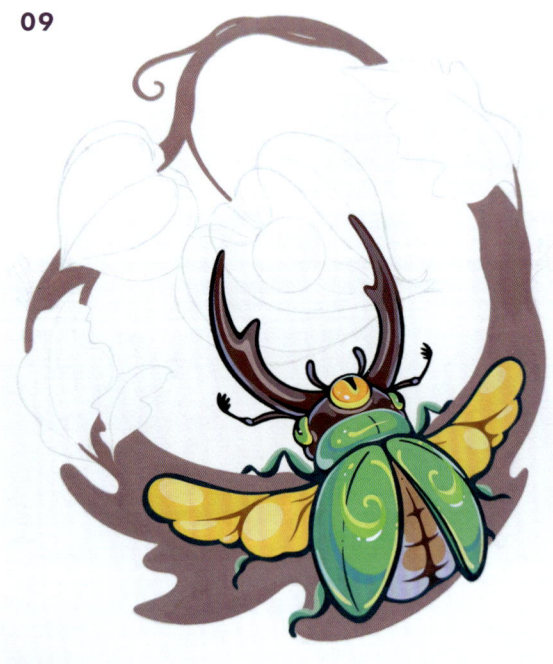

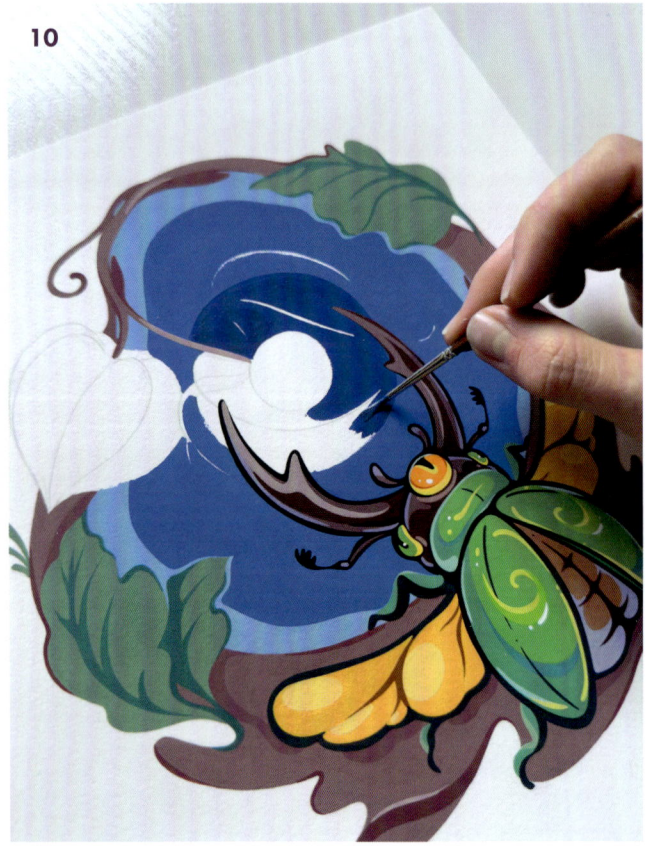

STEP 08: WINGING IT

I begin painting the wings with a base tone made from white, yellow (cadmium yellow), and a little orange (cadmium orange). I make the light spots using a mix of white and yellow. After they dry, I add the contours and draw the legs.

STEP 09: BRANCHING OUT

For the branch, I mix caput mortuum with white and add a touch of madder lake red. The madder lake red gives the branch colour a slightly pinkish tint, making it different from the colour of the beetle's head. I cover the entire surface of the branch and add brighter lines to create a stylized texture. I paint the leaves a dull green so they won't compete with the beetle's green colour.

STEP 10: WORKING IN THREES

The background consists of three shades of cobalt blue: the lightest shade contrasts softly with the branch, the middle shade acts as a transition tone, and the darkest shade, with black added, directs the viewer's gaze to the centre of the composition. I leave thin gaps along the contour of the physalis to preserve its original shape. As you may have noticed, I often work with three colour gradations. Light colour highlights the area, medium colour works for the main body of the shape, and dark colour works for depth and accents.

STEP 11: ADDING THE CENTRAL PHYSALIS

Next, I move on to the physalis. First, I lightly draw its 'skeleton' in white – these will eventually be the main contours that define the shape of the physalis shell. I then paint the physalis berry in three tones: orange, red, and dark red. I leave a white circle of 'glare' to show its shiny surface.

STEP 12: REFINING THE LEAVES

At this stage, the leaves are all one shade of green, which seems boring to me. So, I add another shade that I create using a mixture of cerulean blue, May green, and white, which is reminiscent of mint.

STEP 13: PATTERN-MAKING

I create the pattern on the physalis shell intuitively, simply letting my hand guide the line. I add a little more water to make the strokes smoother and longer. The first layer may be semi-transparent, so it can be repeated after drying. If the line is uneven, I correct it with the colours I used to paint the background.

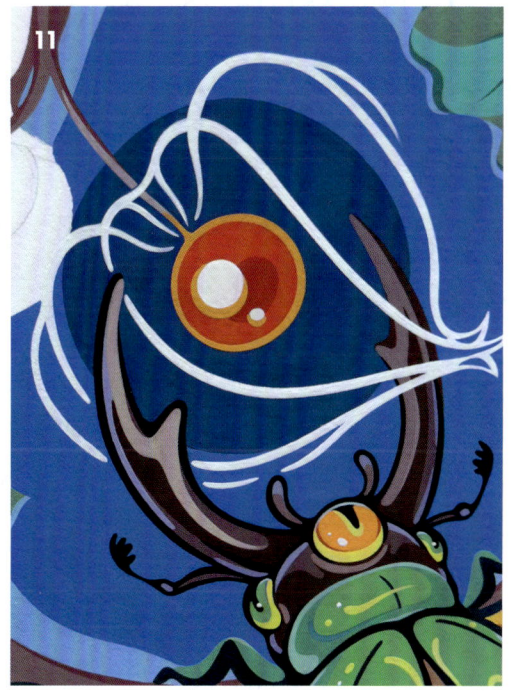

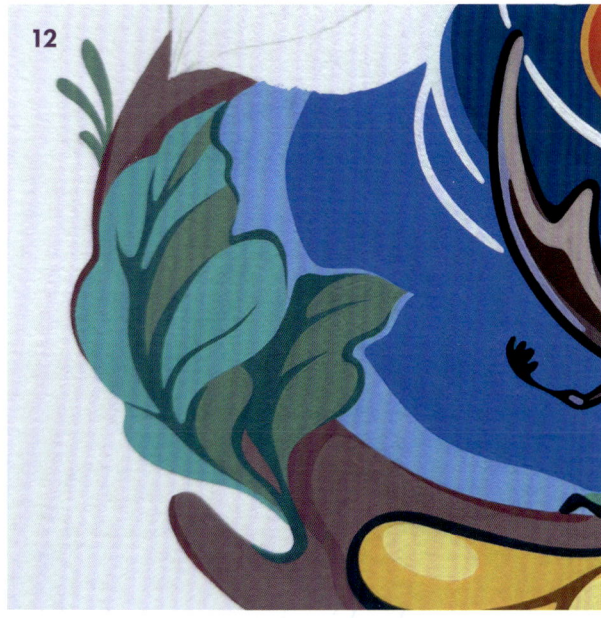

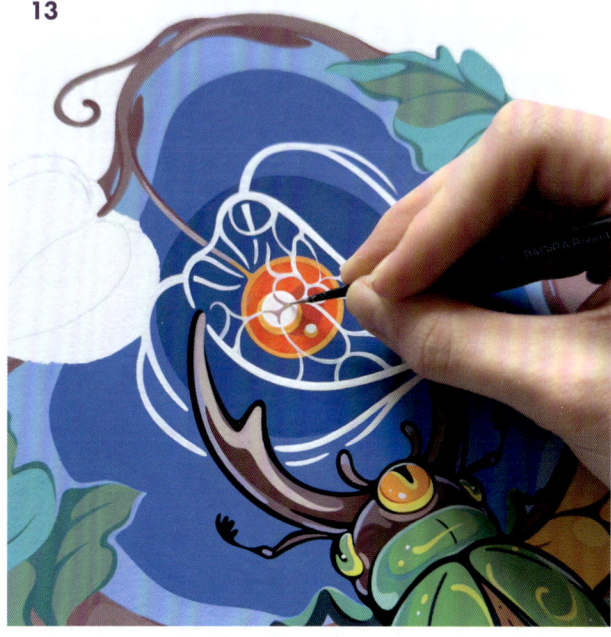

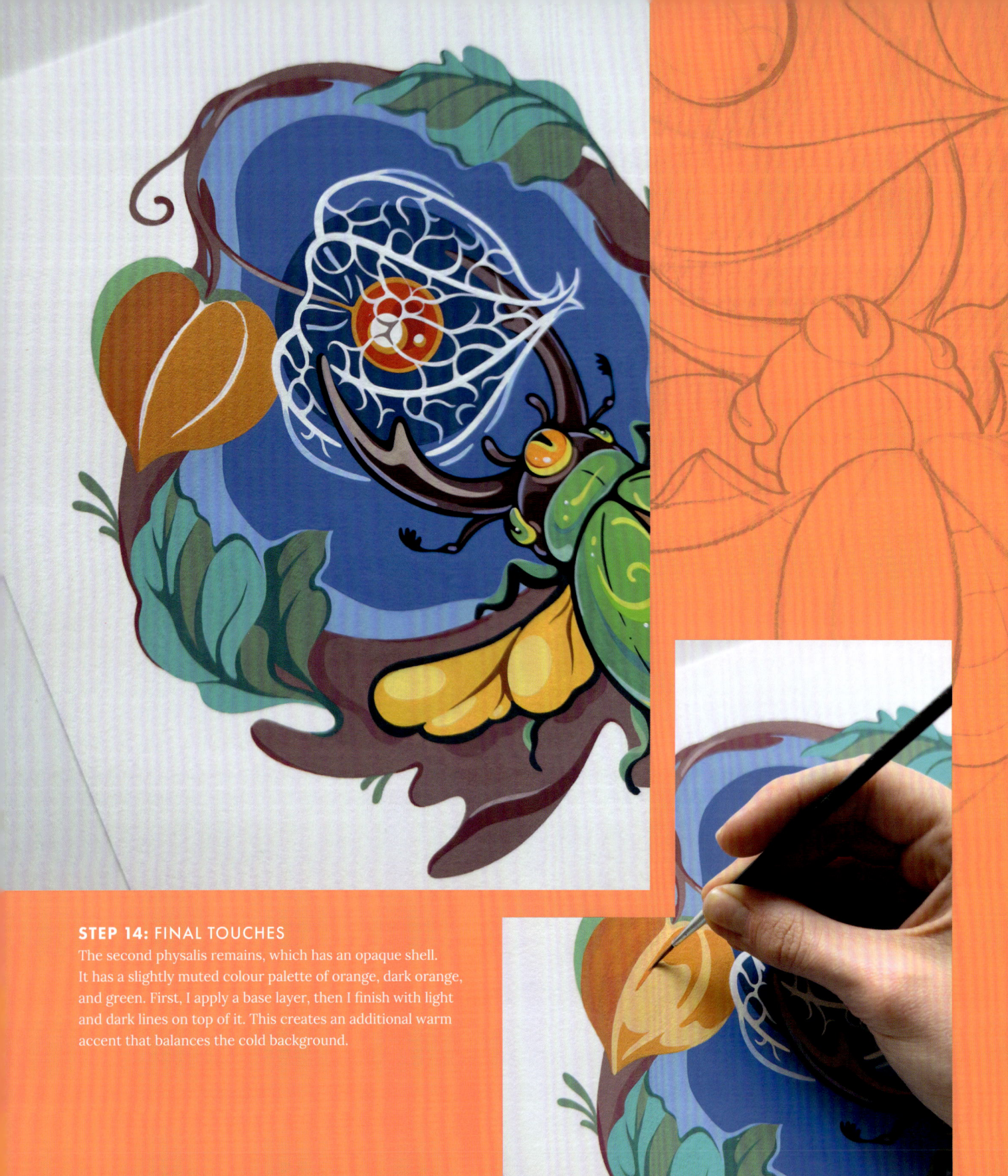

STEP 14: FINAL TOUCHES

The second physalis remains, which has an opaque shell. It has a slightly muted colour palette of orange, dark orange, and green. First, I apply a base layer, then I finish with light and dark lines on top of it. This creates an additional warm accent that balances the cold background.

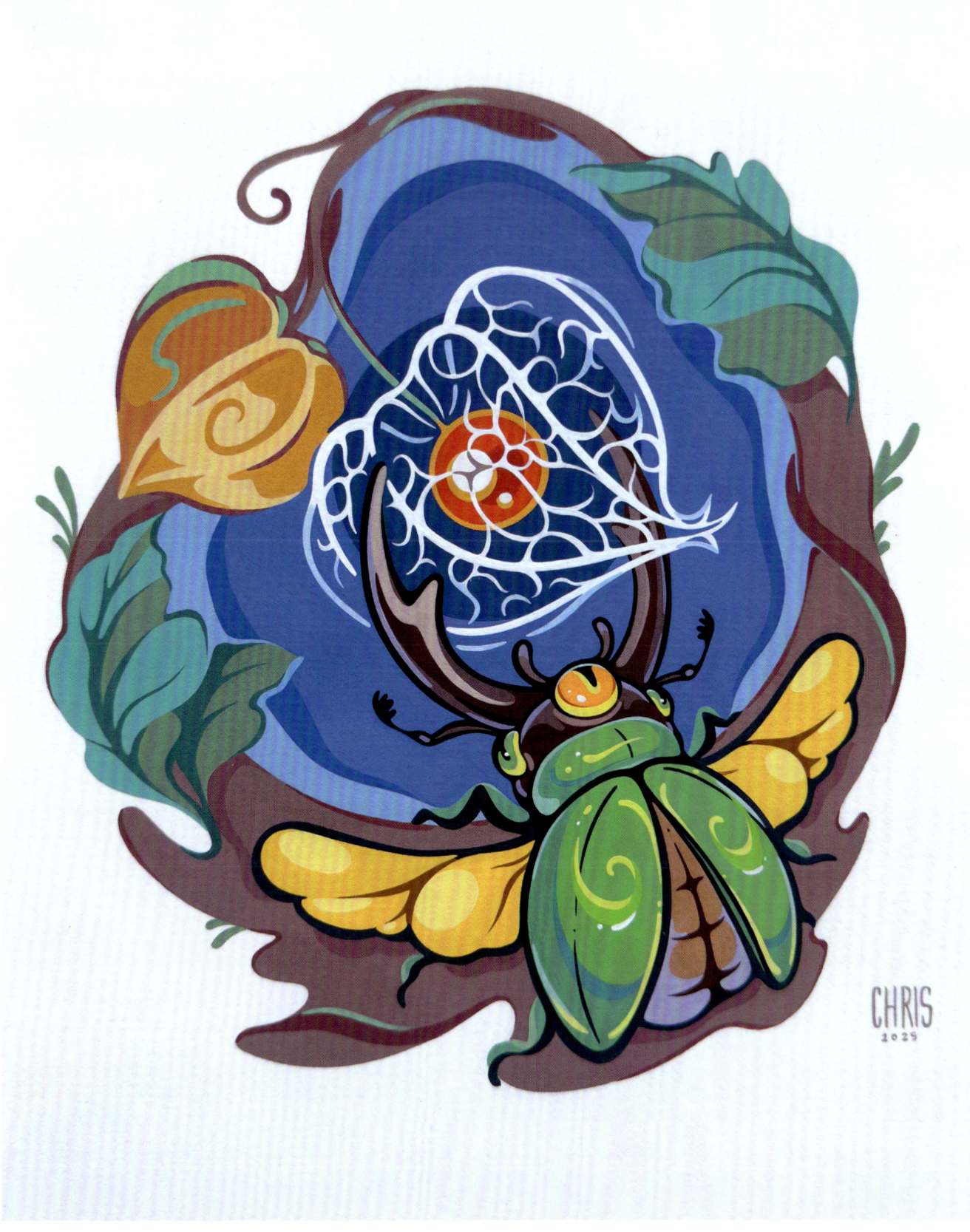

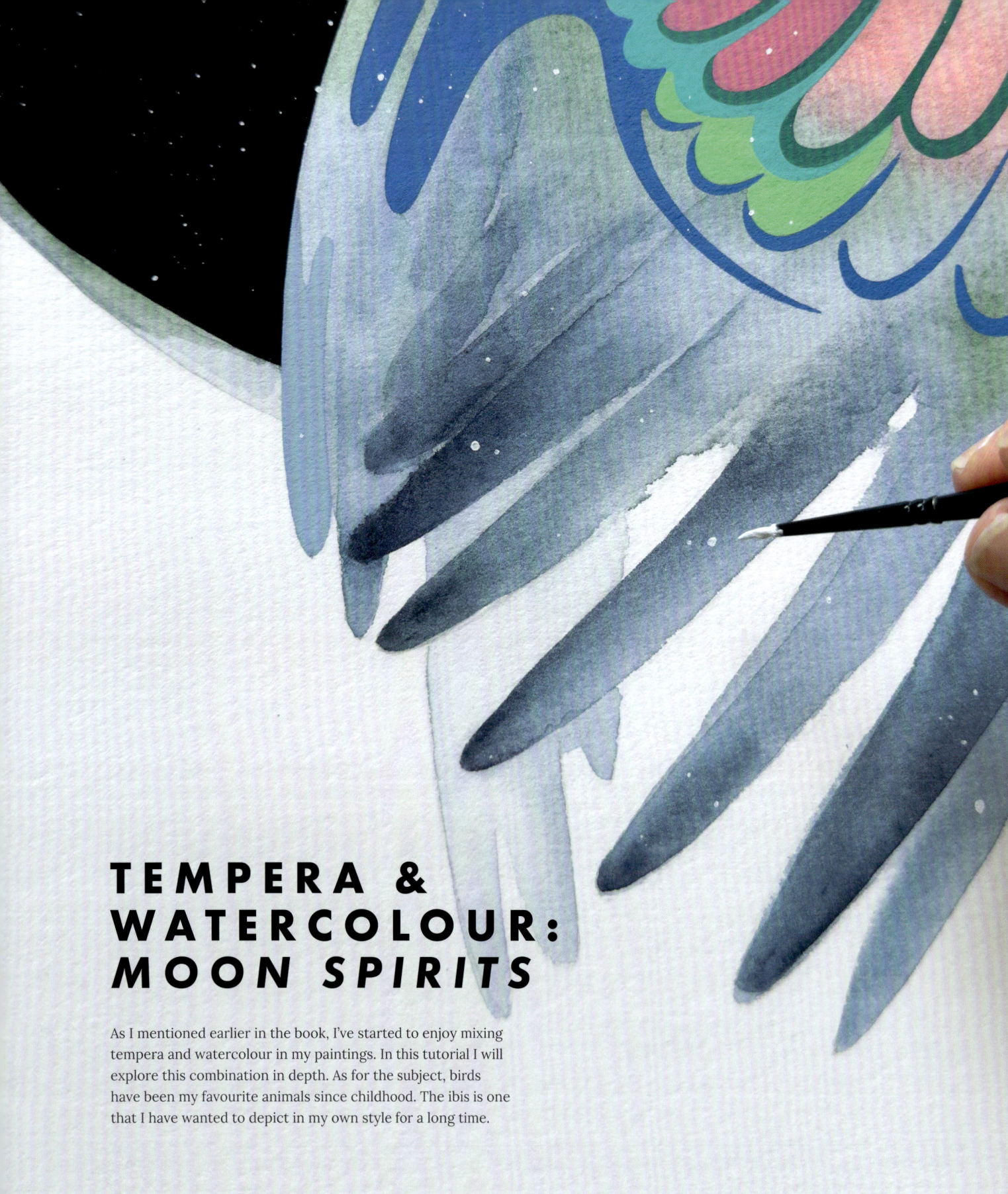

TEMPERA & WATERCOLOUR: MOON *SPIRITS*

As I mentioned earlier in the book, I've started to enjoy mixing tempera and watercolour in my paintings. In this tutorial I will explore this combination in depth. As for the subject, birds have been my favourite animals since childhood. The ibis is one that I have wanted to depict in my own style for a long time.

STEP 01: SEARCHING & SKETCHING

There are different types of ibis, but for this work I choose the rare northern bald ibis, also known as the hermit ibis. I am captivated by its appearance, with shiny feathers creating an otherworldly and mystical effect, and a long, curved beak resembling the shape of a young moon. These two features are the main starting points for developing the idea.

I create several miniature sketches to find the most successful composition, and I decide to include two ibises facing in opposite directions. My key task is to arrange the ibises in the shape of the moon, achieving harmony between their beak shapes and the moon's roundness. Once I have transferred the sketch to a large format, I search for a tonal solution. I imagine the scene as dark, so I carefully balance light and dark elements.

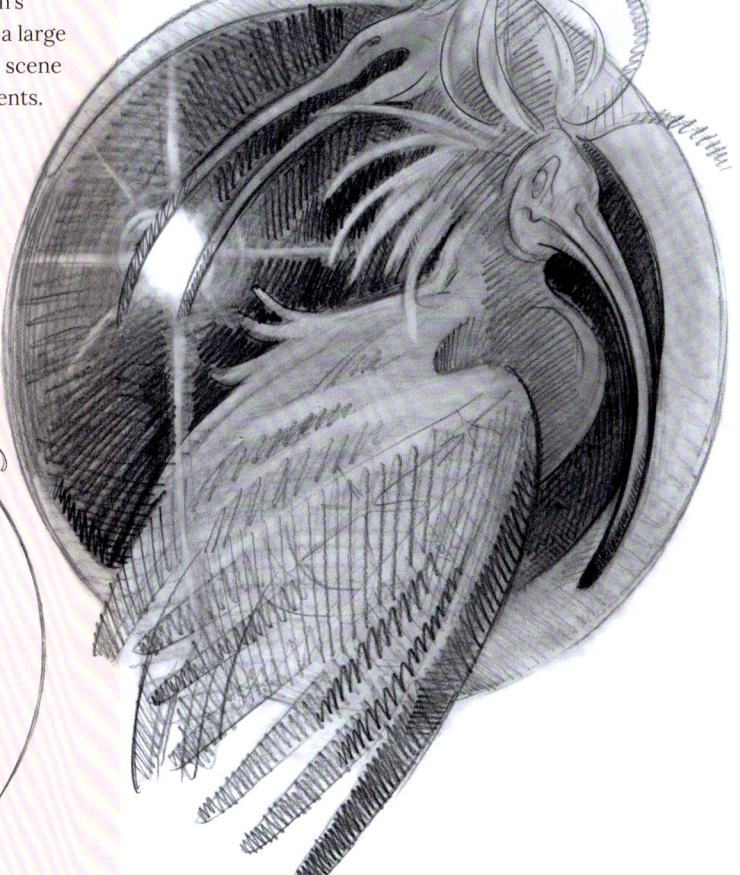

After darkening the background, I decide one of the ibises should hold a star in its beak. It reminds me of a spirit emerging from the night's darkness. This star will eventually be the brightest element in the composition, attracting the viewer's gaze.

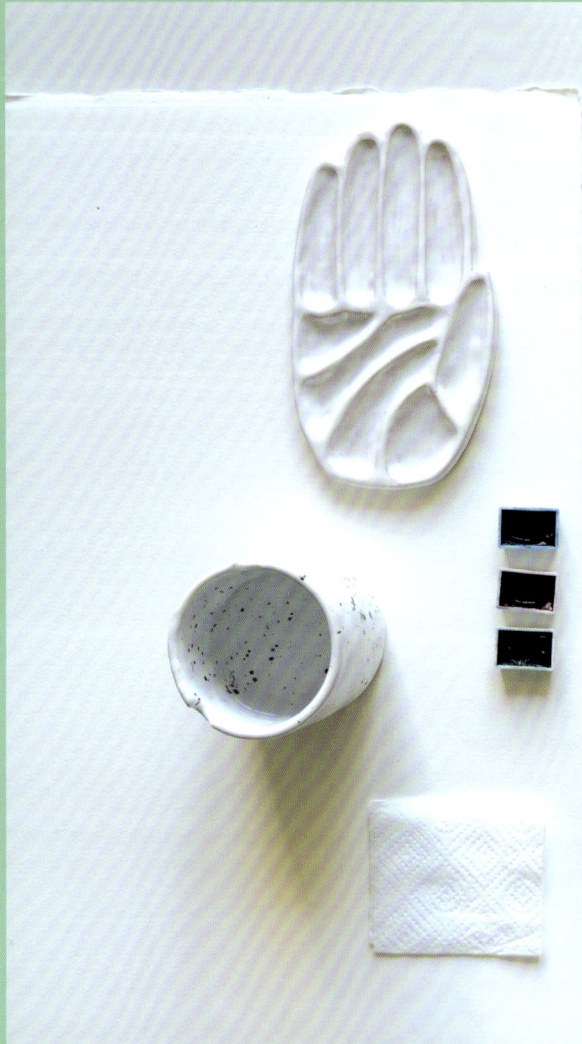
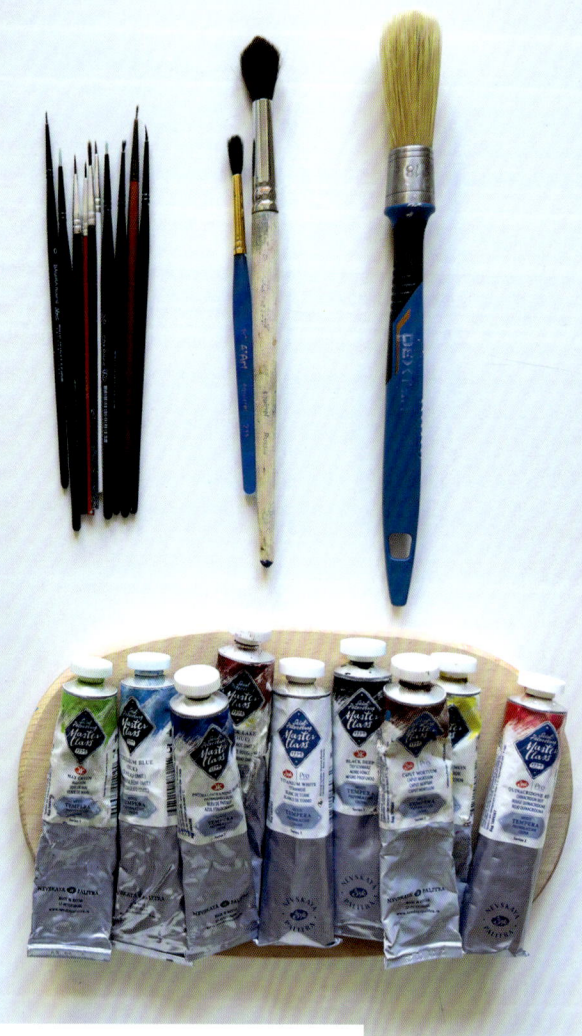

STEP 02: GATHERING MATERIALS

1. Tempera paints

2. Watercolour paints

3. 640 gsm paper

4. Soft brushes (watercolours)

5. Synthetic squirrel hair brushes (tempera)

6. Large brush with stiff bristles

7. Palette

8. Water

9. Napkin

TIPS FOR WORKING WITH WATERCOLOUR

I recommend using cotton paper as it retains moisture well, allowing the paint to spread evenly and create smooth transitions).

STEP 03: WET-ON-WET WATERCOLOUR

Moisten the paper with water. There are two ways to work with the wet-on-wet technique: you can use it locally and only moisten individual areas, or you can moisten the entire surface. I choose to use the local approach, only moistening the areas where I will apply colour. It is extremely important that I do not cross the pencil outline.

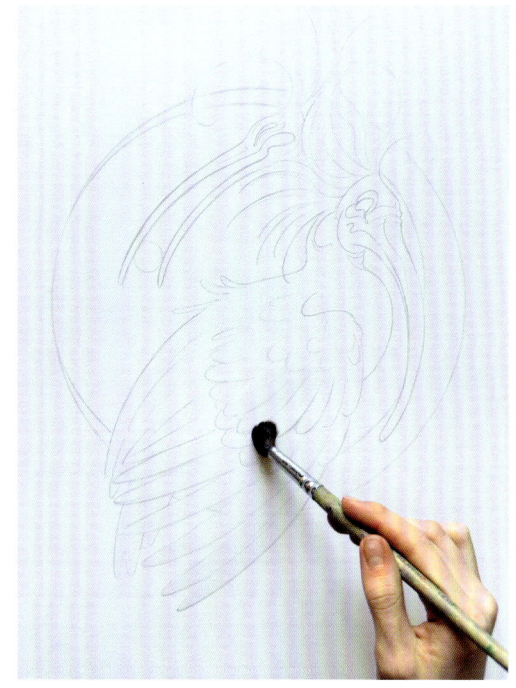

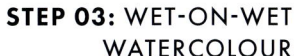

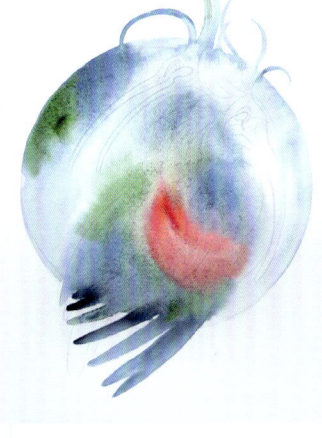

STEP 04: WORKING WITH WATERCOLOUR

I use three colours in this step: indigo, green, and madder lake red light. Starting with the tips of the feathers on the wings, I apply indigo with smooth brushstrokes, allowing the paint to spread over the moistened area naturally. Next, moving upwards, I add green and madder lake red. Each new colour is applied separately with a clean brush, without mixing the paints on the palette. The colours blend directly on the paper, creating natural transitions. I then gradually move on to the background, adding indigo and green. In some places, I apply more paint, and in others I dilute it with more water.

TIPS FOR PAINTING WET-ON-WET

1. Only use clean water to dilute paints. Either change the water frequently or keep several containers of water nearby.

2. Keep a cloth handy to remove excess moisture from the brush. This prevents excess paint or water from getting on the paper.

3. Do not try to correct or refine the areas of colour while the paint is still wet, as this will only disrupt the integrity of the effect.

111

STEP 05: ADDING A SECOND LAYER

The wet technique can be done in one session, then once the paper is dry, you can add more. You can also work with multiple layers, refining individual shapes, shades, and shadows. I add a second transparent layer to individual areas of the feathers, and to the surface of the moon. I also add a more transparent shade of indigo to the tail to separate it from the wing, which has a darker shade.

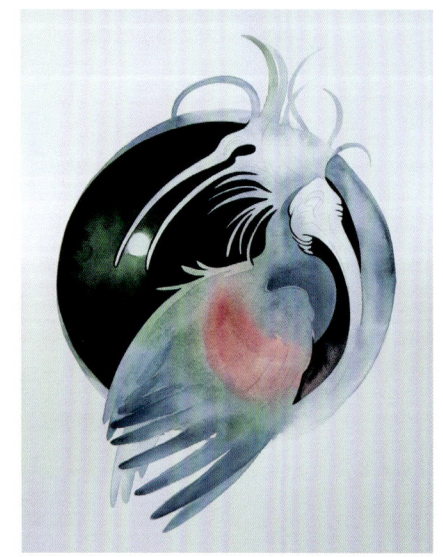

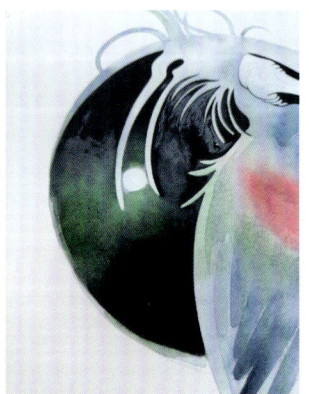

STEP 06: TIME FOR TEMPERA

Once everything is dry, I focus on working with tempera. I fill in the background with black, clearly outlining the silhouettes of the ibises and the moon. I pay special attention to the area of the background around the star. I re-wet this area of the paper, add green watercolour, and then apply watery black tempera around the star while the paper is still wet. I try not to use too many mechanical brushstrokes, allowing the paints to flow naturally. As I go, I'm not entirely sure how it will turn out, but I am pleased with the result. This creates a gentle transition between the transparent watercolour and the dense tempera. It's a good example of how two materials can interact and complement each other.

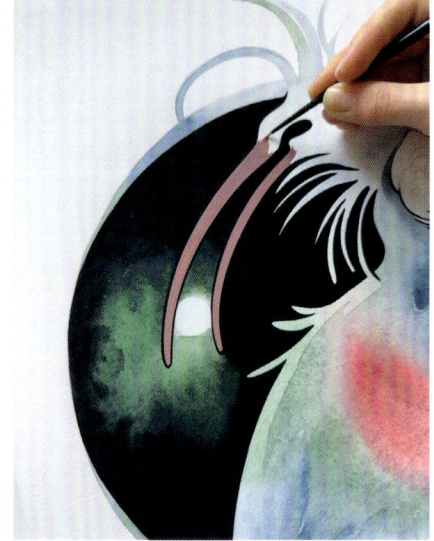

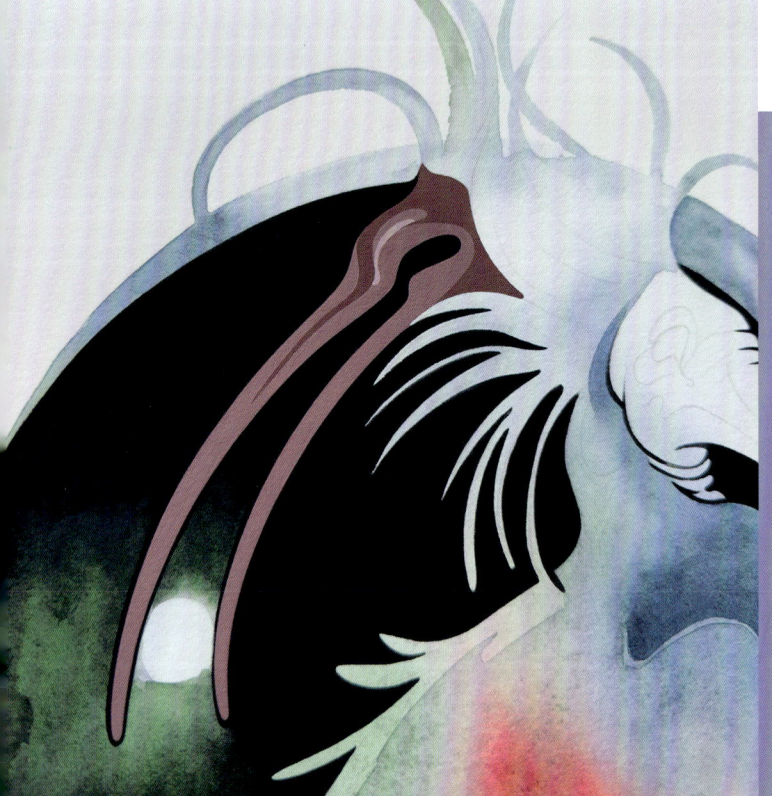

STEP 07: THE BACKGROUND IBIS

I continue working with the ibis in the background. Its colour palette should consist of muted tones. For the face, I mix two shades: caput mortuum with white and a touch of black.

STEP 08: PAINTING THE PLUMAGE

I paint the plumage, known as a 'wispy ruff', on the rear ibis's head in dark blue. Then I move on to the ibis in the foreground. I paint its feathers in a lighter shade of blue, creating smooth, chaotic lines that emphasize the shape of the long, thin feathers. In some places, I leave the lower watercolour layer visible, correcting the lines with the same shade of tempera as the watercolour if necessary, and applying additional layers for clarity.

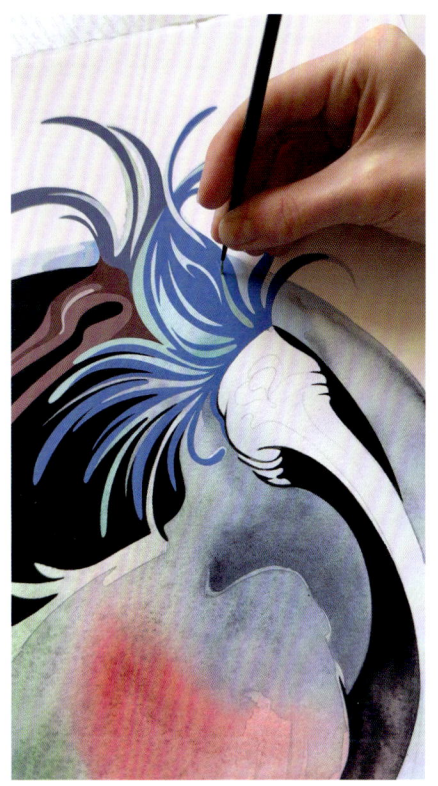

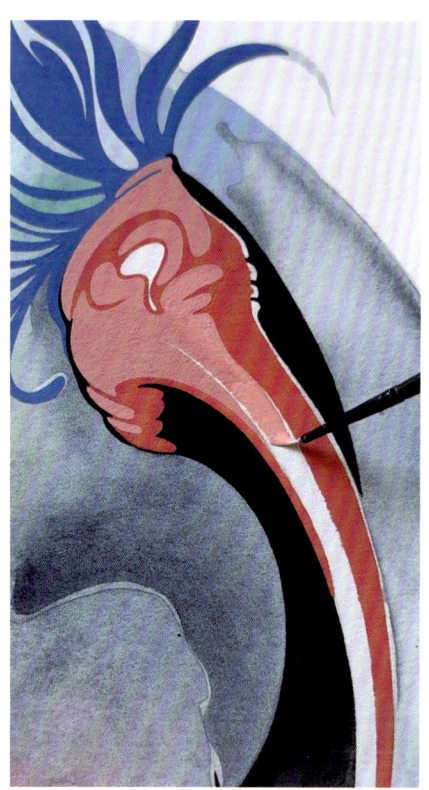

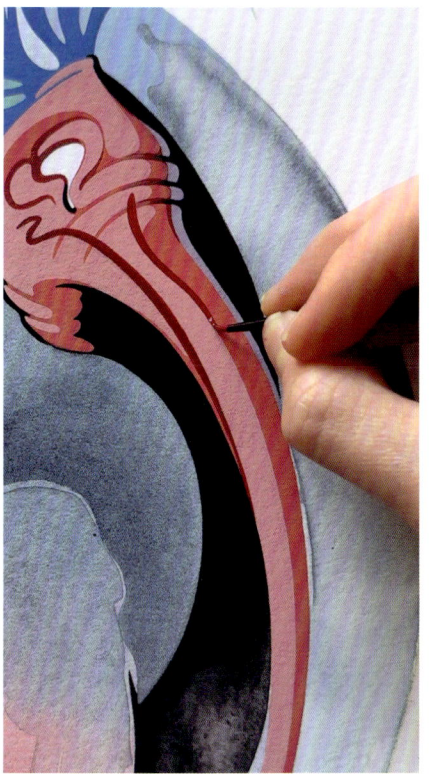

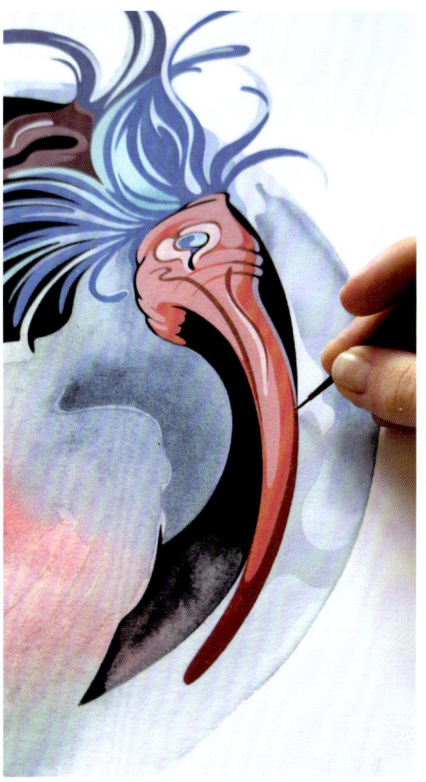

STEP 09: IBIS FACE

To achieve the colour of the foreground ibis's face, I mix three shades using two colours: madder lake red and titanium white. First, I apply a dark shade to the shadowed part of the head, followed by a medium shade. Next, I add a purple highlight to the shadow, then draw the contour lines with pure madder lake red. I draw the eyes afterwards, adding a third, lighter shade of madder lake red around them. I also highlight the contour lines of the beak. At this stage, I also add a few grey and light-grey tempera paint spots to the moon.

STEP 10: DETAILING THE FEATHERS

At this stage, I add the finishing decorative touches to the ibises. I use tempera to apply line work and spots of dark blue, light blue, pink, dark green, and light green. These are similar to the shades used in watercolour, but more saturated.

STEP 11: GLAZING

To paint the star, I mix yellow paint with white. Using the glazing technique, I apply semi-transparent lines, allowing the bottom layer to show through. In some places, I add a thicker layer of paint to enhance the light accent. I fill the centre with white.

STEP 12: SPLATTERING THE STARRY SKY

To create the stars, I use the splattering technique. I dip the tips of the large, stiff brush into diluted white paint, then hold it over my painting. I then pull back the bristles with my fingers and release them so that the paint flies off and forms small, chaotic spots. Before doing this, I make several test attempts on a separate sheet to determine the optimal pressure and distance.

STEP 13: FINAL TWEAKS

In these final stages, I look at the illustration from a distance more often and, as a result, decide to change the colour of the light in the ibis's eye in the background to black. This seemingly insignificant detail makes the image more expressive, in my opinion. Finally, I add another five or six stars manually where I think they are missing.

All done!

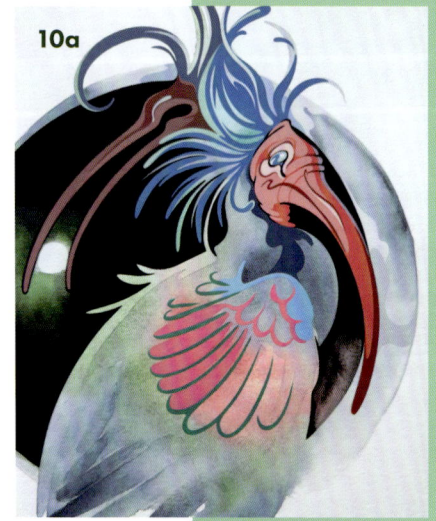

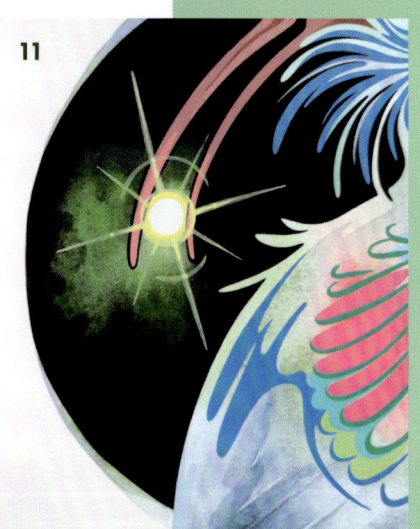

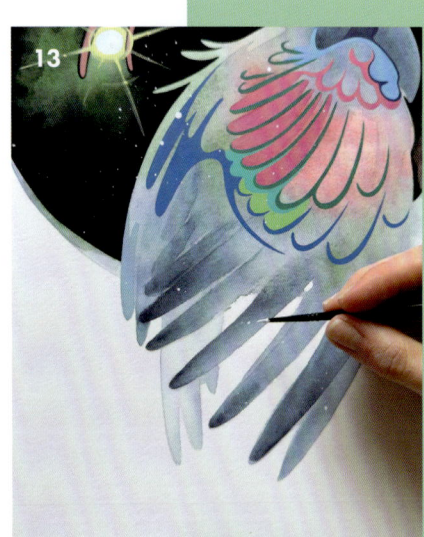

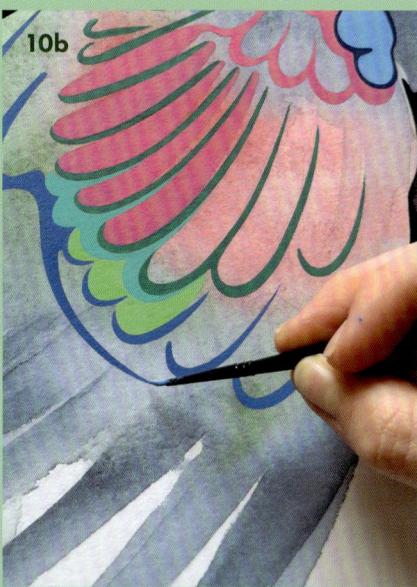

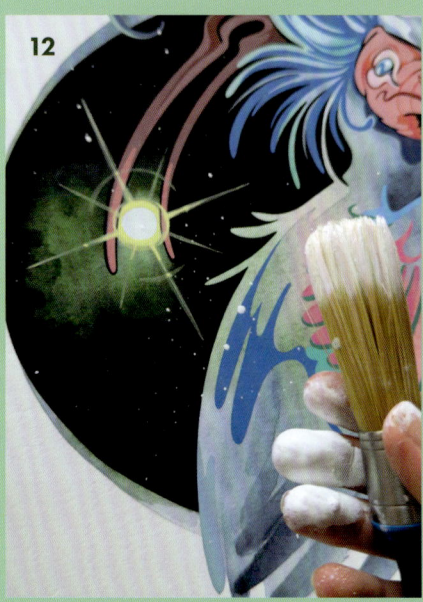

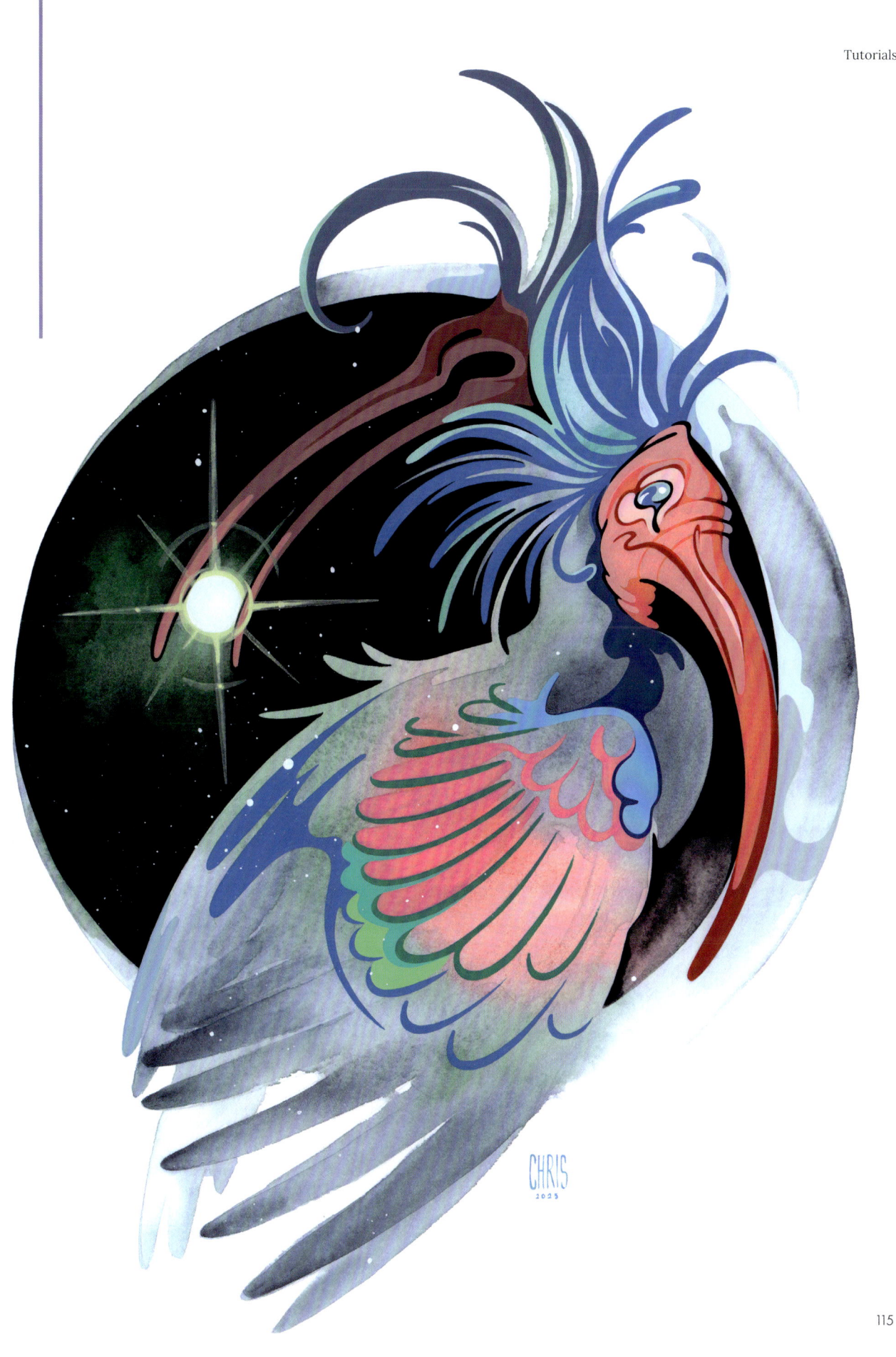

TEMPERA & WATERCOLOUR: OKAME

As I mentioned earlier, different cultures are a source of inspiration for me, so I have decided to create a Japanese Okame mask tutorial. Okame is considered the goddess of joy. She is also known as Otafuku, which translates as 'much good fortune'. Interestingly, the word 'kame' means 'turtle', a symbol of longevity and good luck in Japanese culture.

I want to combine these two motifs by painting a turtle with an Okame mask on its shell, creating a visual and conceptual complementarity.

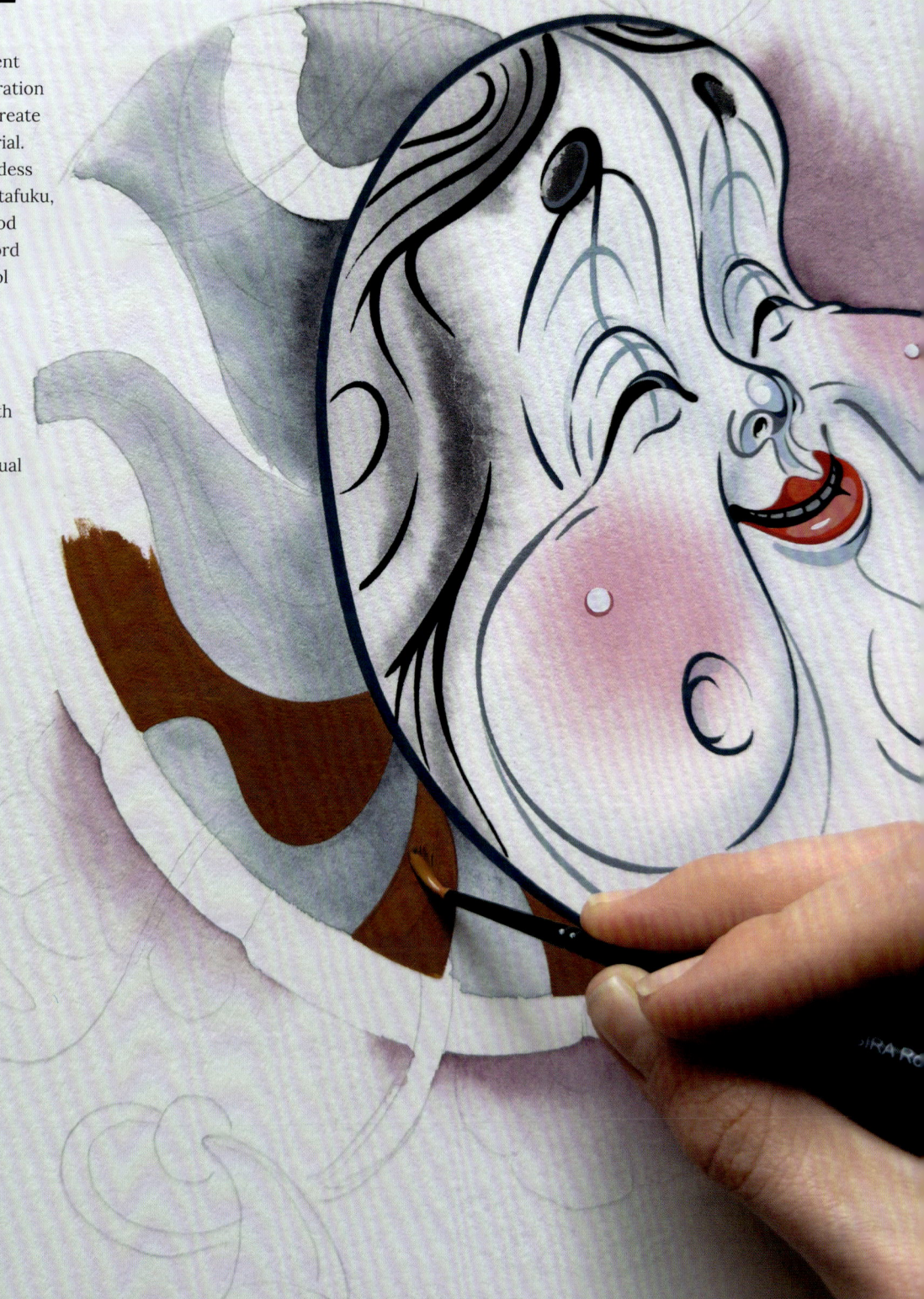

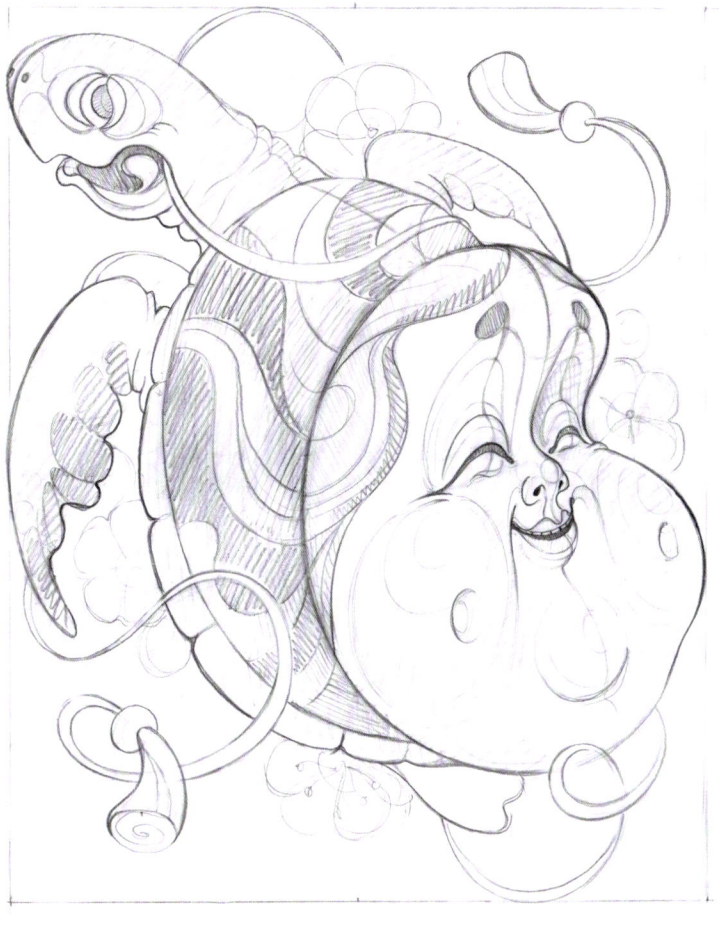

STEP 01: SKETCHING

First, I draw a conditional frame to mark the points of contact on all sides. I don't always use this technique, but I do use it quite often in similar compositions. It helps me to distribute the visual weight and avoid clutter, while keeping the viewer's gaze in the centre.

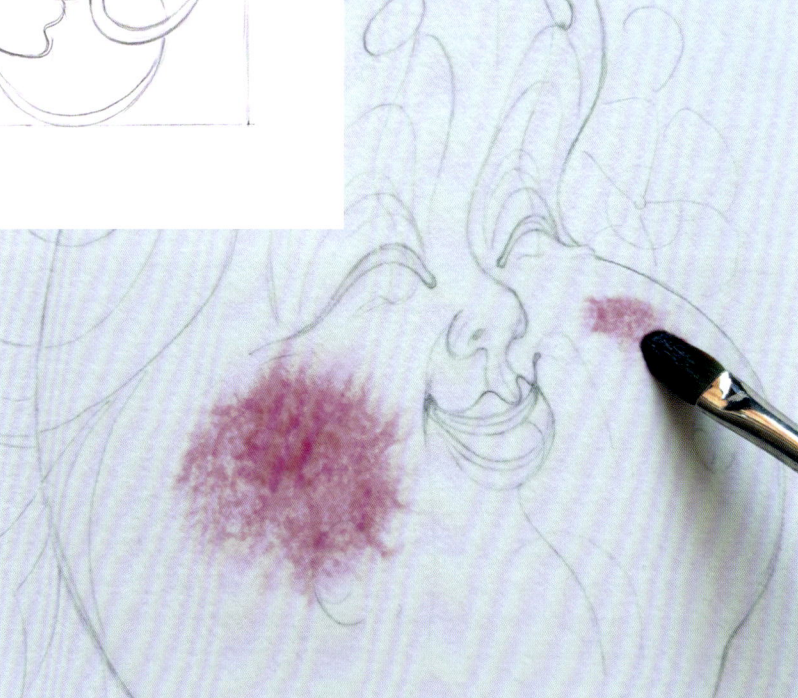

STEP 02: PAINTING A MASK
WITH WATERCOLOUR

The Okame mask traditionally has a white complexion with rounded shapes. This inspired me to use the wet-on-wet technique because I can create smooth, delicate colour transitions. However, unlike the previous tutorial, it is important not to fill the entire watercolour surface. The white paper will act as the 'skin' colour, highlighting certain areas of the face. I begin by painting a pink colour over the cheeks.

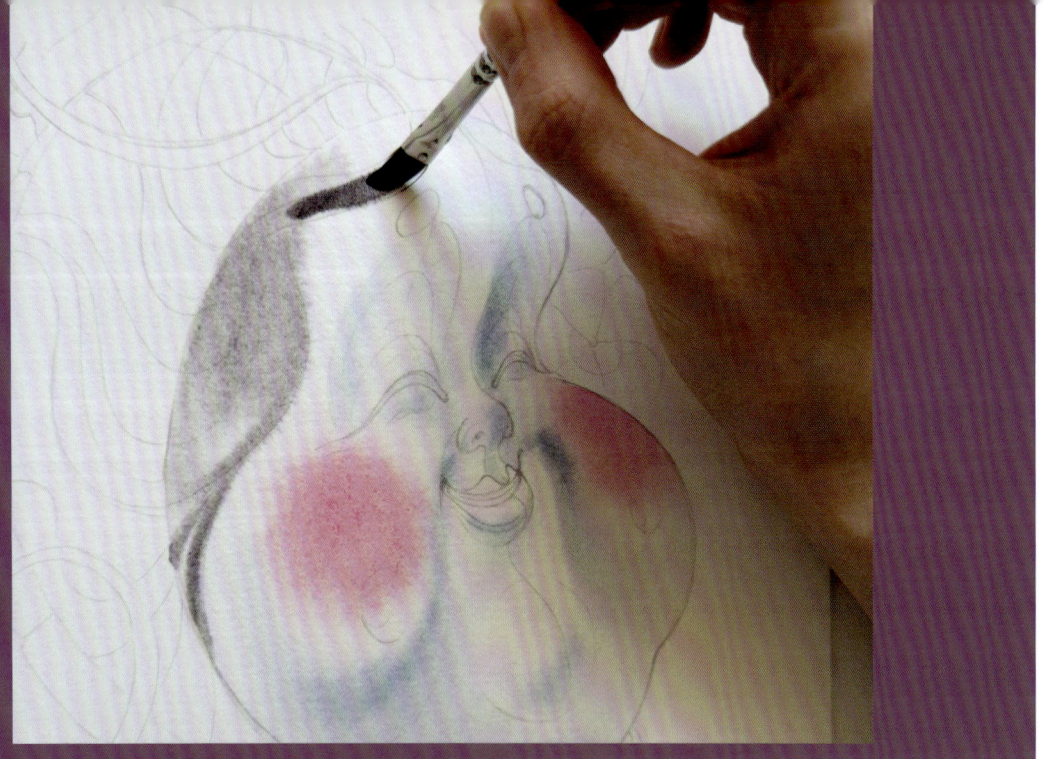

STEP 03: REFINING THE FACE

Using an indigo colour, I paint the shadows on the face with smooth strokes. Okame's hair and eyebrows are black, so I use the colour 'black grape' with a subtle purple tint. While the paper is still wet, I immediately apply two more brushstrokes on top of the first layer, following the shape of the hair, using the same colour but with a slightly higher saturation. I then wait for it to dry completely.

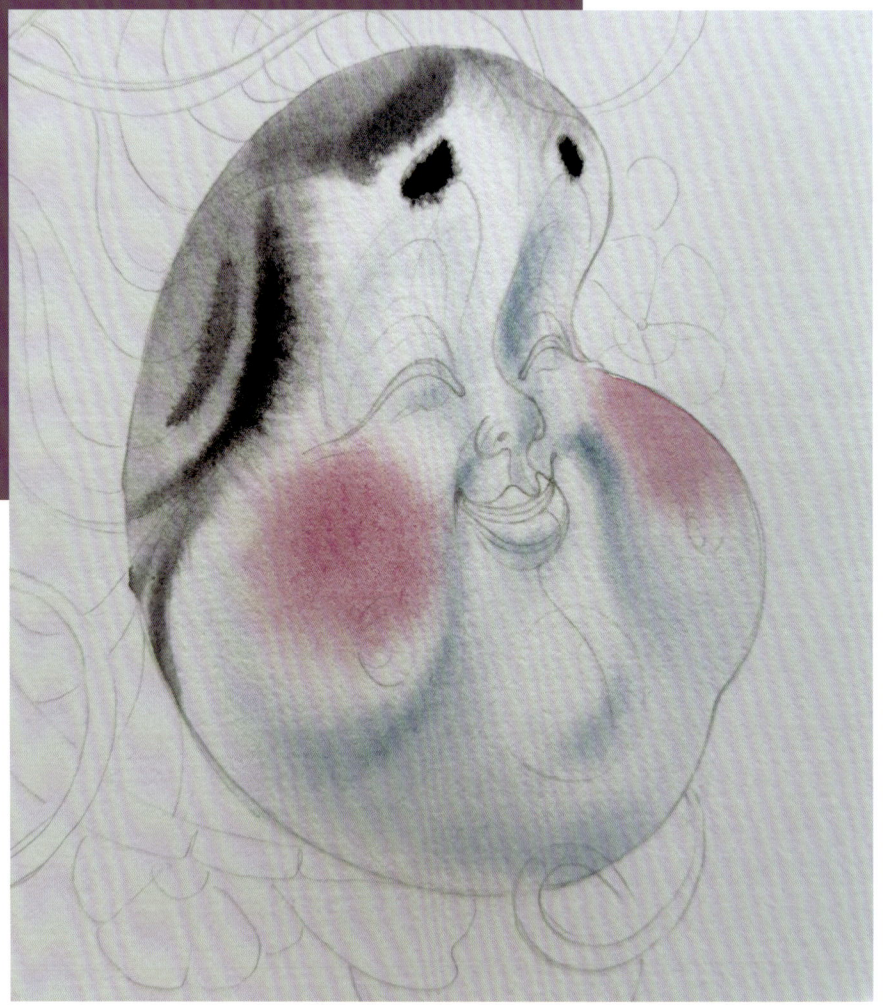

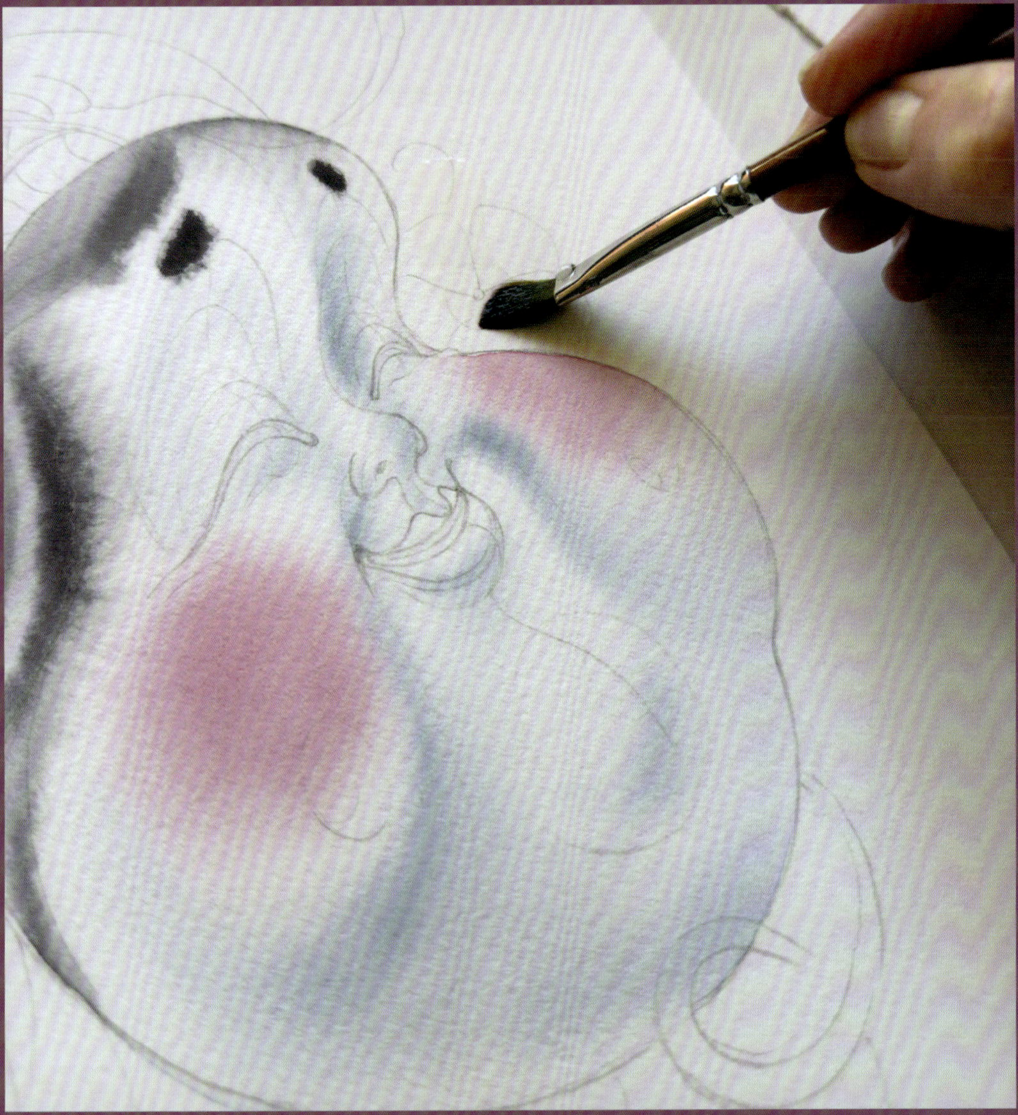

STEP 04: PAINTING THE CONTOURS

Next, I move on to painting the areas where the cherry blossom flowers will appear. To achieve this, I mix carmine with black grape to create a slightly deeper shade. I moisten a section of the paper with the brush, leaving a dry strip next to the outline of the mask. Next, I apply the paint with a thin brush along the contour. The contour on one side of the mask remains clear while the other side blurs because I already made the paper wet. I then apply the same technique to all the other spots where the cherry blossoms will be.

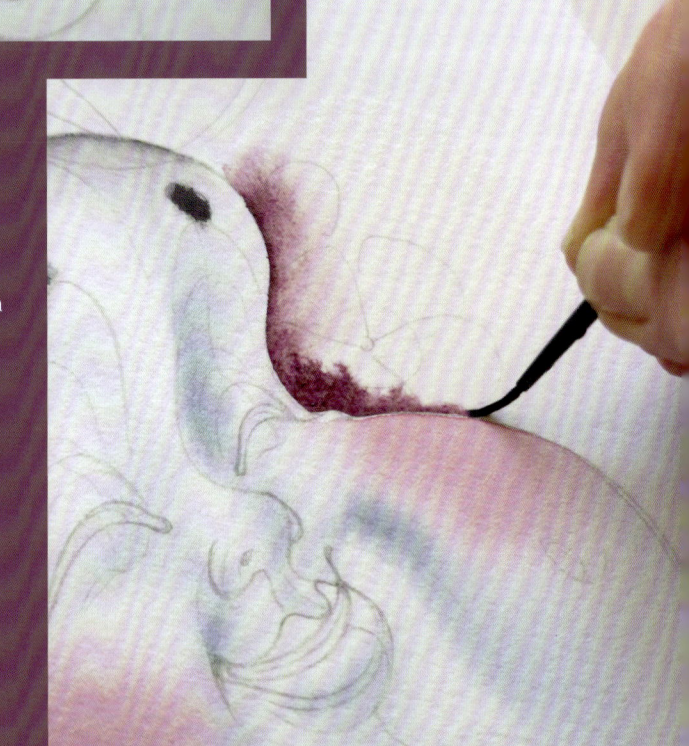

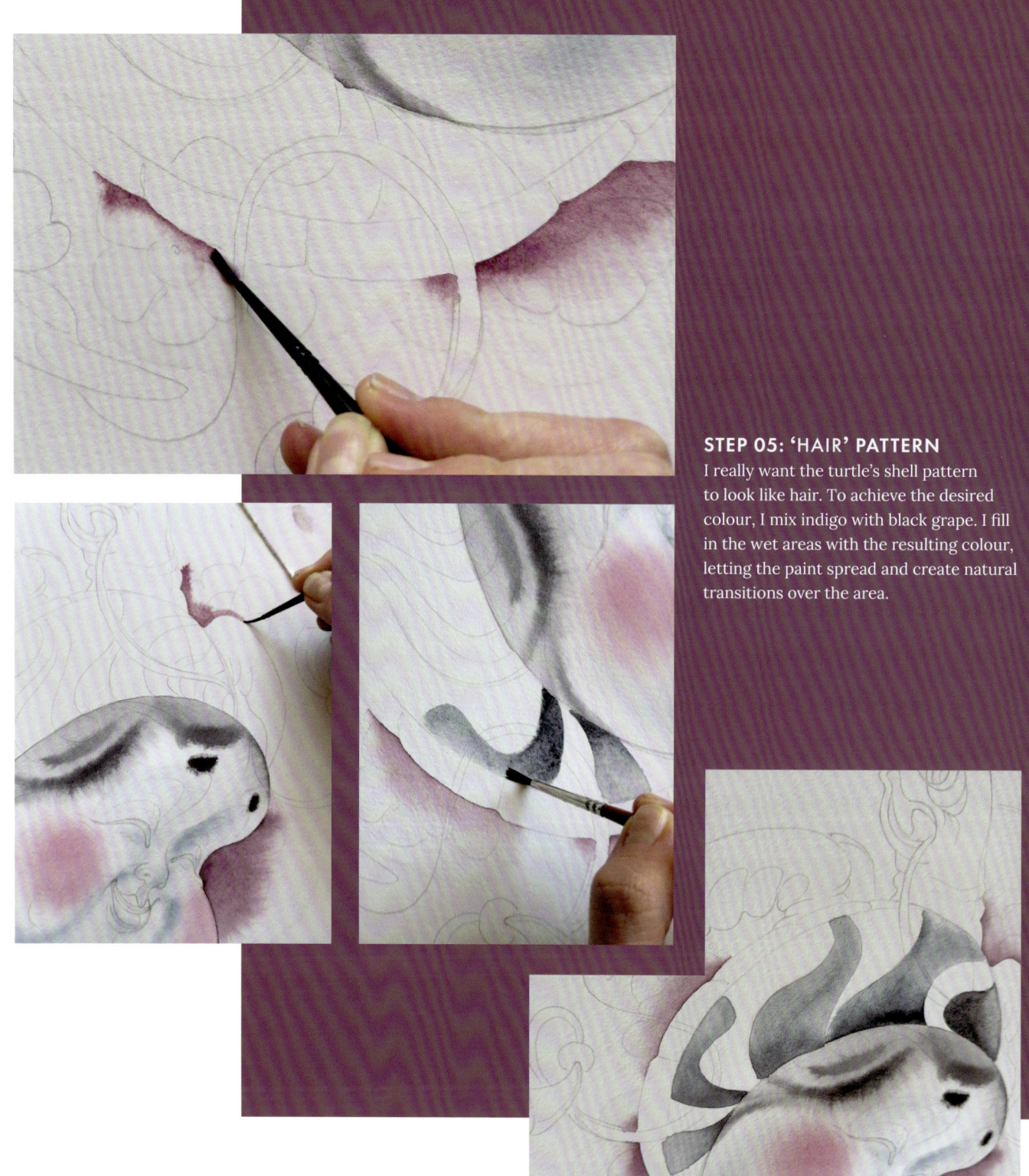

STEP 05: 'HAIR' PATTERN

I really want the turtle's shell pattern to look like hair. To achieve the desired colour, I mix indigo with black grape. I fill in the wet areas with the resulting colour, letting the paint spread and create natural transitions over the area.

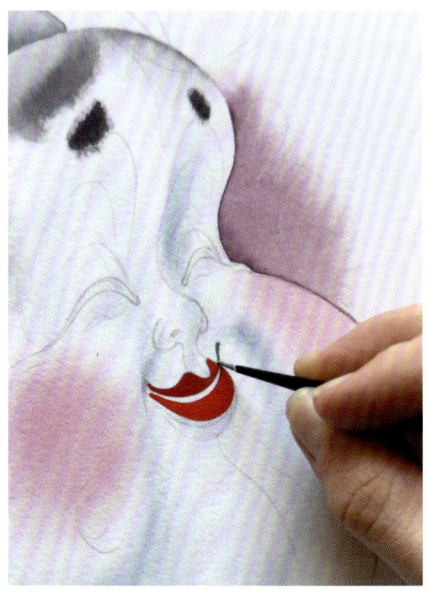

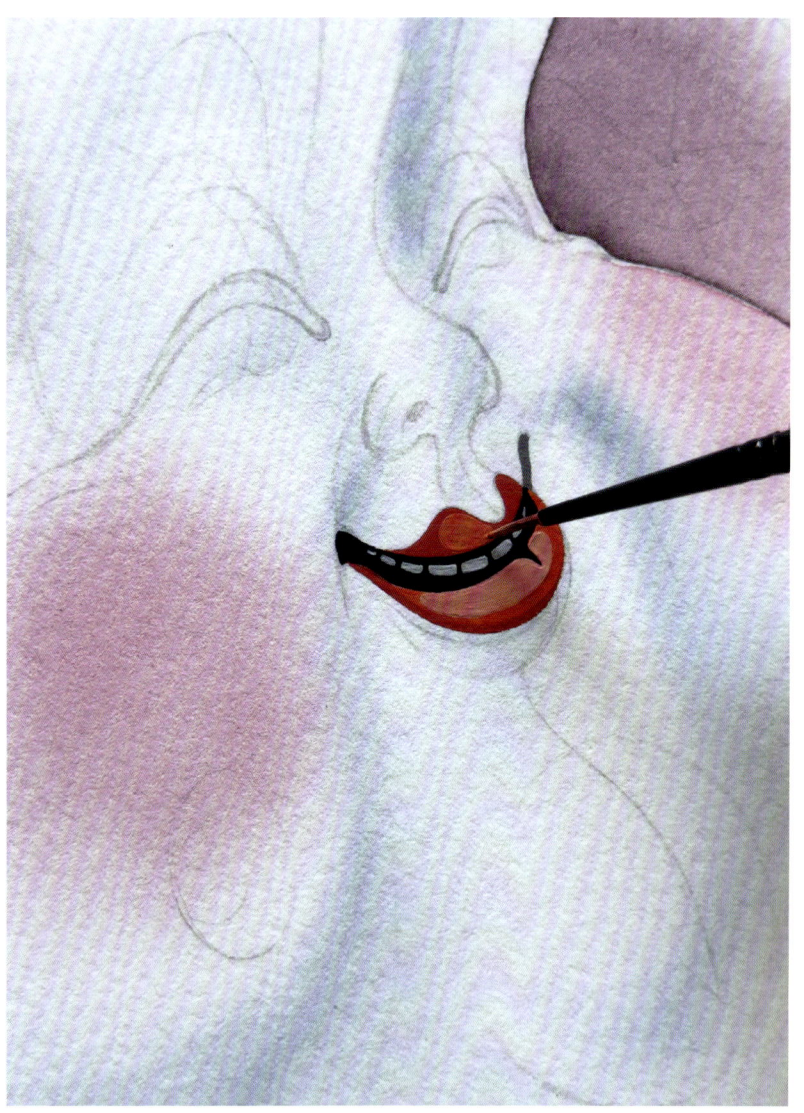

STEP 06: TEMPERA PAINTING

At this stage, I return to the Okame mask to work on the facial features in more detail. I draw the lips and paint the inside black. Then, I shade the teeth grey, wait for them to dry, and adjust their shape with black.

SMOOTHING FINE DETAILS

Brush strokes can dry quickly when you're working on fine details, creating an unwanted texture and making it difficult to achieve crisp lines. To smooth them out, first cover the dried surface with a plastic sheet to protect it. Then gently press the reverse tip of the brush against the problem area to correct any unevenness.

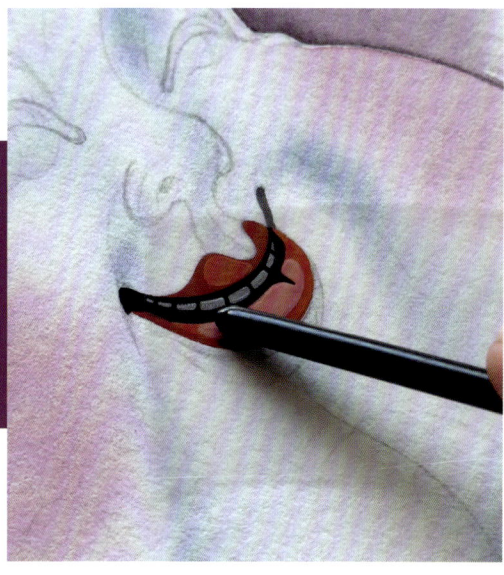

STEP 07: DEFINING THE LINE WORK

I continue working on the details by defining the line work.
I combine lines of different thicknesses and saturations,
using black paint for the hair and dark-blue shades for the
facial features.

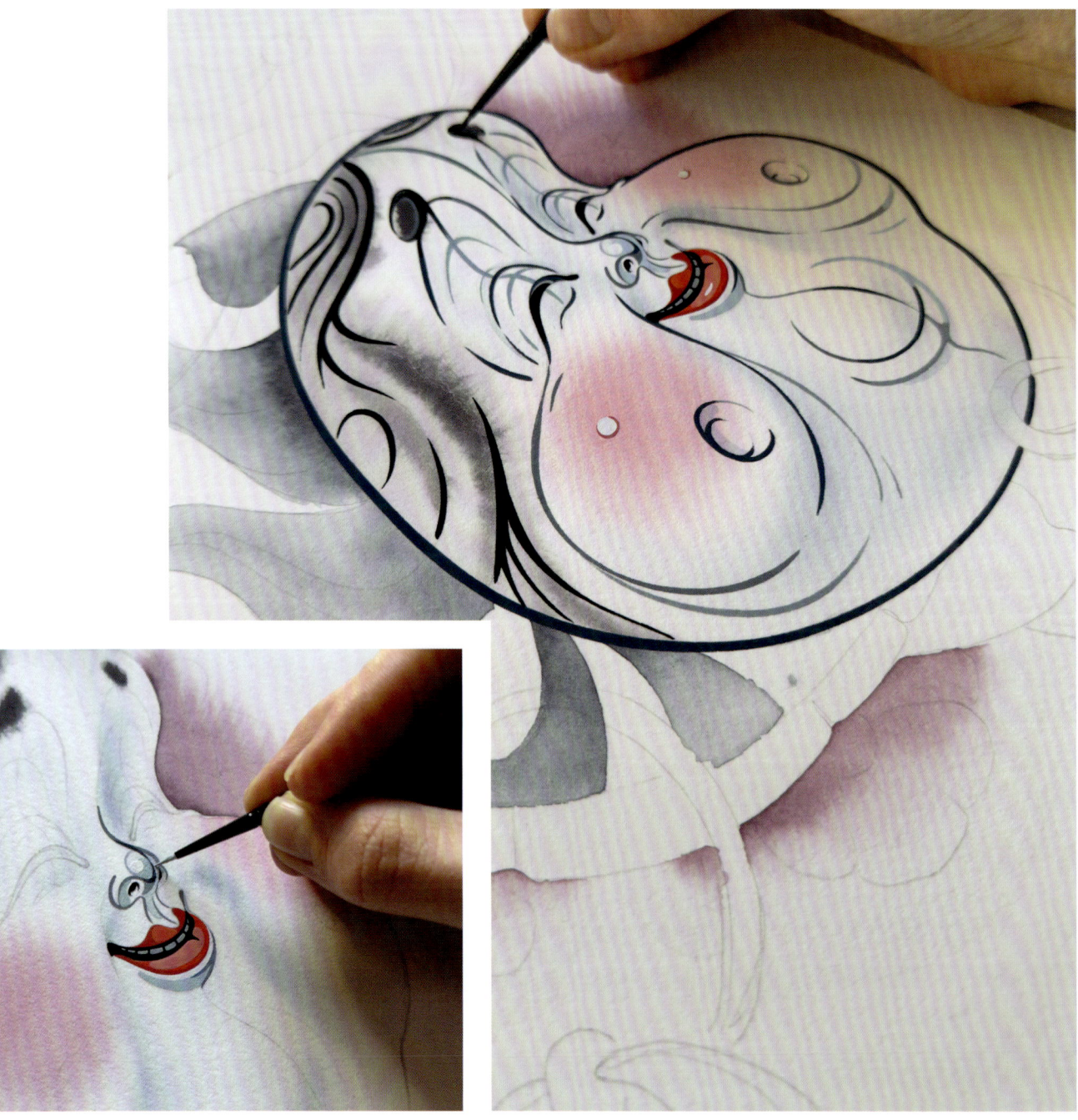

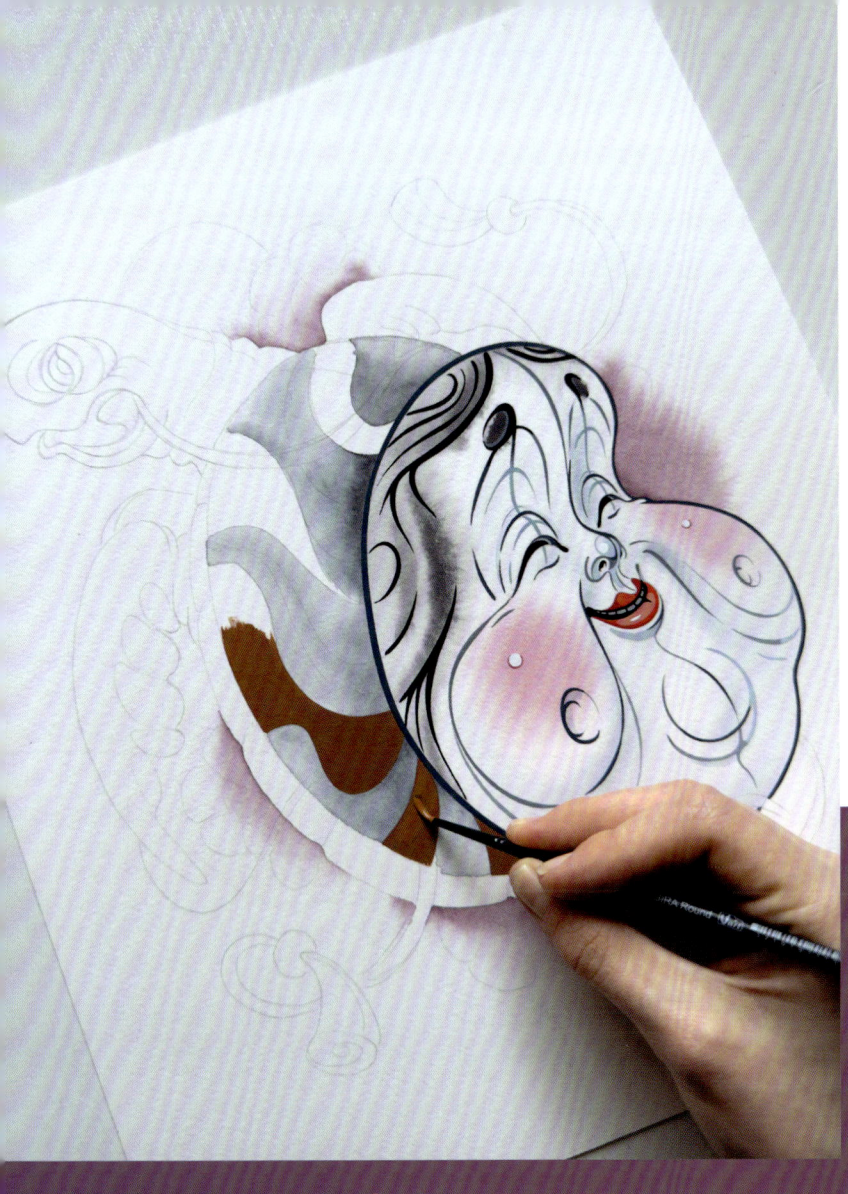

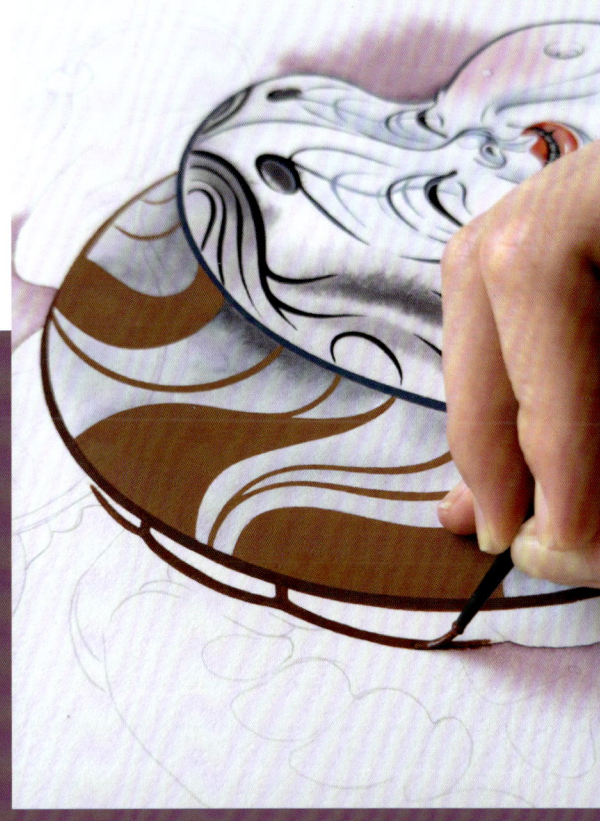

STEP 08: SHELL PAINTING

I use a mixture of burnt sienna, ochre light, and titanium white to fill the inside of the shell. Next, I outline these areas using burnt sienna, and add a lighter tone to the outer shell using a mixture of ochre and white.

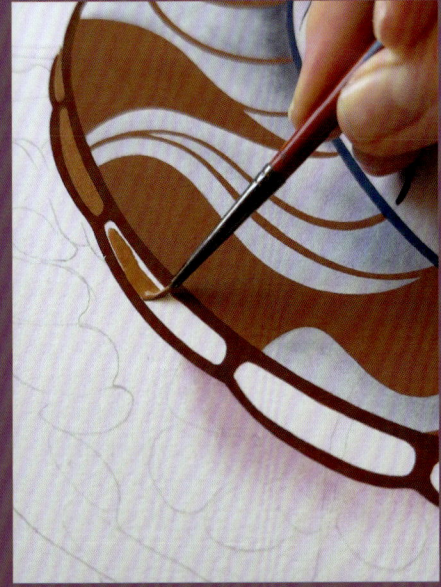

STEP 09: PAINTING THE TURTLE

For the turtle's body, I mix cerulean blue, titanium white, and a little light ochre. I start with the flippers, painting the spots with a more saturated shade. Next, I move on to the head, using purple to outline its shape and fill in the shadowy areas.

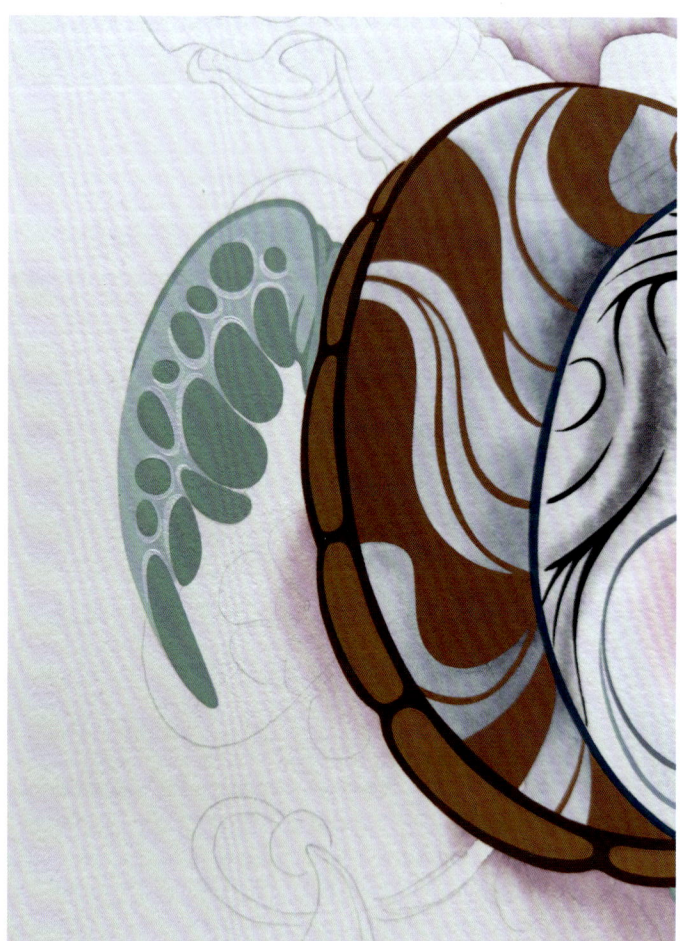

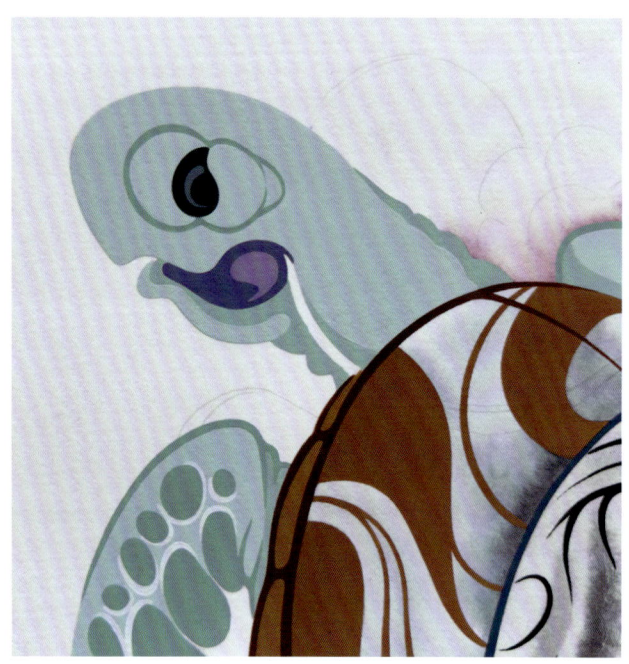

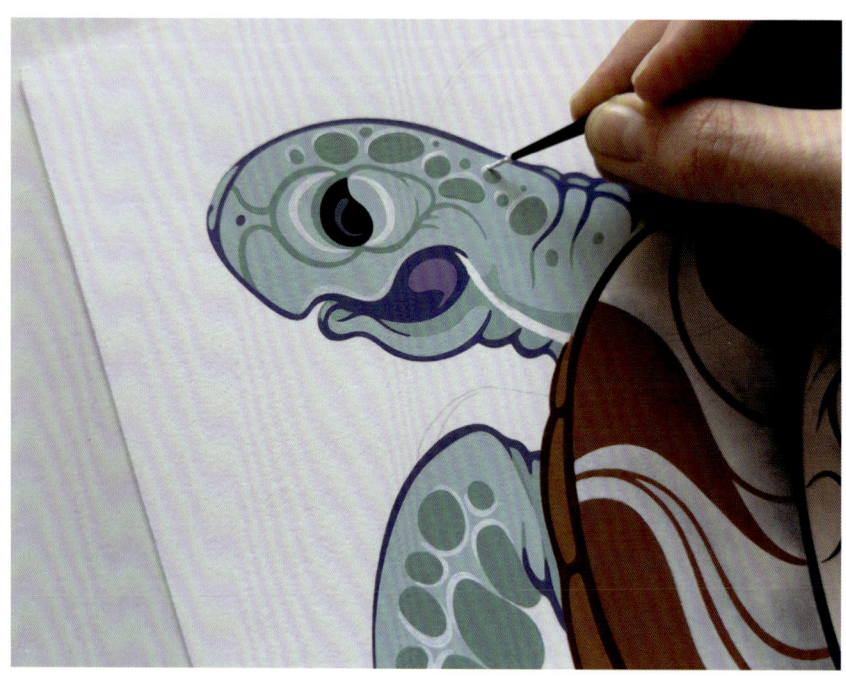

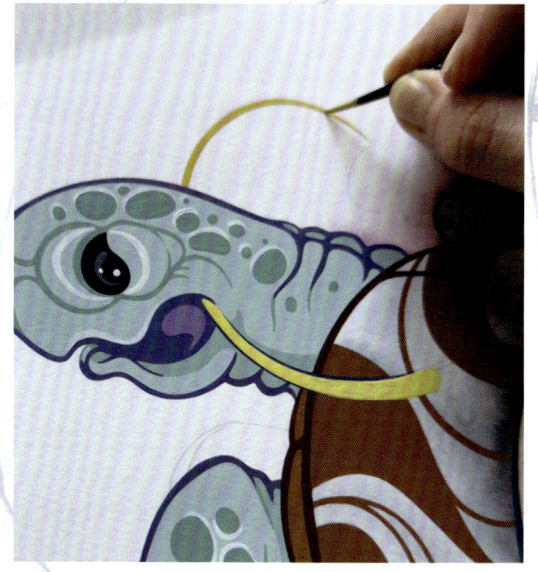

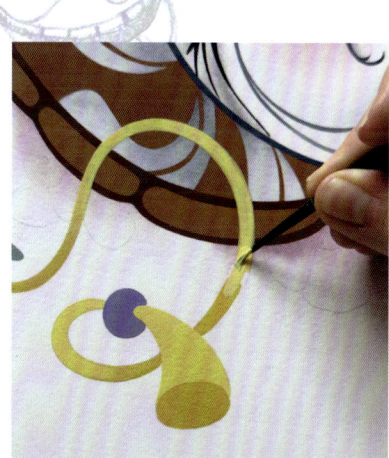

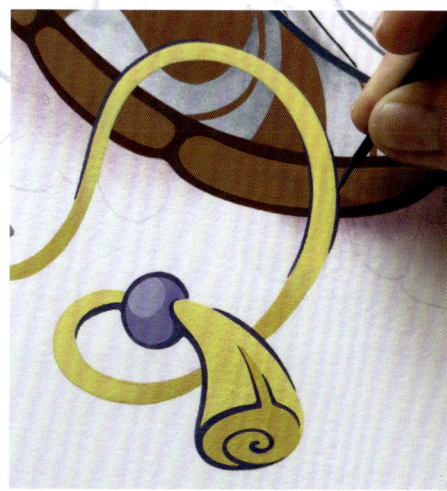

STEP 10: DECORATIVE DETAILS –
JAPANESE CORD

For the cord, I use two shades of yellow to
create tonal transitions and add volume.
I also paint the outline using the same
shade of purple used in the previous step to
create balance.

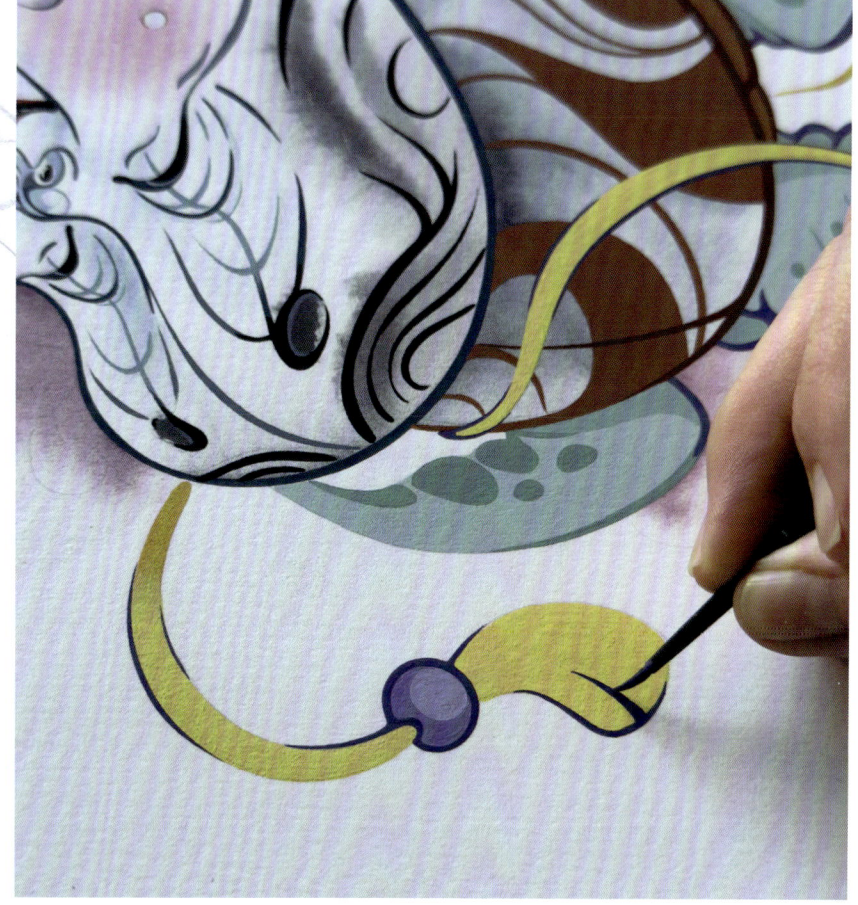

STEP 11: SMALL DETAILS – SAKURA

I finish the illustration by adding some freehand line work. I use paint that is thin enough to last, but not so watery that it smudges. Choosing the right brush is also important. I prefer a pointed, synthetic brush like an imitation Kolinsky brush – it is soft yet resilient, which gives me better control for precise strokes.

STEP 12: TAKE A STEP BACK

It's always important to leave the work for a little while and revisit later for final touches. Then you're finished!

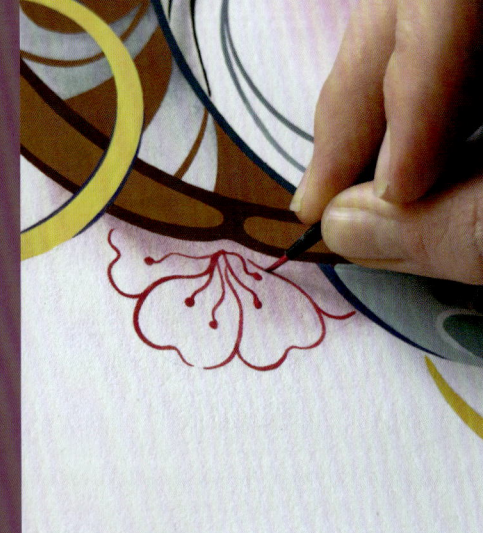

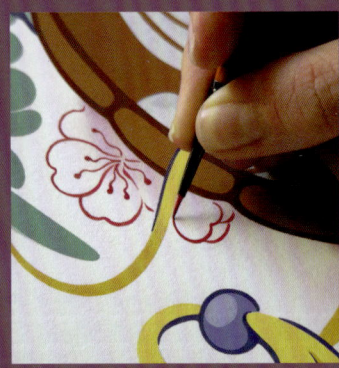

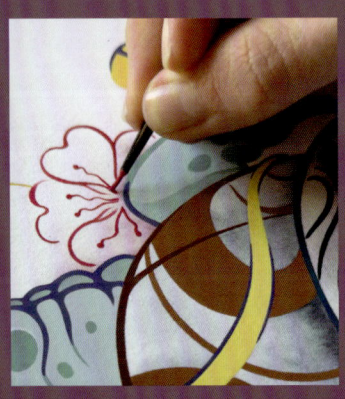

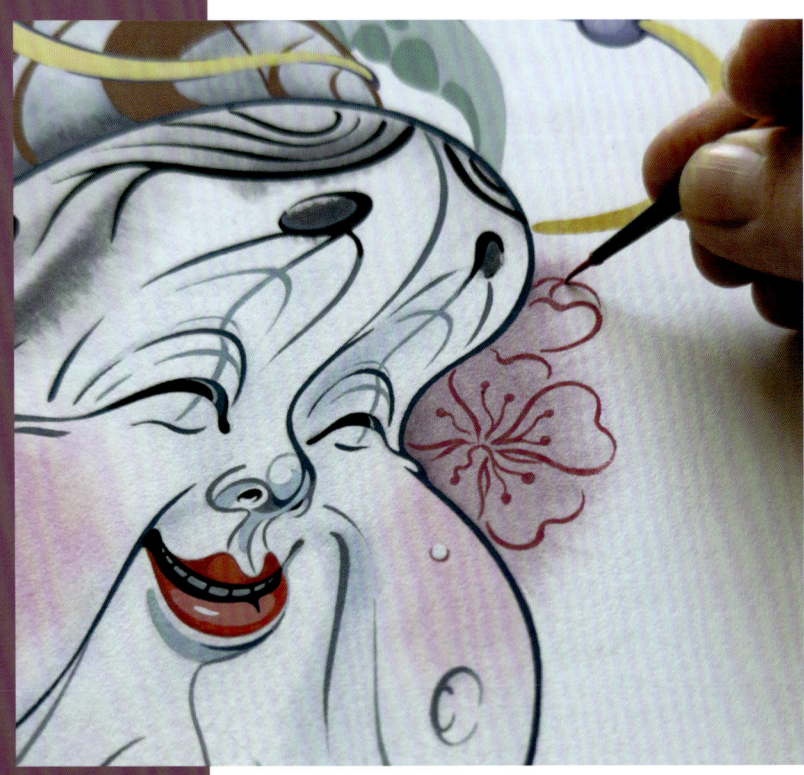

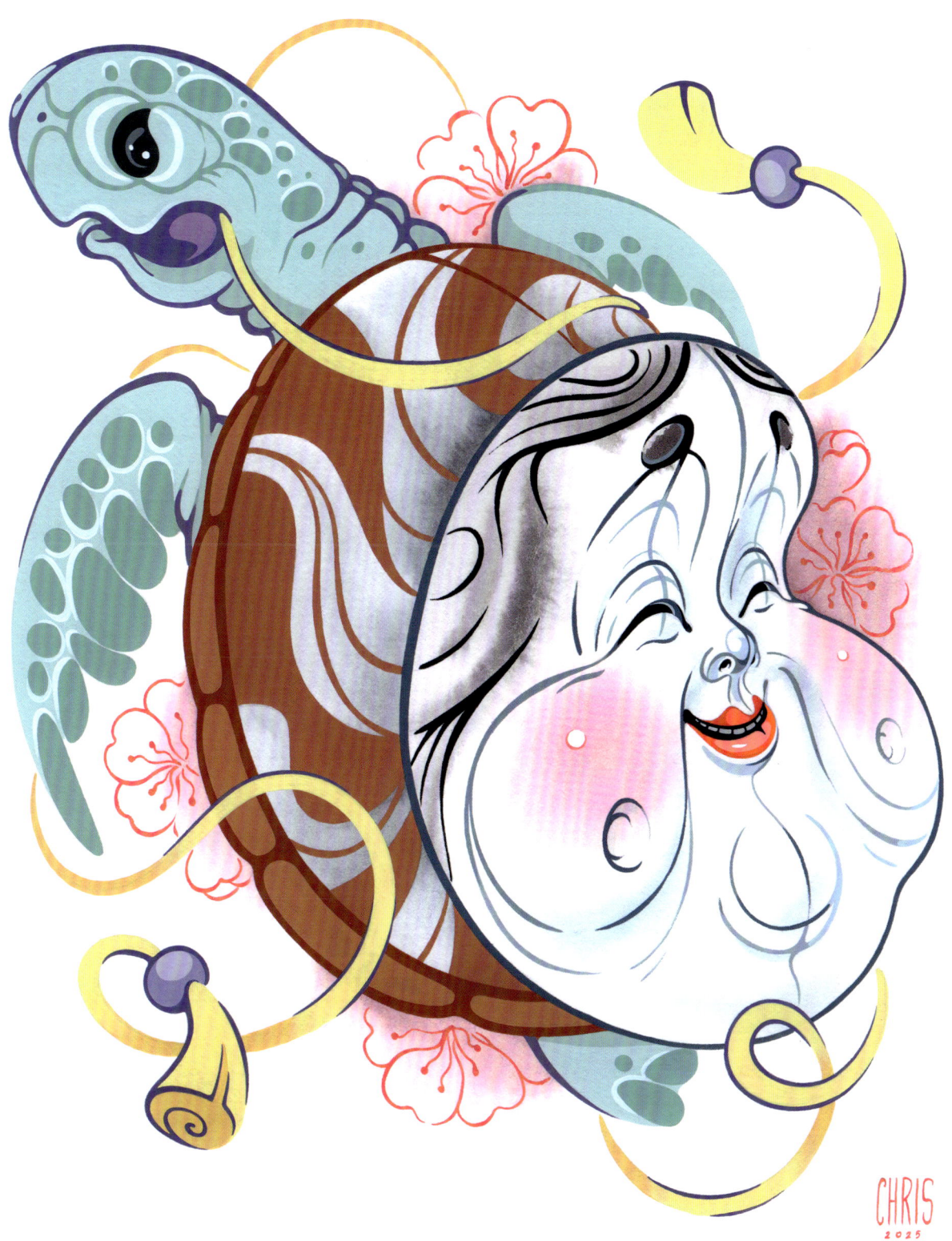

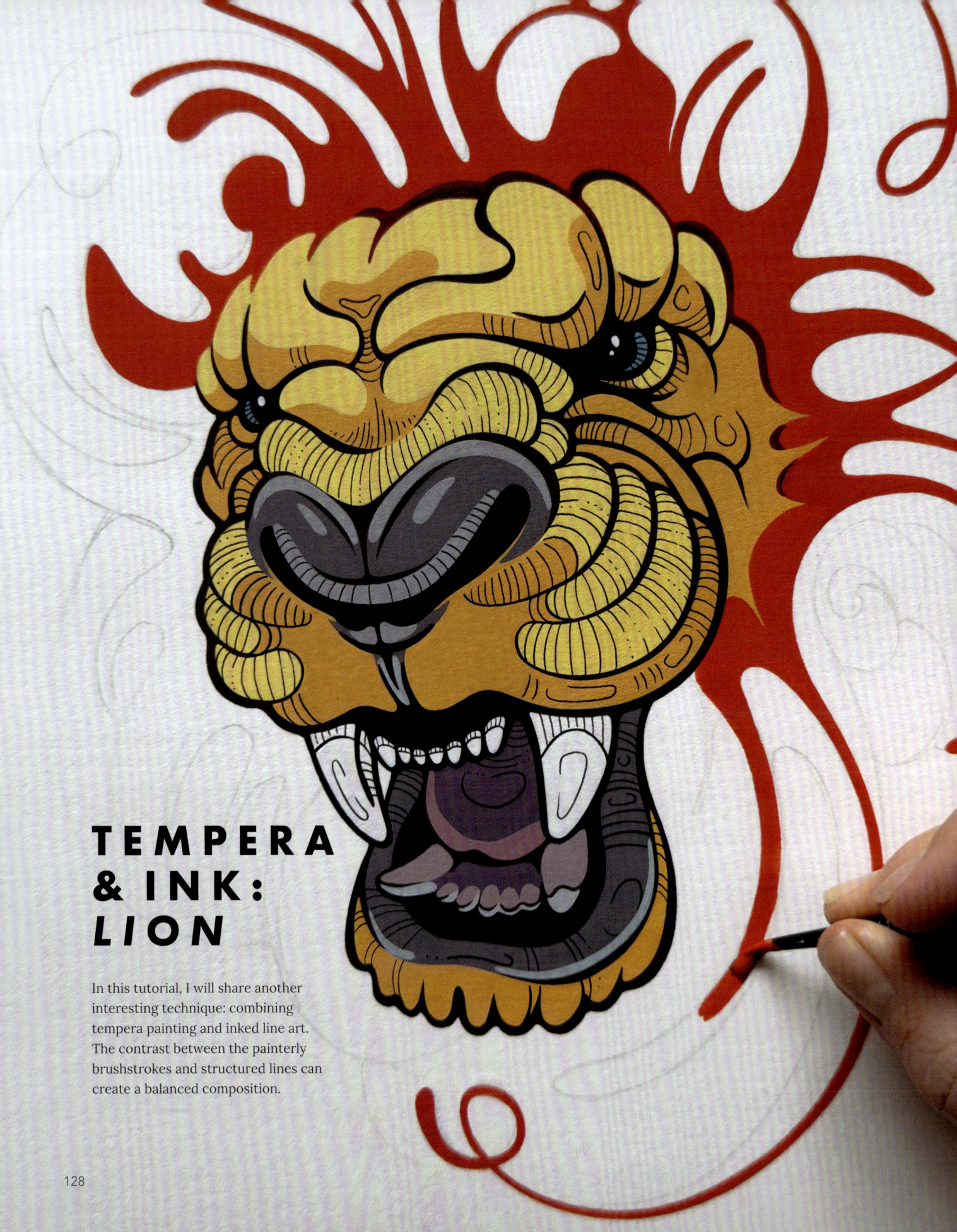

TEMPERA
& INK:
LION

In this tutorial, I will share another interesting technique: combining tempera painting and inked line art. The contrast between the painterly brushstrokes and structured lines can create a balanced composition.

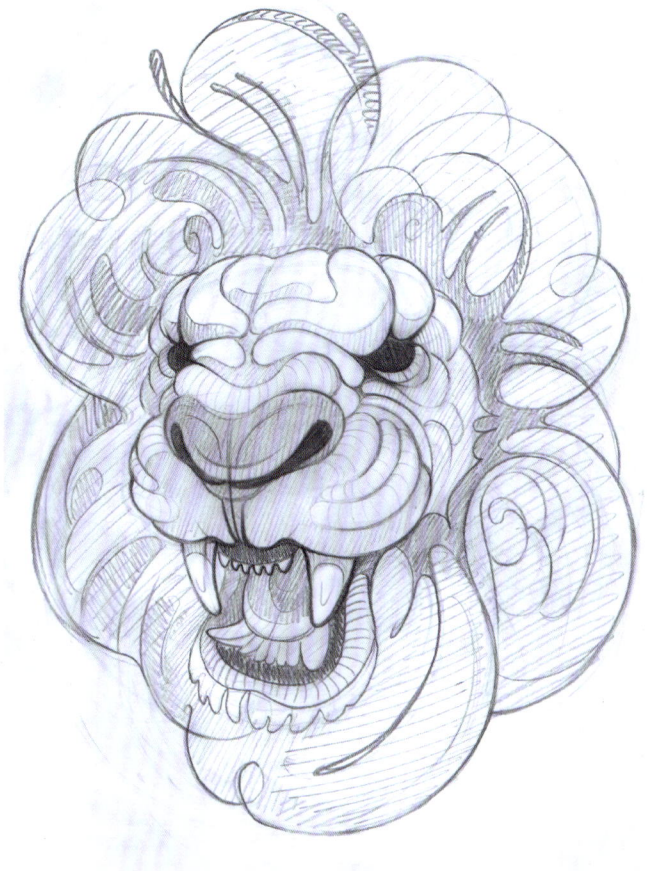

STEP 01: THE SKETCH

For the initial drawing, I adapt a sketch I made of a lion's head, based on an exhibit I saw at a museum. Thinking ahead about the colouring process, I make a few adjustments, refining the facial features and painting the mane in more abstract and decorative shapes than the original drawing had.

STEP 02: PAINTING THE LION'S FACE

I limit the lion's face to two main colours. I start with the light areas, using a mix of cadmium yellow medium and titanium white.

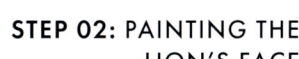

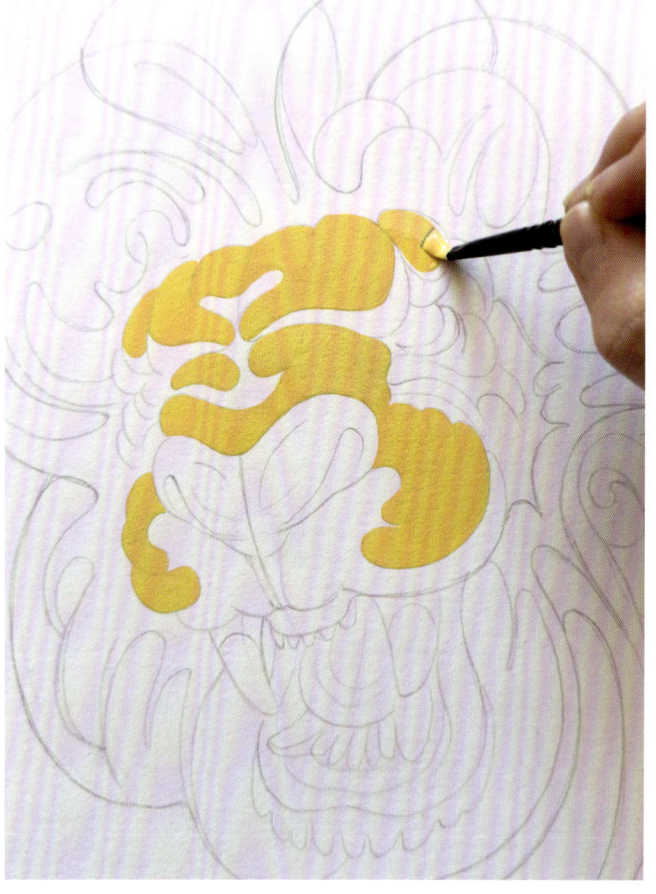

STEP 03: ADDING SHADOWS

I add shadows to the lion's face using a mixture of cadmium yellow medium, cadmium orange, and titanium white.

STEP 04: PAINTING THE NOSE

For the nose colour, I combine white with black and a little caput mortuum to add a brownish tint. To add highlights to this area, all I have to do is increase the amount of white in the mixture.

STEP 05: CONTROLLING HIGHLIGHTS

I add highlights over the first layer. I also use a mixture of caput mortuum mixed with black to add line work.

STEP 06: LINE WORK

After the paint dries, I continue adding lines, using the same dark mixture. If I make a mistake, it's not a big deal – I can fix the lines by using the paint from the layer below.

STEP 07: ADDING DETAILS WITH INK

Once the paint is dry, I use an ink liner with a width of 0.05mm to emphasize existing shapes and add in shadows. I shade around the eyes, nose, teeth, and skin folds. Unlike tempera outlines, liner lines are the same thickness, making the illustration look more graphic.

STEP 08: MOVING TO THE MOUTH

It's important to use muted shades here so that the mouth doesn't draw too much attention. For the tongue, I mix white with quinacridone rose, black, and caput mortuum, which produces a dull pinkish-brown tone. I add a lighter shade on top, then paint the lower teeth grey and brown.

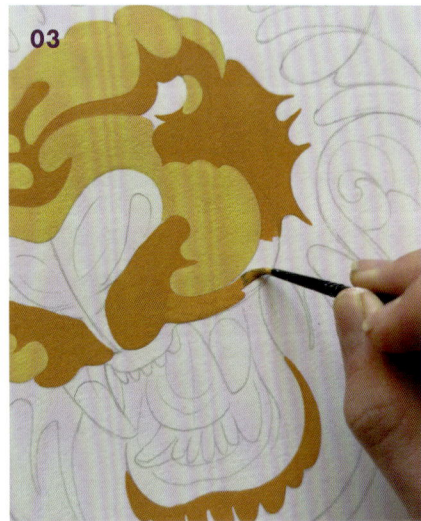

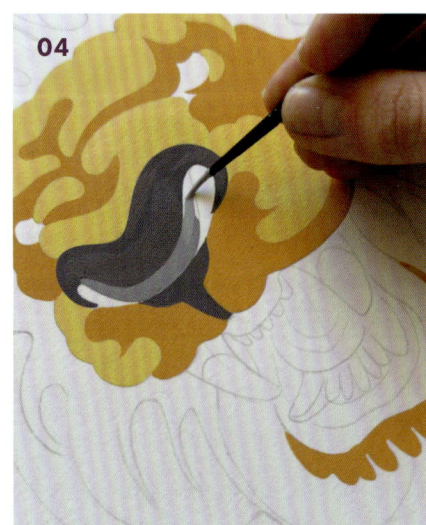

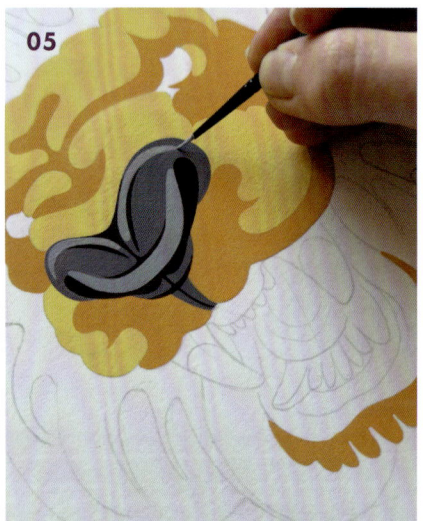

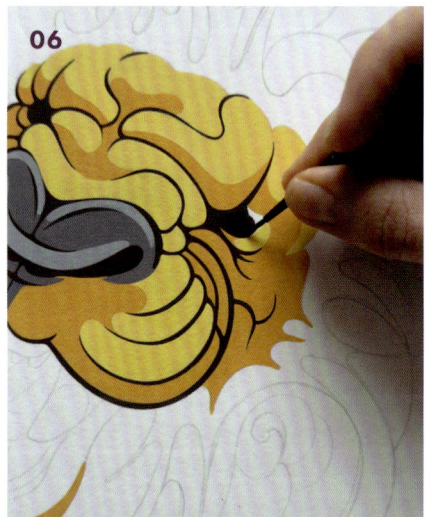

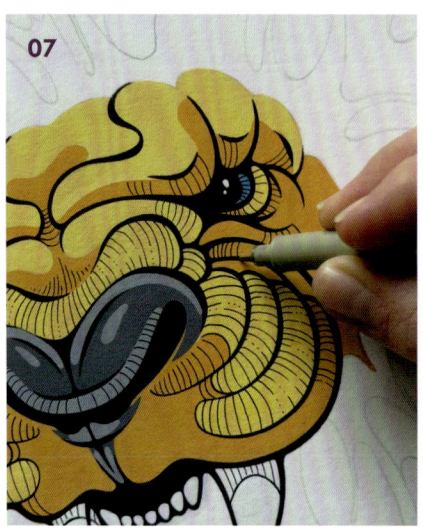

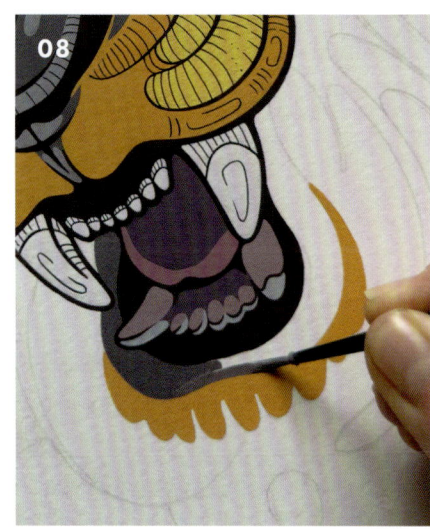

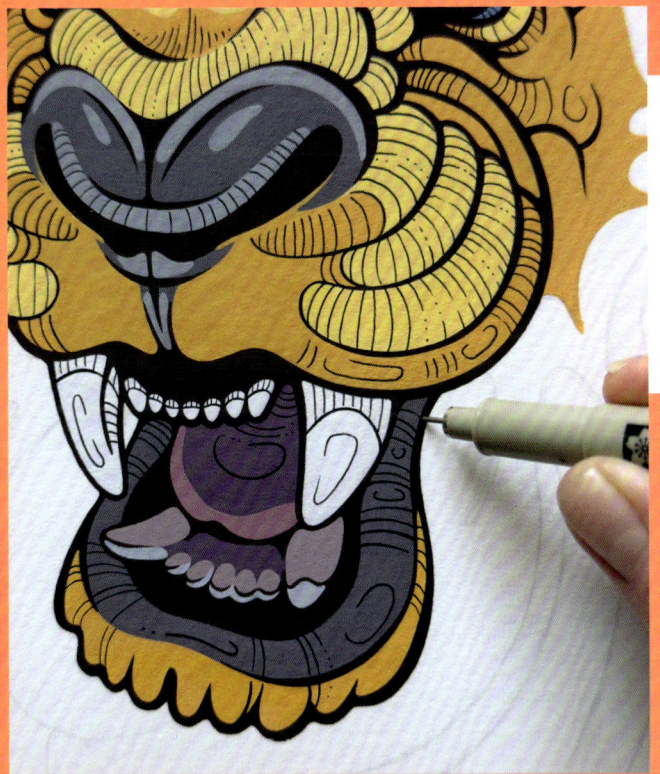

TIP FOR INK DRAWING

Don't try to make the lines perfectly straight right away. Vary the spacing, leave gaps, and add dashes to create a lively, interesting texture. If you control every stroke too closely, the process becomes difficult and stressful.

STEP 09: LION'S MANE

The swirling, chaotic lines of the mane calls for a rich and bright colour, so I choose red as the base.

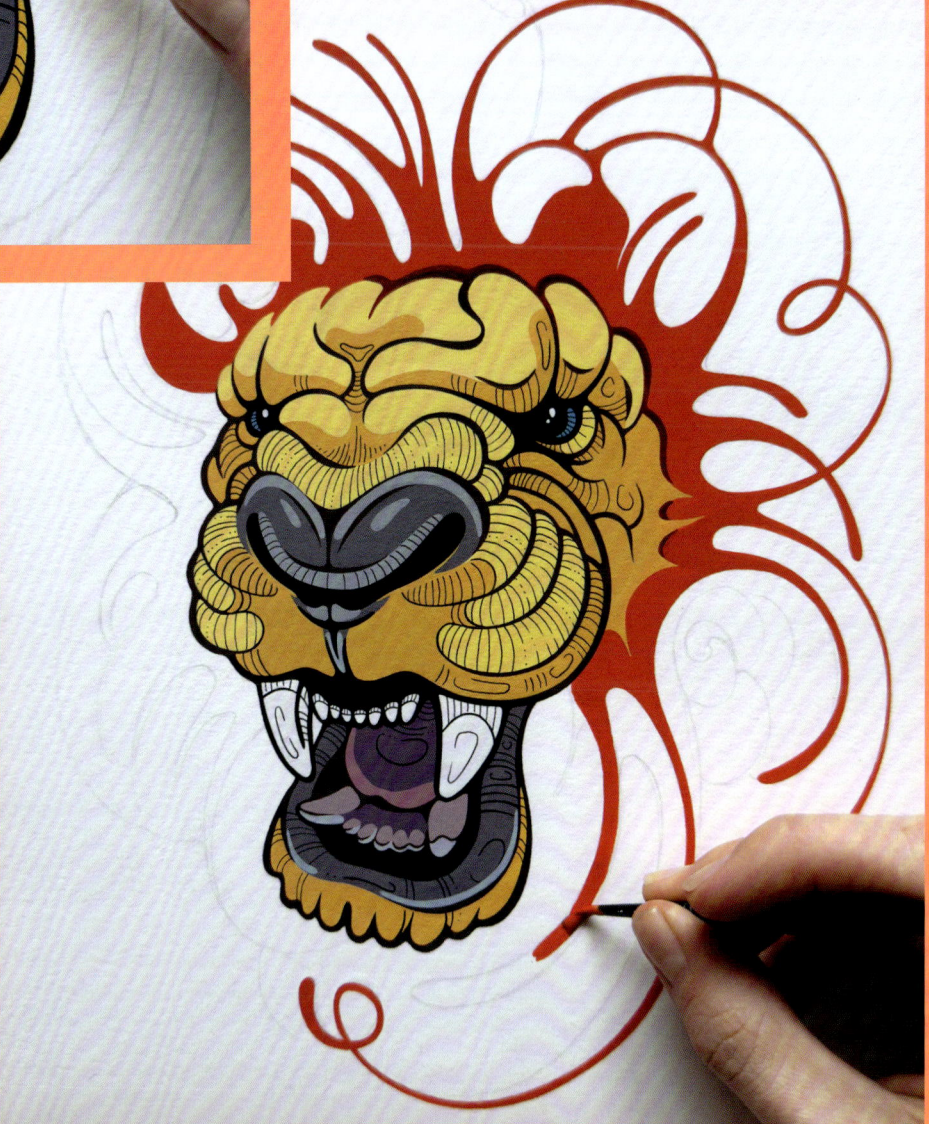

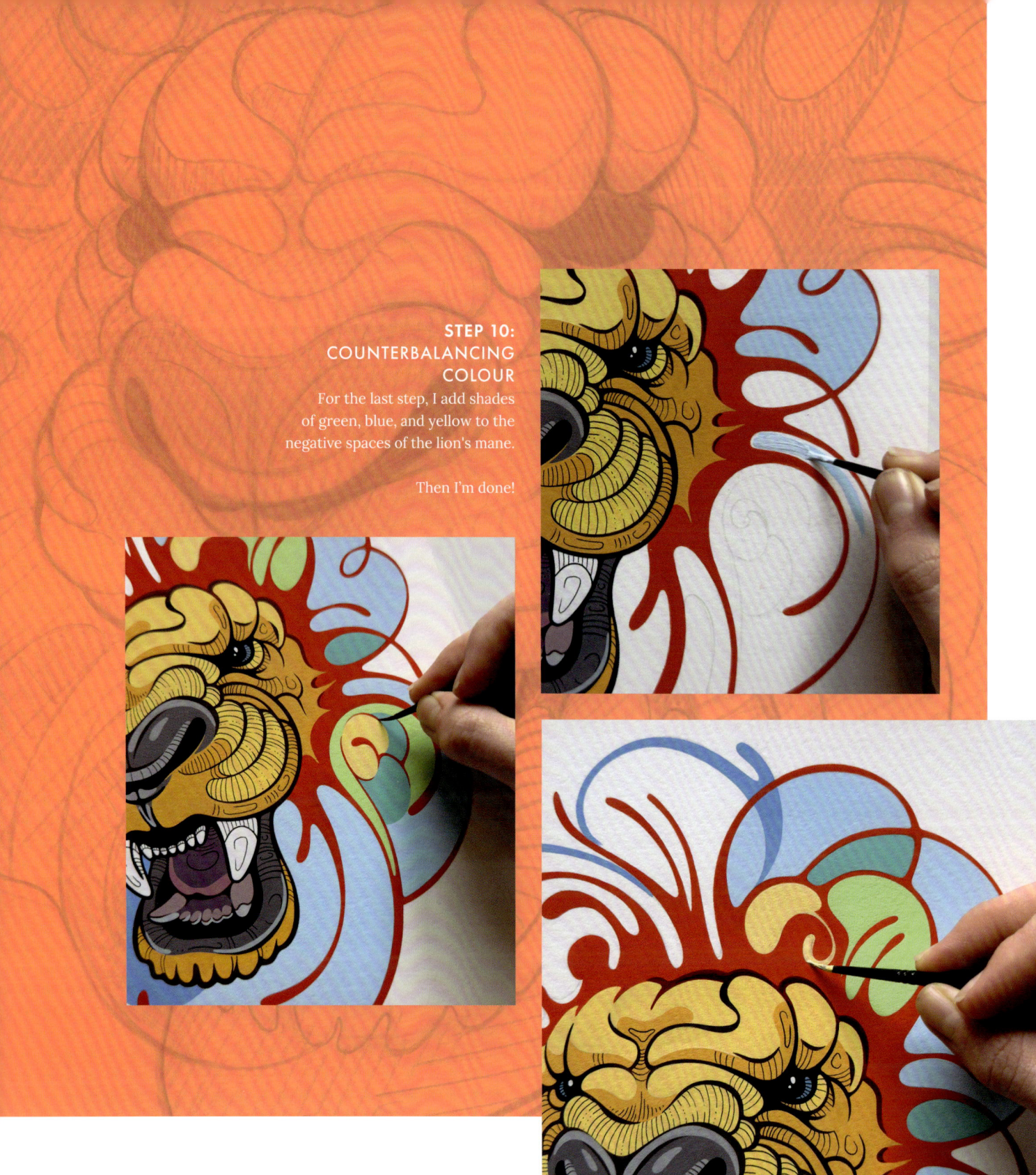

STEP 10: COUNTERBALANCING COLOUR

For the last step, I add shades of green, blue, and yellow to the negative spaces of the lion's mane.

Then I'm done!

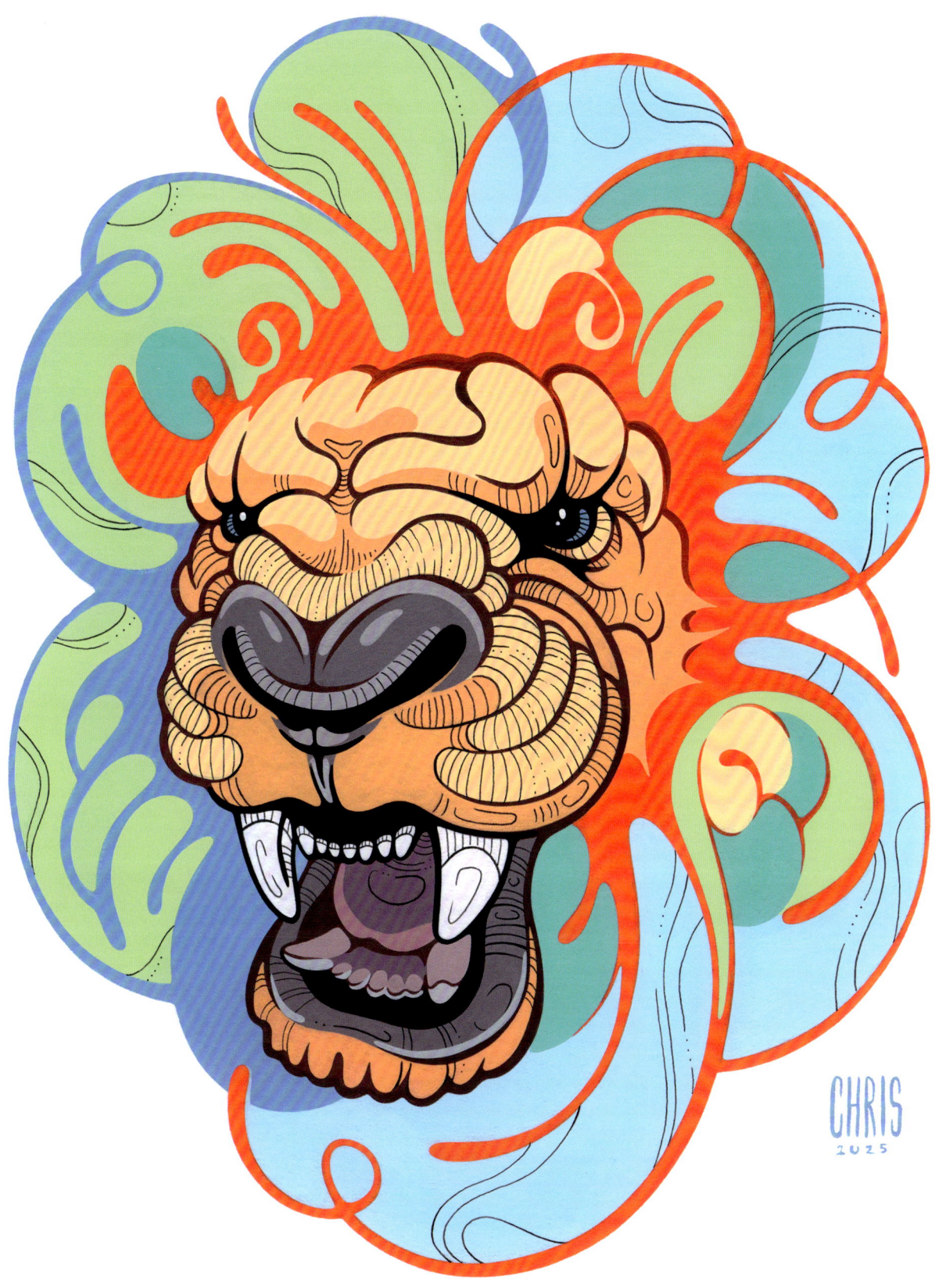

CHRIS
2025

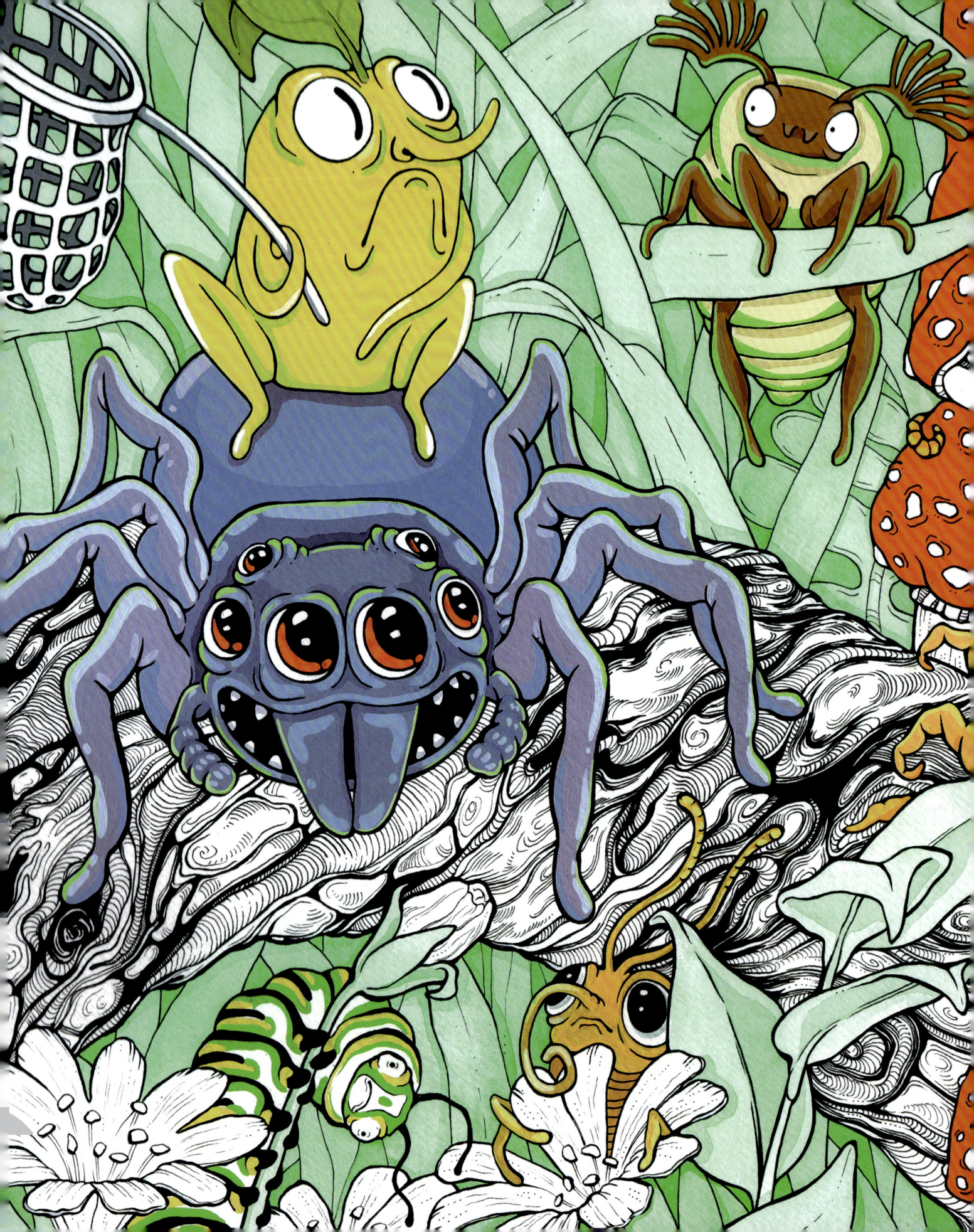

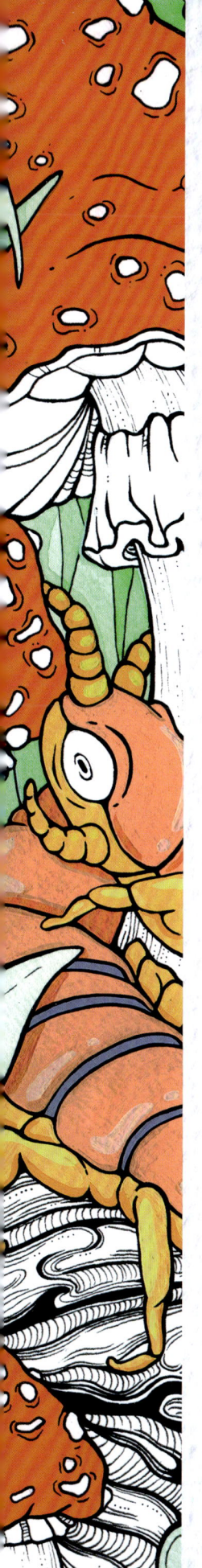

Gallery
Recent works

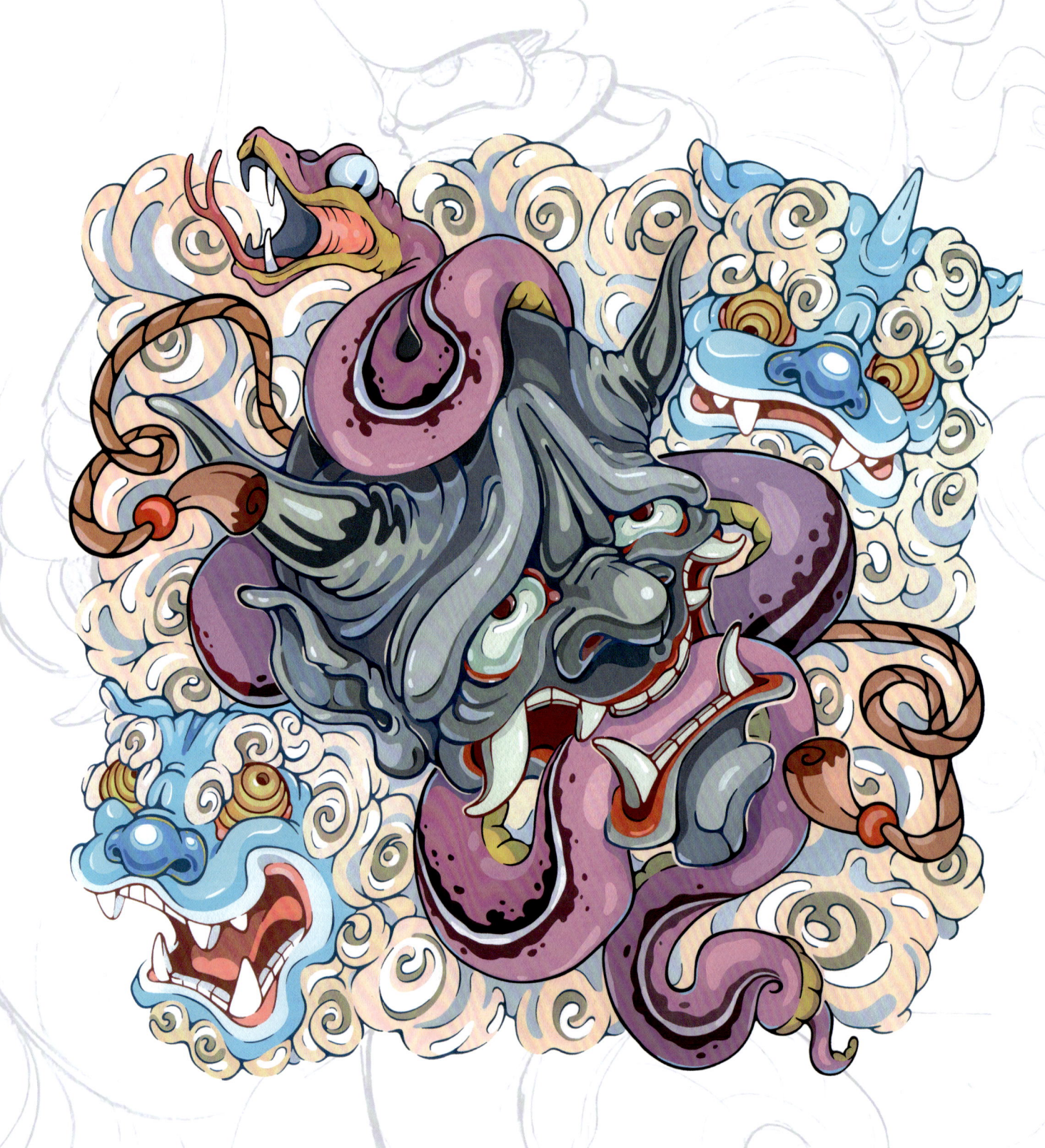

Hannya

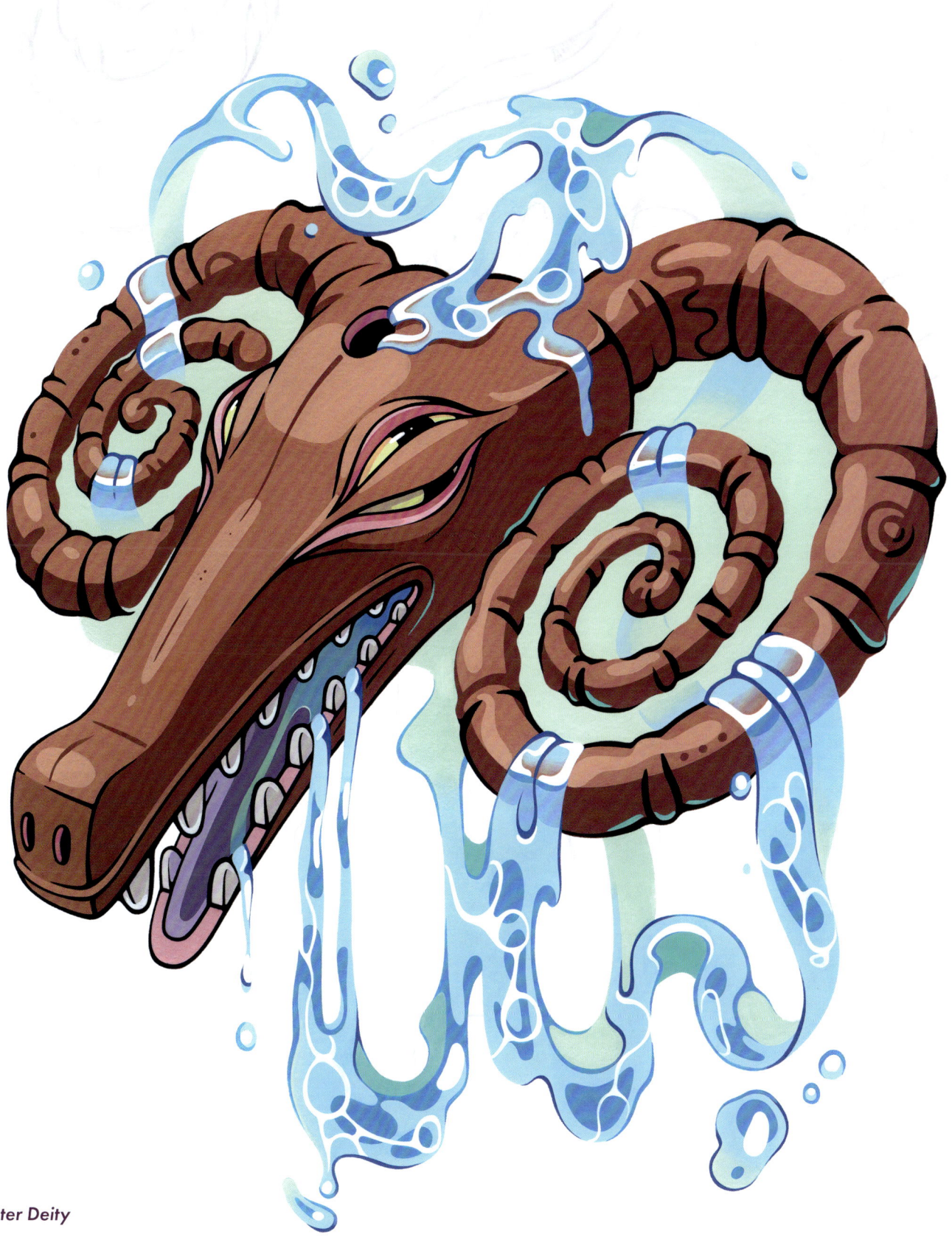

Water Deity

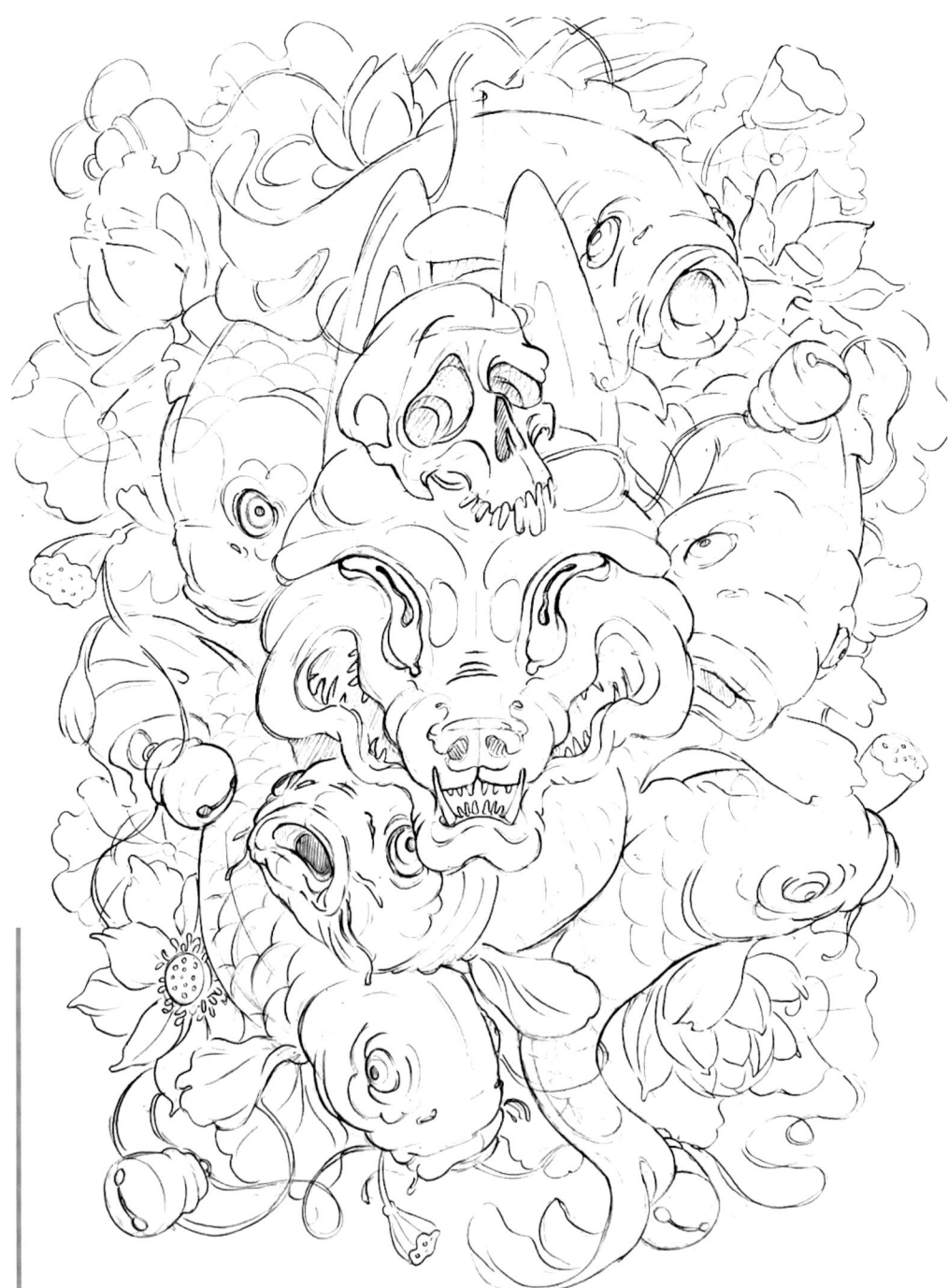

Kitsune: Despite the clear frontal view of the fox mask, everything else I intentionally make asymmetrical to avoid monotonous symmetry. To keep the focus on the main subject, I also simplify the background by using objects that are more similar in form.

The foundation of my compositions lies in the contrast of elements. If I use one large object, I always balance it with several smaller forms.

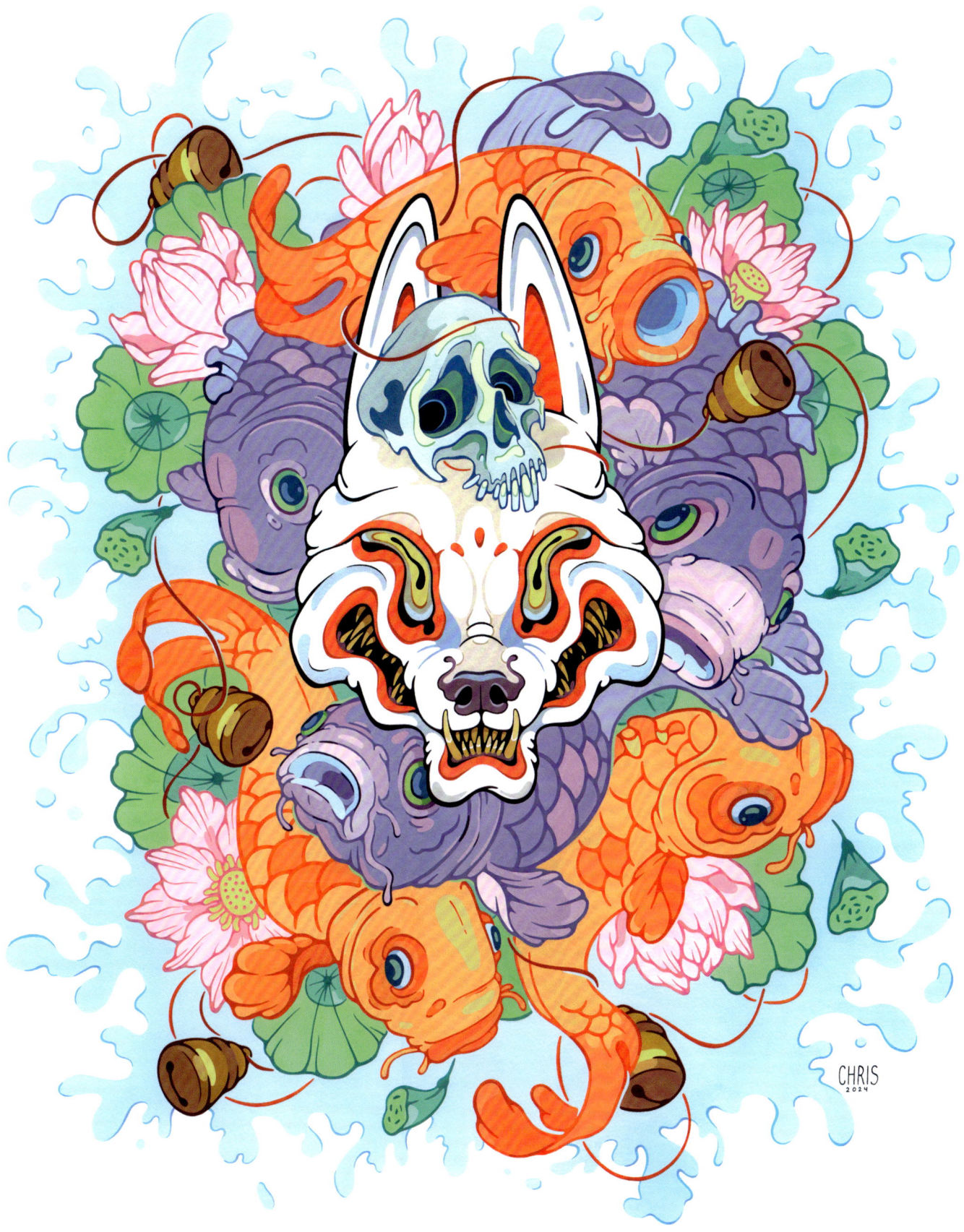

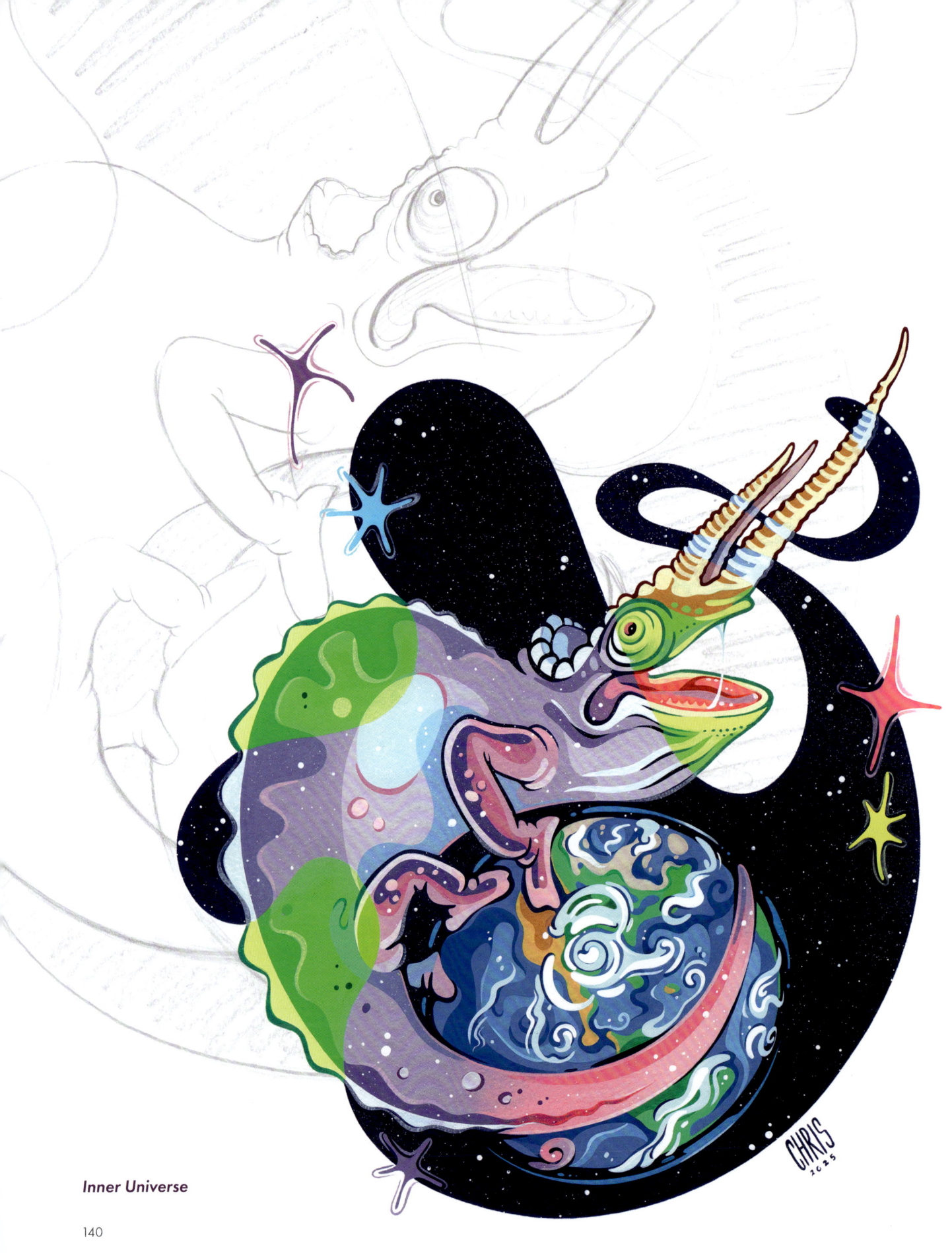

Inner Universe

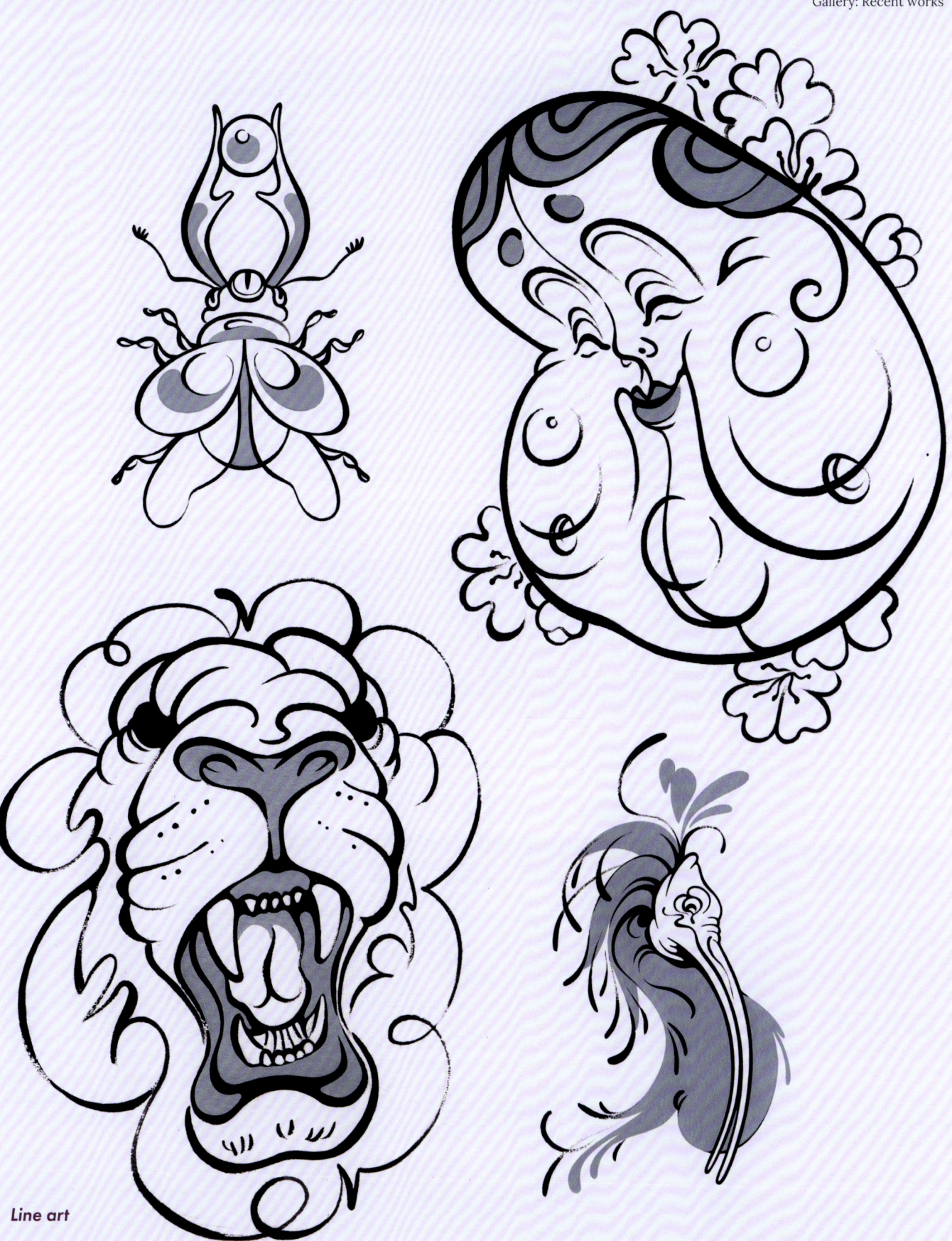

Line art

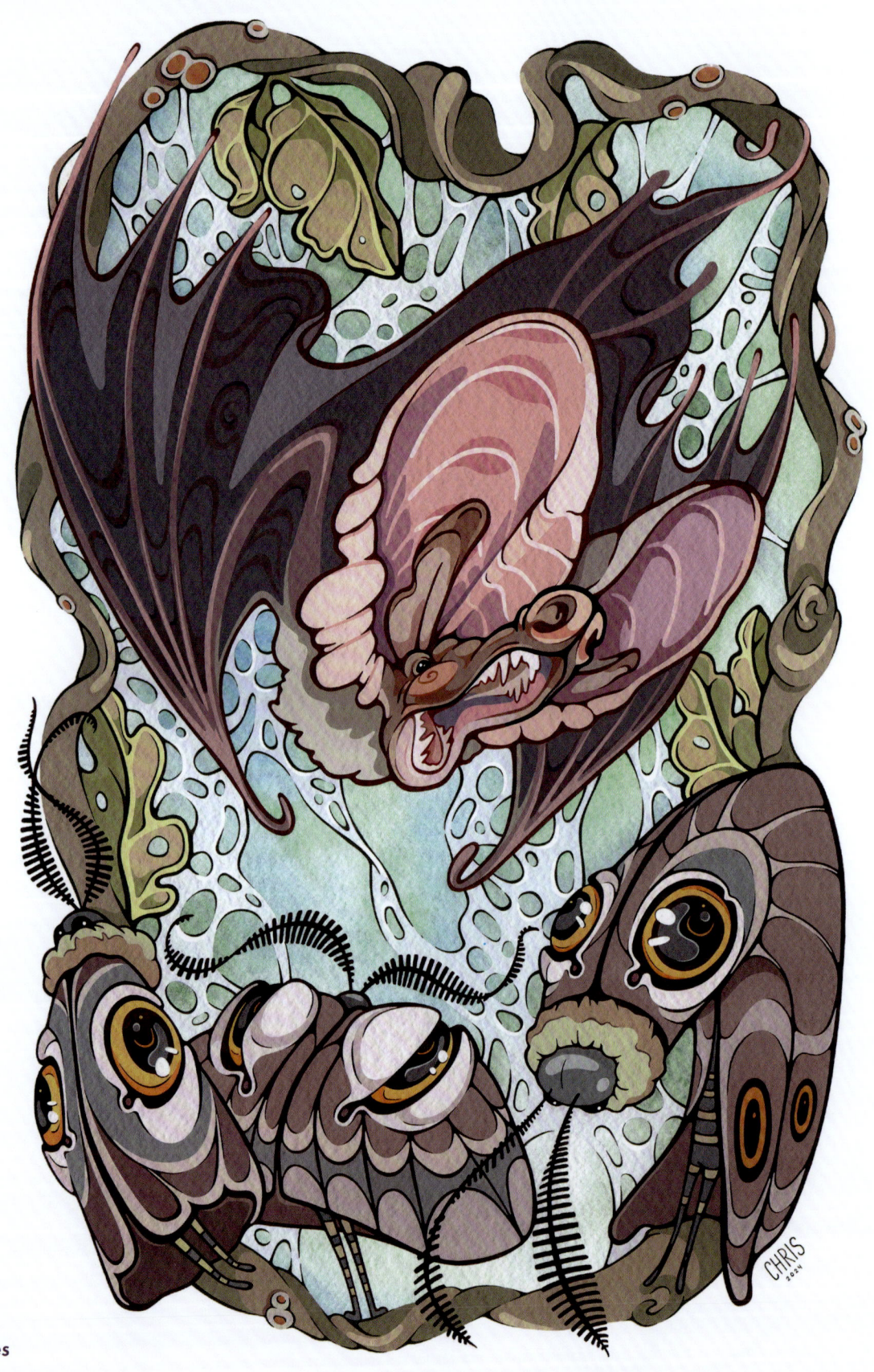

Deceiving Eyes

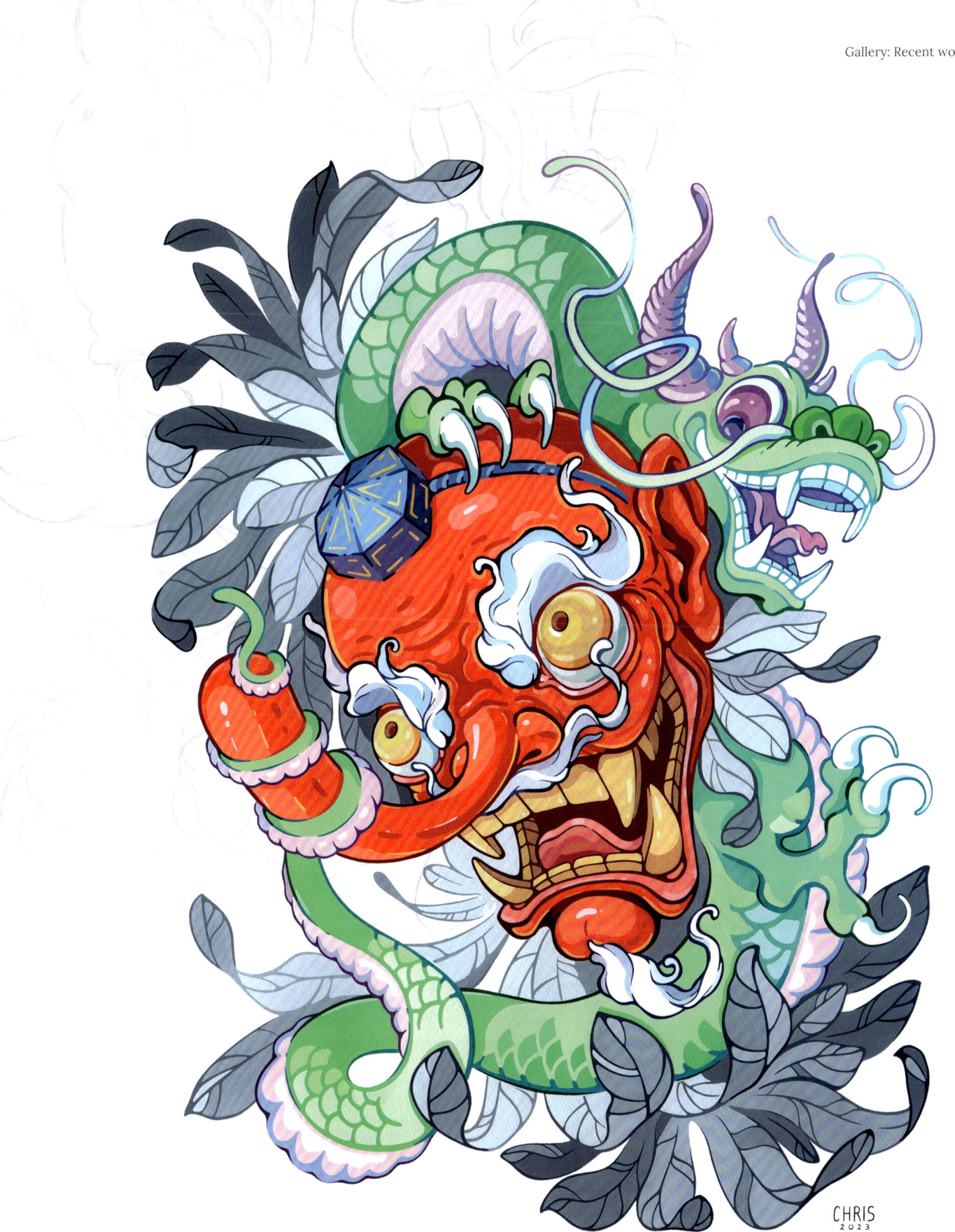

Tengu

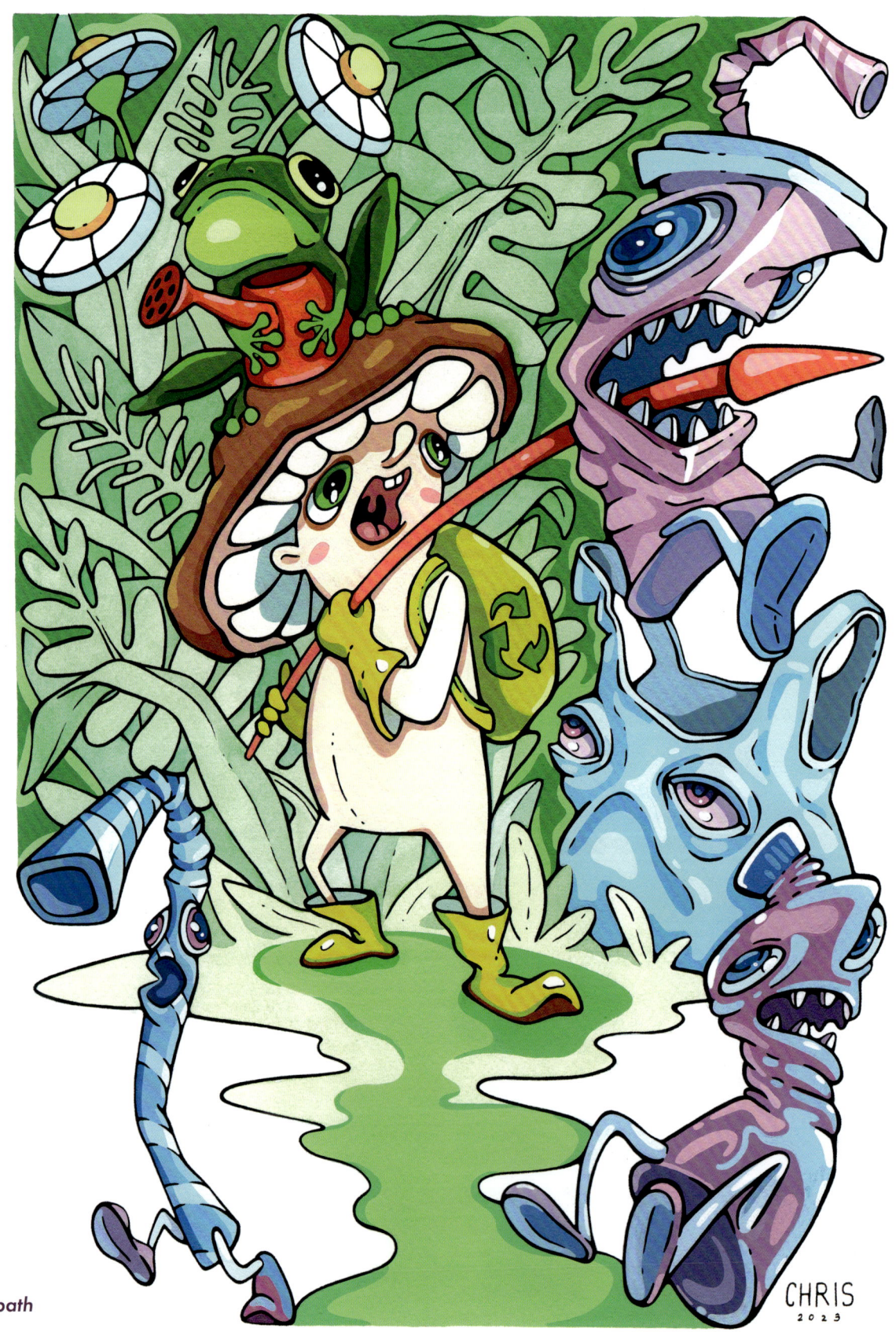

Greenpath

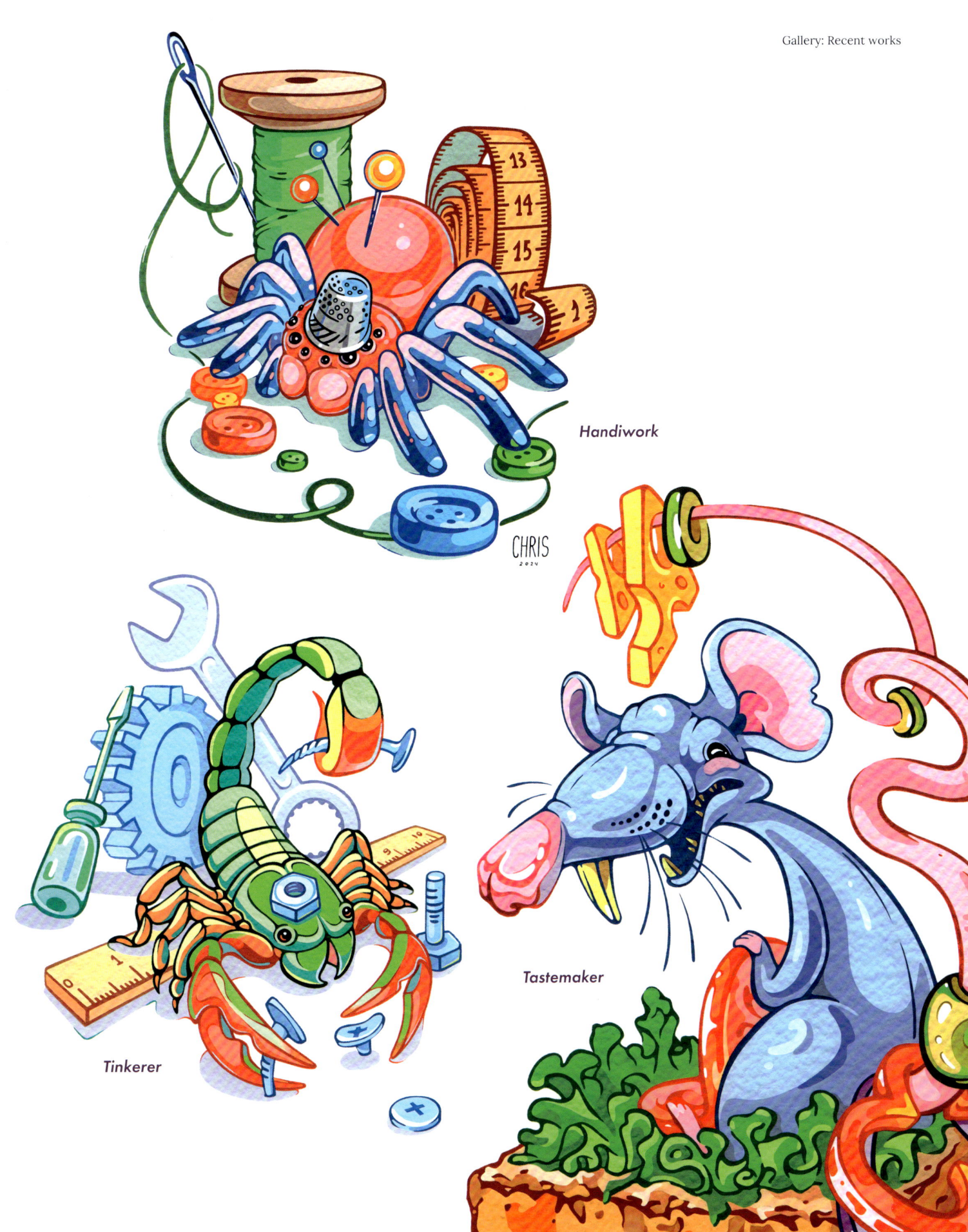

Handiwork

Tinkerer

Tastemaker

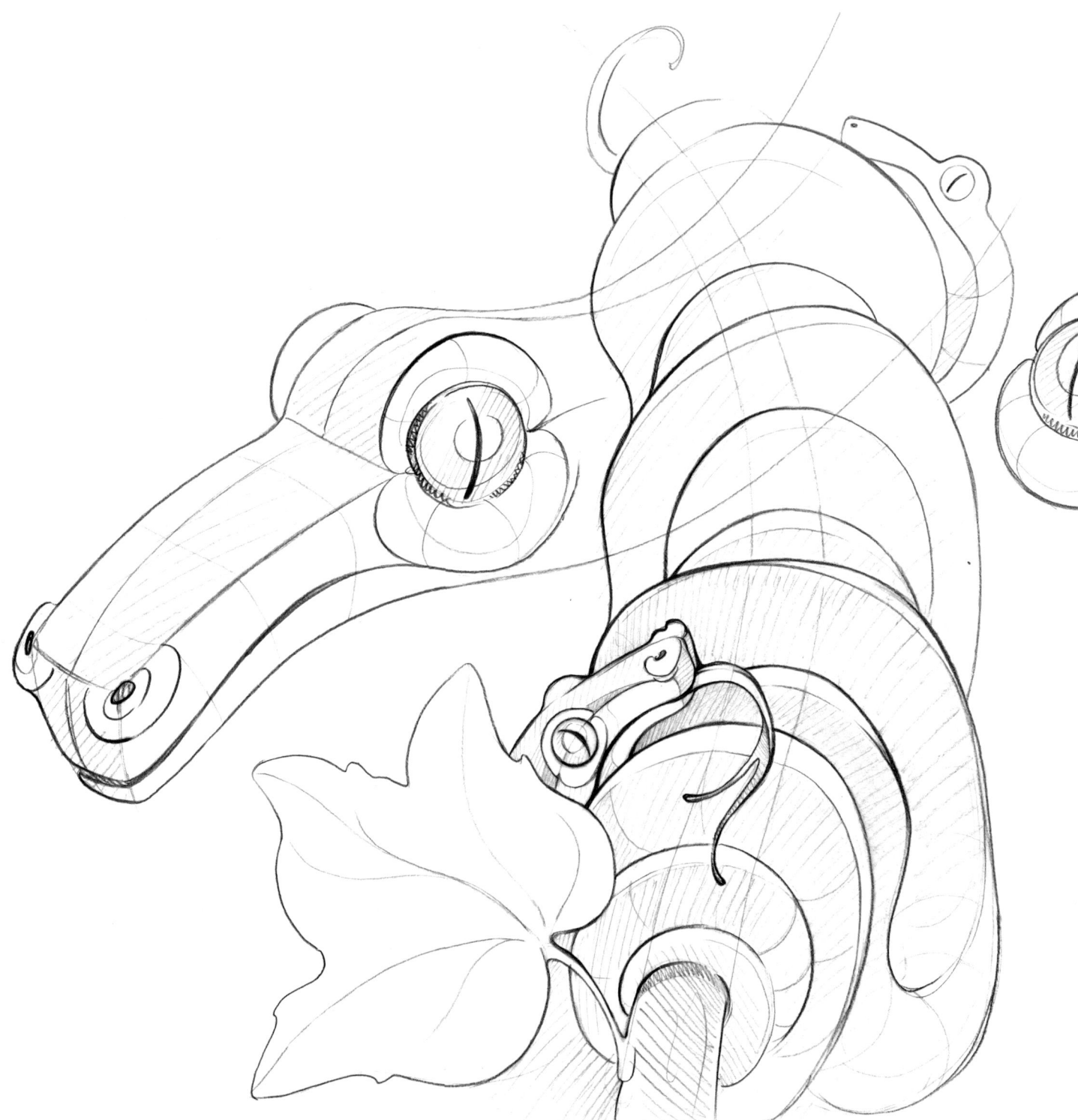

Snake sketch

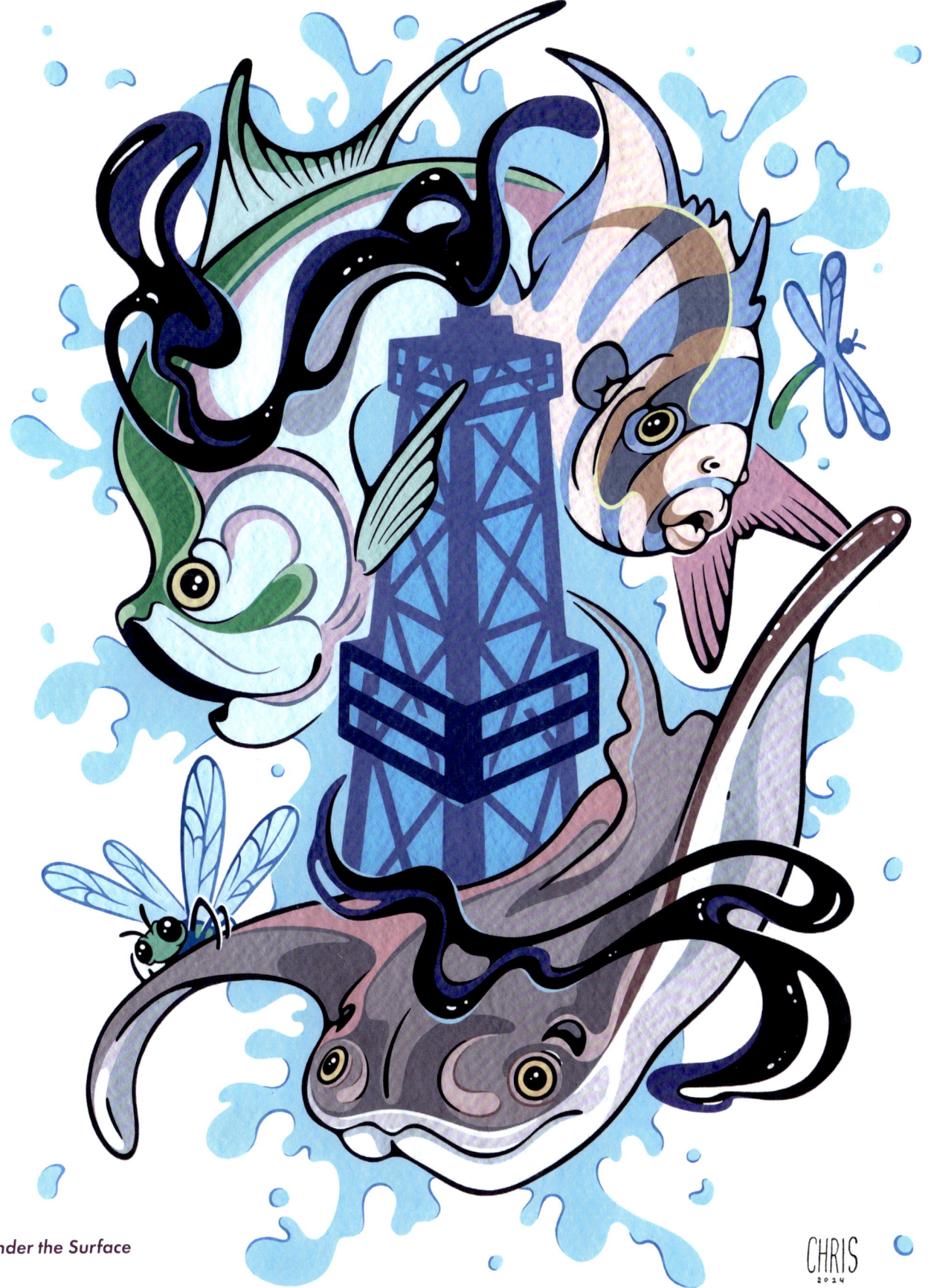

Under the Surface

CHRIS
2024

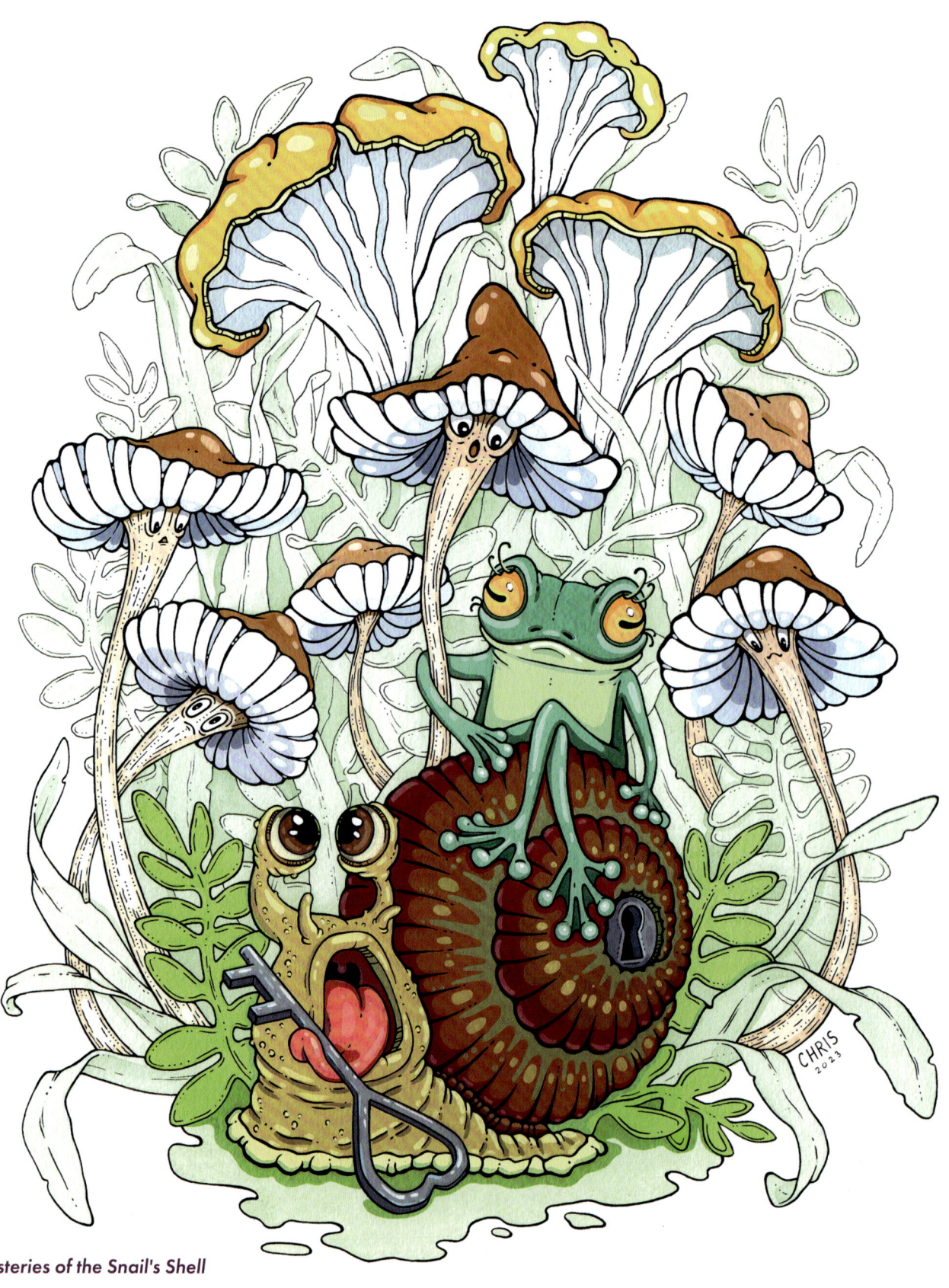

Mysteries of the Snail's Shell

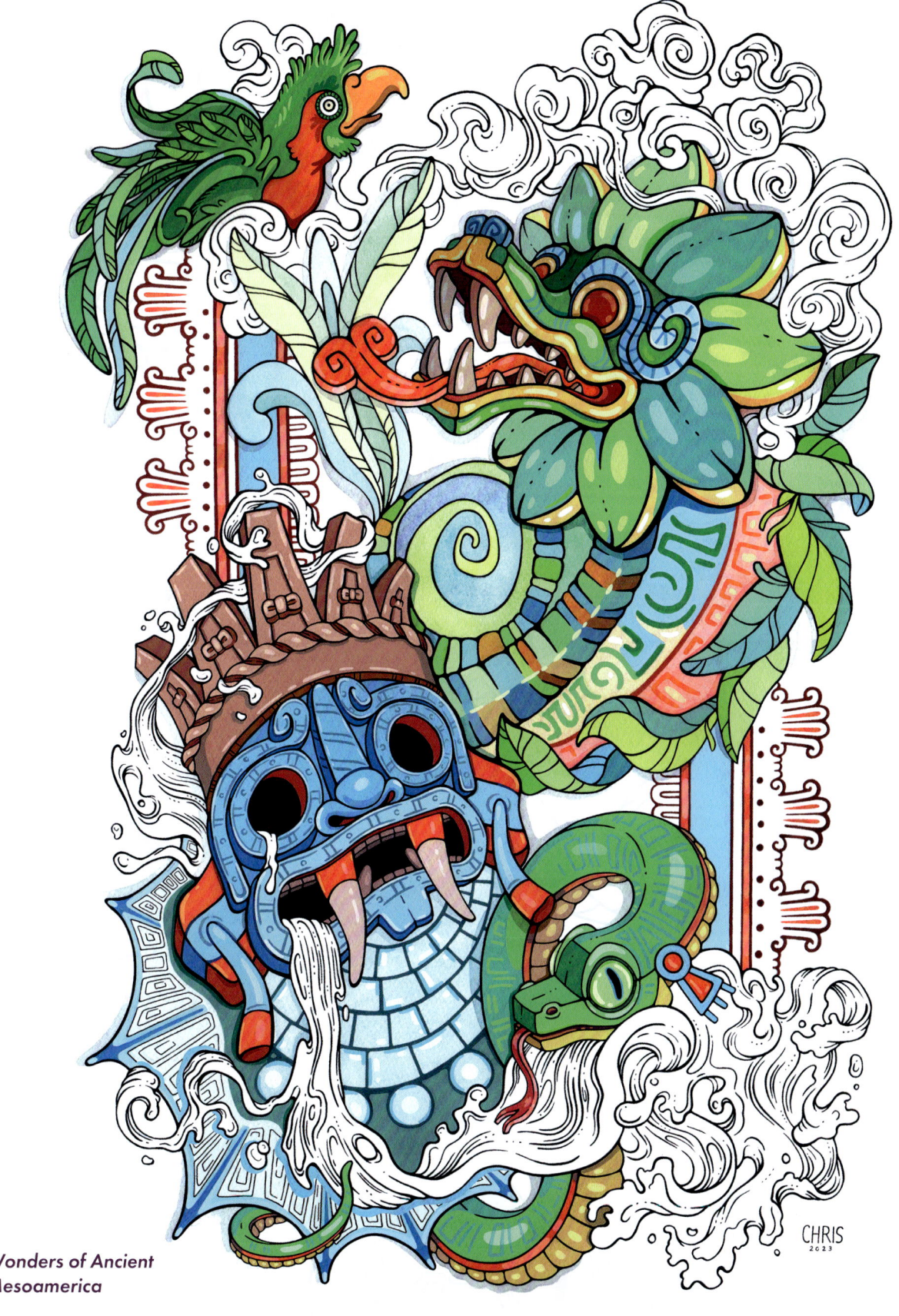

Wonders of Ancient Mesoamerica

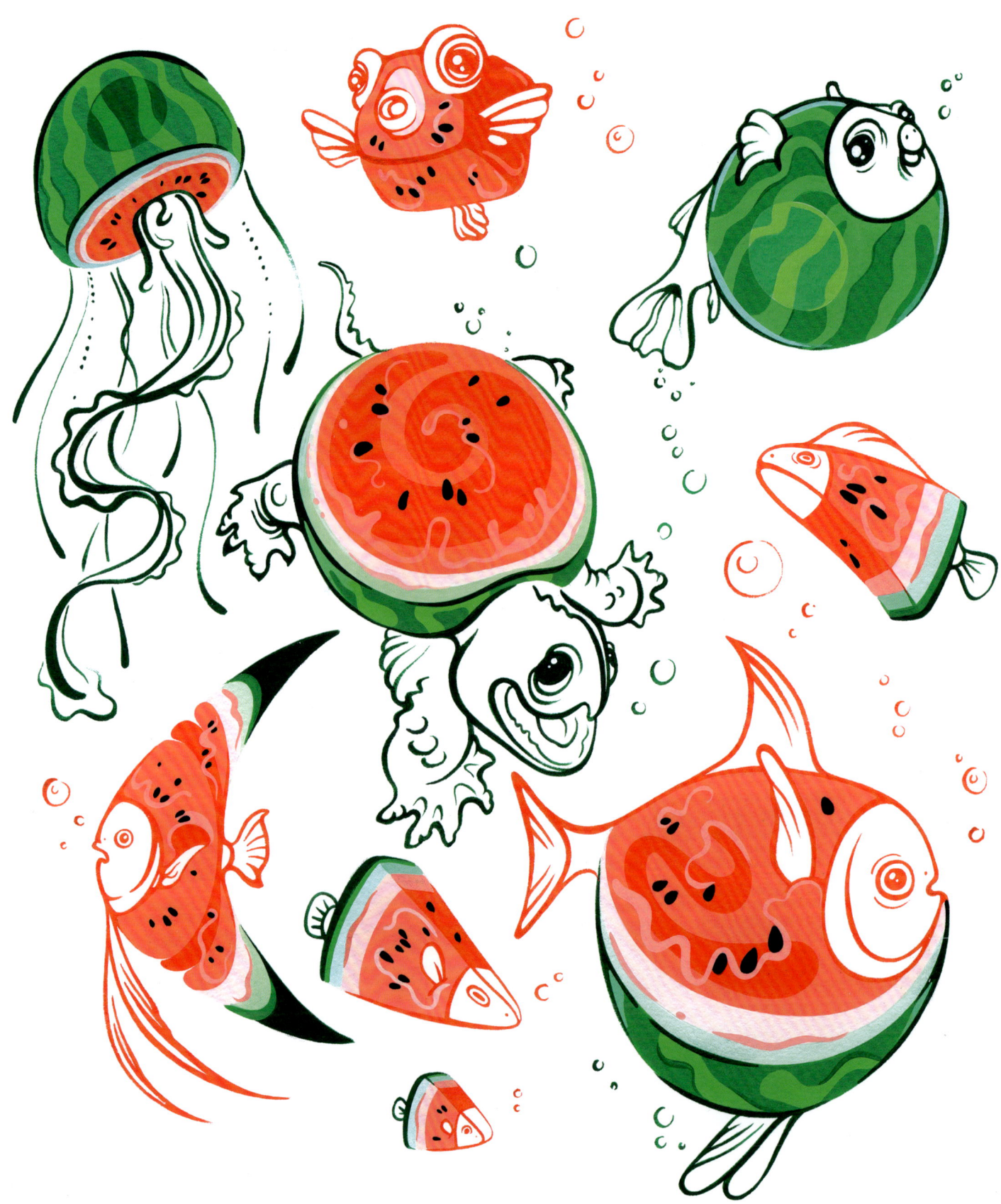

Thank you

I would like to thank everyone who made this book possible, especially Simon who spotted me and suggested that I write this book. Thank you to Rhee, who provided terrific guidance and editing, and to Imi for designing such a beautiful book. And to everyone at 3dtotal Publishing who contributed to the book's production.

Also, a huge thank you to my parents, whose faith and support have accompanied me from the very beginning. Not a day has gone by when I didn't feel it. Thanks to you, my journey began, and thanks to you, I have never stopped.

I am grateful to all my teachers. Each of you invested invaluable experience and knowledge in me at just the right time. Thank you to my friends who have supported my art from the beginning. I don't know how long it would have taken me to decide to show my art to the world if it wasn't for your persistence. Thank you to all those who have been by my side, encouraging me to create new ideas.

For me, creating art is deeply personal and passionate, and it's also a way to share experiences, feelings, and views. I'm so happy to inspire people from all over the world with my work, and honoured to receive so many words of support from you – you all inspire me, too. And to you, dear reader – thank you for trusting me, choosing this book, and sharing in this passion.

3dtotal Publishing

**3dtotal Publishing is a trailblazing, creative publisher specializing
in inspirational and educational resources for artists.**

Our titles feature top industry professionals from around the globe who share
their experience in skillfully written step-by-step tutorials and fascinating,
detailed guides. Illustrated throughout with stunning artwork, these best-selling
publications offer creative insight, expert advice, and essential motivation. Fans
of digital art will enjoy our comprehensive volumes covering Adobe Photoshop,
Procreate, and Blender, as well as our superb titles based around character
design, including *Fundamentals of Character Design* and *Creating Characters for
the Entertainment Industry*. The dedicated, high-quality blend of instruction and
inspiration also extends to traditional art. Titles covering a range of techniques,
genres, and abilities allow your creativity to flourish while building essential skills.

Well-established within the industry, we now offer over 100 titles and counting,
many of which have been translated into multiple languages around the world.
With something for every artist, we are proud to say that our books offer
the 3dtotal package:

LEARN · CREATE · SHARE

Visit us at store.3dtotal.com
3dtotal Publishing is part of 3dtotal.com, a leading website
for CG artists founded by Tom Greenway in 1999.

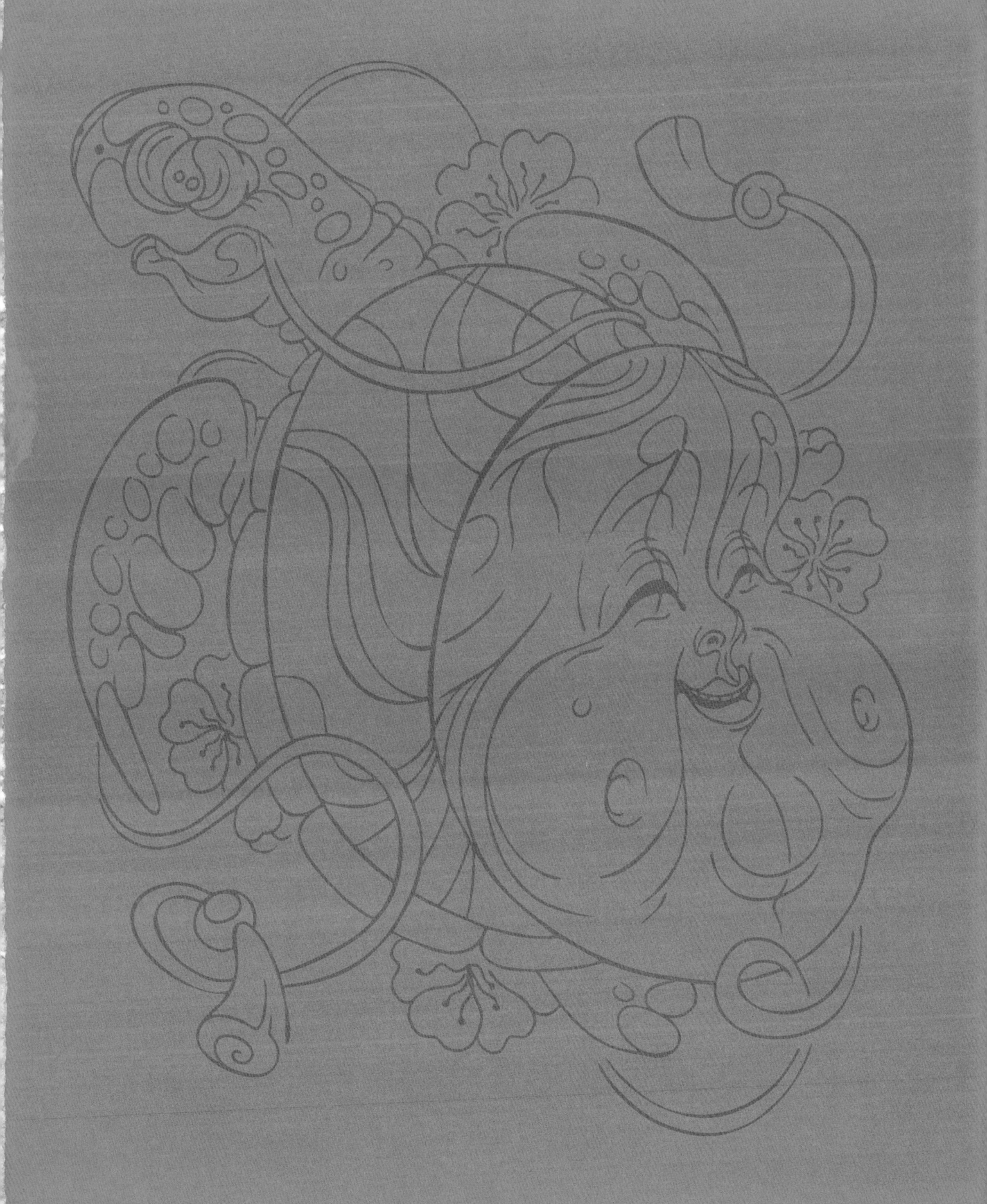